SECOND EDITION

THE
CONTENT STRATEGY
TOOLKIT

Methods, Guidelines, and Templates for
GETTING CONTENT RIGHT

MEGHAN CASEY

New
Riders
VOICES THAT MATTER™

IN PRAISE OF
THE CONTENT STRATEGY TOOLKIT

"A good content strategist knows how to solve content problems. An excellent content strategist knows how to identify the right problems to solve. What makes Meghan Casey an absolute *superhero* is that she's seen just about every content problem there is, and she's here to help you navigate yours, one manageable step at a time.

The Content Strategy Toolkit is just that. It delivers practical, easy-to-use methods for breaking down complexities at every stage of your content strategy journey. And reading it is like having a conversation with Meghan—her writing is so personable, and her advice seems tailor-made just for you.

Most importantly, this book bravely digs into what's often at the root of most organizations' content challenges: a lack of alignment on what matters and why. Once you get that alignment, successful content follows. Sounds overly simple, but it's true.

Whether you're tackling a one-time content project or gearing up for lasting cultural change, let Meghan be your guide. I've learned more from her than any other expert in the field."

—Kristina Halvorson
Owner of Brain Traffic and the Confab and Button Conferences;
Author of *Content Strategy for the Web*

"I'm excited to replace the well-thumbed copy of Meghan's book on my shelf with a brand-new edition, with new chapters about content design and content playbooks, and a WEALTH of online workshop activities! If you work in content strategy or content design, or you know someone who does, you need this book."

—Andy Welfle
Co-author, *Writing Is Designing: Words and the User Experience*

"When I moved from building an agency content team of two to leading an enterprise-sized practice, the tools and templates in the first edition of Meghan's book helped us standardize our processes and work more effectively (and efficiently) with partners. This second edition goes deep into three integral topics for content leaders—assembling cross-disciplinary teams, evaluating processes, and building a content playbook. If you're looking to build a new practice or retool an existing one, this book will help you succeed."

—Natalie Marie Dunbar
Author, *From Solo to Scaled: Building a Sustainable Content Strategy Practice*

"Meghan calls her book a toolkit and I cannot think of a more apt description. It's a wildly useful set of examples, techniques, and activities you can use immediately. I've been doing the content strategy thing for many years and looking through her book still makes me go, 'WHOA.'"

—Keri Maijala
Content Design leader at LinkedIn and the second person Meghan followed on Twitter

"I don't think I've ever come across a book as useful and helpful as this one. Meghan Casey's superpower is breaking down incredibly hard, complex work into clear methods and instructions you can put to use right away. If you're a content pro, you'll find yourself coming back again and again."

—Michael Metz
Founder, Leading Like You and co-author,
Writing Is Designing: Words and the User Experience

"*The Content Strategy Toolkit* is on my shortlist of essential content design and strategy books based on its sheer utility. If you've got a content problem and don't know where to start, jump into Meghan Casey's book and you're sure to find your starting point. The second edition includes practical info to help you navigate even more content strategy challenges."

—Kate Agena
PhD, content design and strategy leader at McAfee

"The path from content strategy to great, meaningful content can seem mysterious and daunting. The first edition of *The Content Strategy Toolkit* was the road map we had been waiting for. The second edition takes us even further. This book details every part of the process without being overwhelming. Having a strategy is one thing, but making it a reality requires diligence. You'll be glad you have this toolkit with you for the long haul. It's easy to overlook the organizational change content strategy often requires, but this book covers all the messy practical realities in a pleasant and organized fashion. If you want your content strategy to succeed in the real world, buy this book now. And then we'll all get to benefit from better content in the wild."

—Erika Hall
Author of *Just Enough Research and Conversational Design* and co-founder of Mule Design

"Meghan's only gone and done it again. The magic of *The Content Strategy Toolkit* is that it makes the theoretical practical, and this edition takes that even further with ready-to-use digital tools. The first book was a total must-have for every content and UX person's bookshelf, and this kit of excellence needs to be pride of place just next to it."

—Candi Williams
Content Design Leader

"The first version of *The Content Strategy Toolkit* helped me show up as a pro early in my career. Version 2's enhanced focus on cross-functional collaboration makes it an even more practical and tactical investment for anyone aspiring to grow as a content design and strategic leader."

—Aladrian Goods
Content Design Manager, Intuit

"*The Content Strategy Toolkit* is a staple in the go-to library of content strategists the world over, and for good reason. Through her extensive efforts, Meghan has synthesized multiple careers' worth of experience into a single, referenceable utility that is focused on immediately actionable learnings. It jump-starts the reader into productivity in the shortest possible time. It's a strategic buy for the aspiring or experienced content strategist."

—Noz Urbina
Founder and Omnichannel Strategist, Urbina Consulting & OmnichannelX

THE CONTENT STRATEGY TOOLKIT: METHODS, GUIDELINES, AND TEMPLATES FOR GETTING CONTENT RIGHT, SECOND EDITION
Meghan Casey

NEW RIDERS
www.peachpit.com
Peachpit Press is an imprint of Pearson Education, Inc.
To report errors, please send a note to errata@peachpit.com

FIGURE CREDITS

Chapter 7, Figure of A HERO'S JOURNEY: Joseph Campbell Foundation. Chapter 12, Screenshots from Hotjar: Hotjar Ltd, Screenshots from Google: Google LLC. Chapter 13, Screenshot of sitemap: Voices for Racial Justice, Screenshots from Optimal Workshop: Optimal Workshop Ltd, Screenshots from DoorDash: DoorDash. Chapter 14, Screenshots from UCare: UCare Minnesota, Screenshots from Medicare: U.S. Centers for Medicare and Medicaid Services, Figure of a businessman working online: Perfect Wave/Shutterstock. Chapter 15, Screenshots from allrecipes.com: Dotdash Meredith, Screenshot of the WYSIWYG editor: CKSource Holding LTD, Screenshot from the Craft CMS Recipe Plugin: nystudio107. Chapter 17, Screenshots from Internet Society: Internet Society.

Executive Editor: Laura Norman
Development Editor: Robyn G. Thomas
Senior Production Editor: Tracey Croom
Copy Editor: Liz Welch
Compositor: Danielle Foster
Proofreader: Dan Foster
Indexer: Valerie Haynes Perry
Cover Design: Sean Tubridy, with Mimi Heft
Interior Design: Sean Tubridy, with Mimi Heft

ISBN-13:   978-0-13-805927-9
ISBN-10:   0-13-805927-6

1 2023

For Kai, Riu, Zulmïra, Alula, Egypt, Mason, and Javonna…
you deserve a better world.

TABLE OF CONTENTS

II ▶ SET UP FOR SUCCESS

III ▶ DIG IN AND GET THE DIRT

V ▶ DESIGN YOUR CONTENT

17 BUILD OUT YOUR CONTENT PLAYBOOK   275

ACKNOWLEDGMENTS

I still can't believe I'm writing acknowledgments for a book that I wrote. But here we are…

Let's start with my Brain Traffic family: Kristina Halvorson (who always tells me I'm awesome and trusts me to do awesome work with Brain Traffic clients), Sean Tubridy (who designed the front of the book jacket and took my headshot and makes me laugh a lot), Tenessa Gemelke (who every year with Kristina brings together the smartest content strategy people on the planet), and Amy Pletch (who gives the best hugs and is always so happy to see me, or so she says).

Before we move on, so many people who have had an impact on my life and career fall into multiple categories and, well, writing acknowledgments is hard. Especially for someone who worries *a lot* about not making anyone feel left out.

Okay, on to an amazing group of friends, colleagues, teachers, and authors I have had the privilege to meet, learn from, and work with throughout my career… Natalie, Candi, Brittney, Jordan, Malaika, Aladrian, Amber, Marchaé, David, Keri, Rebekah, Chris, Jane, Lisa Maria, Corey, Michael, Andy, Scott, Mary Ann, Callie, Julie, Christine, Erin, Jodi, Noz, Eileen, Eaton, Oriana, Katie, Rosie, Lauren, Jennifer, Akilah, and so many more.

To Kev Walsh, I am so sad we never had the opportunity to work together again. You changed my perspective on collaboration between content strategy and development. I still can't believe you're gone.

Moving on to my comrades in the fight for liberation and justice… DiDi and staff and board of Done For DiDi; Shireen and the board at Stop Online Violence Against Women; Kay, Autumn, Monica, Gabi, and the rest of the board and staff at Voices for Racial Justice; Kevin, Kahlee, and the board at Until We All Are Free; Jason and The Institute for Aspiring Abolitionists; Northside Awesome Board of Trustees with reverence to Mr. Cottman; Valerie with reverence to Philando; Sumaya with reverence to Isak; Katy; Angela; Aisha C.; Aisha G.; Robin W.; Wintana; Aurin; Anika; Leslie; the Susans; Nitasha; Ann Marie and Mikka; the jail support, court support, encampment, and transportation crews; Montez, José, and our solidarity committee; and, of course, Minneapolis Twitter for speaking truth to power every single day.

Then, there's just a full-on consortium of family and friends who have offered their encouragement, believed in me, inspired me, or cared for me….

To my best gym pals Traci, Katherine, Robin, and Hannah.

To my sisters, Jackie and Erin, the middle sister loves you and appreciates you more than she could ever put into words. Ironic, huh?

To the rest of my immediate and extended family—Bill, Katie, Jake, Lizzie, Sean, Tanya, Evelyn, Carrol, Alan, Rachel, Maddie, Kyle, Hank, and Olivia—I'm glad to love and be loved by you.

To Tony, thank you for your support these last 20 years. And for loving our doggies.

To the Jones, Universe, and adjacent families—Ayo, Niall-Julian, Kai, Riu, Lutalo, Kenna, Plaiqu, Anita, Ray, Valerie, and Mona—thank you for welcoming me with open hearts.

To my chosen family—Zedé, Degen, Zulmïra, Alula, Maddie, Courtney, Mason, Debbie, Javonna, Al, David, Davion, Tawakoni, Naida, Dakotah, Dom—I just really can't imagine life without any of you.

To my love, Warren, who brags about me behind my back every chance he gets.

Thanks to all the people I referenced, quoted, and borrowed from throughout the book (and in my practice). And to everyone who reviewed the book and wrote material in praise of the book.

And last, but not least, thanks to the entire team at Peachpit. Extra especially, my deepest thanks to my absolutely amazing development editor Robyn Thomas. When Laura asked if I wanted to work with her again, it took me all of a nanosecond to say "YES!" Thank you for keeping me grounded and validating that my well-being, the well-being of my loved ones, and the well-being of my community deserve to be prioritized.

ABOUT THE AUTHOR

 Meghan Casey owns Do Better Content Consulting. She helps a wide variety of clients—from startups, nonprofits, colleges and universities, Fortune 50 companies, and everything in between—solve the messy content problems most organizations encounter every day.

Meghan has also helped several agencies and clients build their capacity to do content strategy. Perhaps her proudest moments are when content strategy practitioners tell Meghan that the first edition of this book helped them launch their content strategy career, tackle a difficult content project, or get a promotion.

A regular trainer and speaker on content strategy topics, she once inspired participants to spontaneously do the wave in a workshop setting. Yep, that really happened. Meghan has been working with content and communications since 1996, after receiving her Bachelor of Arts degree in writing from Concordia College. She also holds a Master of Arts in nonprofit management from Hamline University.

INTRODUCTION

Hi. I'm glad you picked up this book. I wrote the first edition because I had often wished for a playbook to help me solve my clients' content problems. There is a ton of great stuff out there, but I wanted it all in one place.

I should probably level set how I think about content strategy. This tried-and-true definition is still a go-to when I'm talking with people who already kinda get it.

> "Content strategy plans for the creation, publication, and governance of useful, usable content."
>
> —Kristina Halvorson
> President of Brain Traffic and author of *Content Strategy for the Web*

When I'm talking with people outside the various digital disciplines (like my clients' stakeholders or my brother Bill), I'll often say something like:

Content strategy helps organizations provide the right content, to the right people, at the right times, *for the right reasons.*

"For the right reasons" is the most important phrase in that definition. Without clarity about the why—the purpose—it's almost impossible to meet user needs or achieve business goals. Content strategy defines content purpose, and then guides planning for the creation, distribution, and maintenance of that content.

I'm still a fan of the original content strategy "quad" introduced by Brain Traffic way back in 2009:

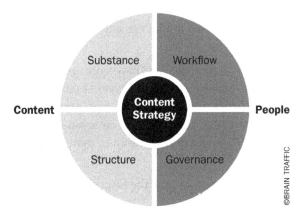

While Brain Traffic has updated the quad a couple times since then, I still think it makes sense in the context of this book. It binds together everything that goes into creating successful content experiences with the content purpose at the center.

Surrounding the content purpose are four quadrants:

- **Substance** defines what content the organization should produce, how it should sound, and why it's meaningful or relevant to users.

- **Structure** refers to how content is organized and displayed so users can find and use the content they need.

- **Workflow** is how content flows through the organization—from ideation to distribution to ongoing maintenance.

- **Governance** details how the organization makes decisions about content to ensure that it's on-strategy.

As you work your way through *The Content Strategy Toolkit*, keep in mind that this book is not meant to tell you everything you should do on your project and how to do it—although it just might work out that way. It does offer you some proven instruction, tools, and templates that you can use as is or adapt for your needs. Some of the tools in the kit are going to apply to your situation, and some aren't. Some might apply, but only if you tweak them based on your own experience and situation. Please tweak them freely! And share how you tweaked them! And maybe even write the next book!

WHY A SECOND EDITION?

A couple years ago, my acquisitions editor Laura Norman asked me if I wanted to write a second edition. At that time, I didn't think I had anything new to say. So I declined and went about my business.

But the more I thought about it, the more I realized I did have more to say. As the field evolves, so does my practice. As I have taken on new types of projects and collaborated with new people, my content strategy horizons have expanded. (I mean, I never would have thought two years ago that one of my favorite parts of my job would be collaborating with back-end developers on content modeling. But it is!)

So, what's new? Along with refreshes of content from the first edition, there's a bunch of new stuff, including:

- A new chapter about assembling your cross-discipline team

- A new chapter on preparing your organization for content-related change

- A whole section on content design versus one chapter

- A new chapter on building a content playbook

- Some new tools like the Content Operations Assessment Guide

- Workshop exercises, some old and some new, that you can immediately use in Miro or Mural

- An *extensive* Airtable database with so many tabs (thanks to my friend and colleague Jane Newman for collaborating on this!)

I'm really geeked. And I hope you are, too!

WHO THIS BOOK IS FOR

It's for you! Seriously, if you picked up this book, chances are good you are:

- An aspiring content strategist

- An experienced content strategist who's always learning

- A manager building a content strategy team

- A designer, developer, marketer, or communicator who wants to make content strategy a part of your process

- A project manager who will be working with a content strategist for the first time and wants to understand what it is we do and how to build it into their project plan

- An educator teaching a class on digital design and content

- A family member or friend who doesn't know what the heck I do, but is proud of me for writing a book

If you're not on this list, that's OK. You can still read it.

HOW TO USE THIS BOOK AND GET THE TOOLS

If you're new to content strategy or if you're working on your first content strategy project, I recommend you read the book sequentially. It can serve as a starting playbook for your project (in fact, my friend and fellow content strategy practitioner Scott Kubie suggested I call this edition *The Content Strategy Playbook*). Just keep in mind that you may need to adapt or pivot.

For those of you who have a few content strategy projects under your belt, the book can be an encyclopedia. You might reference it for ideas at specific times in your project or for an idea from one of the included tools.

As you're reading or flipping through the book, you'll notice some hints and tips. An explanation for each is included in these examples:

HINT *These usually provide you with information on where to find additional resources or other things you might consider.*

TIP *These provide information to help you with the current task (tips-of-the-trade if you will).*

Text that appears in angle brackets and in italics is a placeholder used to demonstrate a concept. Here's an example: You assume that *<company>* will complete the site inventory and that *<agency>* will use the inventory to conduct the audit.

Each chapter contains one or more tools with explanations related to how they apply that chapter's tasks. You can find them easily because the pages with tools on them will stand out when you flip through the book. Here's an example:

CONTENT STRATEGY TOOL 8.1

CONTENT ECOSYSTEM MAPPING GUIDE

Download the guide and spreadsheet/Airtable template to document your content properties and types and relevant details about them.

TIPS

- Some of the stuff in Scott's guide is more relevant to the next chapter on content processes. Feel free to start documenting it now.

- Include everything you think might be relevant (rather than leave something off).

- Modify the information you include to match your project needs.

- You might find content that no one knows anything about, which makes you a hero in my book. If you found it, their audiences might too.

WHERE TO GET IT

Download the spreadsheet at www.peachpit.com/register.

WHERE IT CAME FROM

Scott Kubie (www.kubie.com) & Meghan Casey (www.dobettercontent.com)

Or you can use the appendix to find which tools are in each chapter in case you need a quick review.

You must register your purchase on peachpit.com in order to access the tools:

1   Go to www.peachpit.com/toolkit.

2   Sign in or create a new account.

3   Click Submit.

4   Answer the question as proof of purchase.

5   Click the Access Bonus Content link to download the Bonus Content from the Registered Products tab on your Account page.

If you purchased a digital product directly from peachpit.com, your product will already be registered.

ONE LAST THING

I don't really have much more to say. It just seems rude to send you off with a set of instructions.

So, let's get started. Get comfy. Grab a cup of coffee or whatever else you'd like to drink. Find some sticky notes and a highlighter. Keep your computer handy to download any must-have-right-now tools. (Hmmm, this is sounding like a set of instructions.)

Most of all, enjoy!

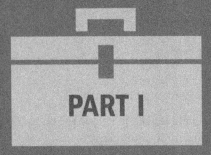

PART I

GET BUDGET
AND BUY-IN

One thing that hasn't changed since the first edition of *The Content Strategy Toolkit* was released in 2015 is that, most often, the first step in a content strategy project is convincing others in your organization that a content strategy project is necessary. But first you must uncover the problems with the content.

Then, you can translate those problems into business opportunities. These opportunities are what you need to persuade the powers-that-be to OK the time and resources to manage content well.

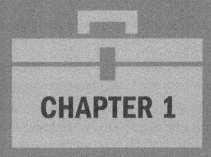

CHAPTER 1

IDENTIFY PROBLEMS AND OPPORTUNITIES

Your company, organization, or client likely has problems with web content. Those problems have probably impacted your productivity, profit margins, growth, or other metrics that reflect success. That's why you bought this book. Or maybe someone gave you this book because you've been entrusted to find and fix content problems.

That's the bad news. The good news is that all of us who work on the web have the same or similar problems. And those problems are opportunities to do something worthwhile, like make the Internet a better place.

In this chapter, I give you some ideas and tools for determining what's wrong with your content, what role your workflow might play in what's going wrong, and how to turn your content problems into opportunities to do great work for the organizations you work with.

FIGURE OUT WHAT'S WRONG WITH YOUR CONTENT

You might want to dig into what's wrong with your content for several common reasons:

■ You're about to embark on a website redesign, and you've decided to take a content-centric approach, starting with content strategy. Yay, you.

■ Your website redesign is underway—launch is imminent—you've realized the content is a mess, and you don't want to launch a beautiful new site with crappy content. I'm really, really sorry.

■ You're migrating to a new content management system (CMS) or using a CMS for the first time, and you have to get all your content from where it is now to the CMS. While you're at it, you want to fix the content you've wanted to fix for a long time. Smart plan.

■ You're working on adding more structure to your content so it can be displayed in various ways and on multiple devices and screen sizes. So you're going to clean it all up as you implement the content models. Structured content—exciting.

■ You just know deep down in your heart that your content could and should better meet the needs of your organization and its audiences. And you are determined to make it so. Onward, content warrior.

Whatever the impetus, chances are you have a pretty good idea of what's wrong on some level but haven't been able to adequately document and quantify those issues. Your hunches are usually the best place to start—sort of like an experiment.

HYPOTHESIZE WHAT'S WRONG

The first step of documenting what's wrong with your content is to record your hypotheses, just as you would in an experiment. Here are some example hypotheses to get you thinking:

■ The majority of the content on your site is for *<audience a>*, but you're really trying to increase conversions with *<audience b>*.

■ Your content isn't written in a way that represents your brand, or it doesn't elicit the reactions or perceptions you want your key audiences to have.

- You don't think you've provided good enough meta descriptions—your content ranks well, but you don't get the clicks you think you should.

- Your calls to action aren't very strong or may not exist at all—users aren't doing what you hope they'll do after visiting a page.

- You don't think your content supports the reasons people visit your site or use your application—people most often visit to do *<this thing>*, but most of your content is about *<that thing>*.

- Your site contains a lot of outdated content, such as wrong information or links to pages that no longer exist.

- The content is not very readable or accessible—it's long, it's not organized well, important information is buried, it uses a lot of jargon, and charts and images don't have relevant metadata.

- Visitors can't find anything on your site or instructions in your application aren't clear, so you get a ton of customer support calls and emails.

Documenting your hypotheses is super important because it helps you focus on what you want to learn about your content and what method you'll use to learn it.

CHOOSE YOUR METHODS

Once you've documented your hypotheses, you can decide how you'll prove or disprove them. Not all hypotheses can be proved or disproved using the same method, which is why I recommend combining the methods from the following three sections to get the broadest look at what's wrong.

CONTENT AUDIT

You can conduct a content audit yourself or hire a content strategist to help. In a content audit, you typically look for things you can evaluate objectively: what audience the content is for, what the intended purpose of the content is, whether links are broken or go to the wrong place, whether pages aren't accessible through the navigation, how long the content is, how easy it is to scan and understand the key message(s), and whether pages have the appropriate metadata for search engine optimization. See the **Content Strategy Tool 1.1** for an example audit.

CONTENT STRATEGY TOOL 1.1

AUDIT PLANNING TIPS AND TEMPLATES

Download the audit template workbook so you don't have to start from scratch (see the "How to Use This Book and Get the Tools" section in the Introduction for instructions on downloading tools from www.peachpit.com/register to help you work smarter). It contains templates for the audit sheet (where you can collect your data) and a fancy summary sheet with formulas that pull in data from your audit sheet(s). If you've fallen in love with Airtable like I have, start with the Airtable template. Oh, you don't know about Airtable? Let me tell you! It's like if a spreadsheet had a baby with Tony Stark (you know, Iron Man). Easy to use like a spreadsheet, but with so much database functionality.

TIPS

- If you're auditing more than 1,000 pages of content, use a site crawler such as Content Insight to import the site structure and URLs.
- Consider whether you need to audit every page of your website or whether a representative sample will give you what you need.
- You might want to use more than one sheet in your audit, especially if you are auditing more than one property or if breaking down your data by section will be useful.

WHERE TO GET IT

Get the audit instructions, Google sheets workbook, and link to the Airtable template at www.peachpit.com/register.

WHERE IT CAME FROM

Lots of people: Lauren Pope (www.lapope.com), Meghan Casey (www.dobettercontent.com) with Airtable support from Jane Newman

ANALYTICS REVIEW

With an analytics review, you can look at things like pageviews, user paths through content, common search terms, devices and browsers used, and traffic sources.

USER TESTING

TIP

Disproving your hypotheses may make you feel as though you failed. But really, the opposite is true. Instead, you've discovered an area in which you're doing better than you thought, and you can focus your efforts on the stuff that really needs help.

Getting insights from actual users is a great way to add some subjectivity to your assessment. You can look at things like how content makes a user feel, how easy your content is to understand, how easy it is for users to complete a task on your site or in your application, and how findable key content is. See the **Content Strategy Tool 1.2** for an overview of a content testing method.

Table 1.1 includes a few examples from the previous hypotheses list.

CONTENT STRATEGY TOOL 1.2

A SUPER SIMPLE USER TEST

The fine folks at GOV.UK have been rocking content strategy and content development for several years now. This super simple user test gives some great insights about your content.

STEPS

1. Choose a few key pages from your site and print copies for each participant and one for you. Or for remote testing, copy and paste the text into a Google Doc that you can share with participants.

2. Ask participants to read the content or have their screen reader read it if they have a visual impairment. Have them highlight in green the content that makes them feel <confident, smart, ready to act>, and highlight in red the content that makes them feel <less confident, confused, hesitant>. For participants with visual impairments, ask them to pause the screen reader and talk you through their perceptions.

3. Take a deep breath and look at the intensity of the green and red highlights to see where your content is doing pretty well and where it really needs work.

4. Once you have results from all participants, start with a clean copy and highlight everything your participants highlighted in the corresponding colors, noting commonalities and divergence between participants and any additional context from your discussions.

TIPS

- Ask participants to highlight for only one set of adjectives (such as more confident, less confident). Pick the set that is most important to your organization.

- When analyzing the results, pay attention to the content with the most highlights, which represent patterns.

WHERE IT CAME FROM

Pete Gale, @petegale, GOV.UK (www.gov.uk)

TABLE 1.1 **CONTENT ASSESSMENT HYPOTHESES AND METHODS**

HYPOTHESIS	AUDIT	USER TESTING	ANALYTICS
The majority of the content on our site is for *<audience a>*, but your business goals are to increase conversions with *<audience b>*.	X		X
The way our content sounds is not consistent across our content, and much of it does not match our brand voice and tone.	X	X	
Visitors have a hard time finding what they need on our site even though the information is there.		X	X
Instructions for completing tasks in our application are cumbersome and unclear, resulting in lots of calls to/chats with customer service.	X	X	

SET UP YOUR EXPERIMENTS

Now that you know what methods to use, you can get specific about what to measure and how to measure it. For each method, document what you'll look for to prove or disprove your hypotheses and how you'll document or gather the findings.

AUDIT

You should start with the audit, but before jumping into it, get really specific about the criteria you'll use to assess your content. I put together an audit charter with a matrix that details the criteria and the evaluation scale. This matrix is especially helpful when you have multiple people working on the audit. It also helps you explain your findings to your stakeholders or clients.

HINT
You might be able to reuse some of what you come up with here when you develop your scorecard for measuring content performance later. And the assessment, or at least some of it, can be used as a baseline. More in Chapter 11.

TIP   Save yourself a spreadsheet headache by setting up data validation for the values in your audit. Slicing and dicing the data is much easier when the values are consistent throughout the audit sheets. Or if you use Airtable, your data validation is built in, making sorting and filtering a breeze.

Table 1.2 provides an example of an audit criteria matrix.

TABLE 1.2 **AUDIT CRITERIA**

ATTRIBUTE	CELL VALUES	RESEARCH QUESTION	WHAT YOU'LL LOOK FOR
Audience	▪ C-Level ▪ Manager ▪ Media ▪ Unclear	Who does the content appear to be written for?	▪ Call to action (CTA) that suggests a role ▪ Level of complexity ▪ Nature of the content
Voice and tone	▪ Yes ▪ Somewhat ▪ No	Does the content portray the desired voice and tone?	▪ Content that clearly embodies our defined voice and tone attributes of x, y, and z
Clarity	▪ Yes ▪ Somewhat ▪ No	Is the message conveyed clearly and effectively?	▪ Descriptive title and headings ▪ Logical information hierarchy ▪ Plain language ▪ Persuasive CTAs
Readability	▪ Yes ▪ Somewhat ▪ No	Does the content employ writing, style, and formatting best practices?	▪ Simple, short sentences ▪ Little to no jargon ▪ Headings and lists ▪ Active voice
Accessibility and inclusivity	▪ Yes ▪ Somewhat ▪ No	Are best practices for accessibility and inclusivity being followed?	▪ Appropriate alt text ▪ Descriptive link text ▪ Text alternatives for visual content ▪ Inclusive language ▪ Inclusive imagery

ANALYTICS

 TIP
I'm not an analytics expert, but the folks at Google are. Chances are you use Google Analytics on your site, and it has a ton of resources for using its tools online.

You can learn so much from your analytics that you may be tempted to just start mining the data and hope you find some good insights. A better approach is to decide what specific questions you want answers to first. Depending on what you want to know, you might be able to use your audit sheet to collect the data. For example, if you want to know which pages were viewed most, you can add a column for that in your spreadsheet.

Once you know the questions, record how you'll document what you learn. **Table 1.3** provides an example of research questions and documentation details.

TABLE 1.3 **ANALYTICS RESEARCH PLAN**

RESEARCH QUESTION	DOCUMENTATION
What do users do after visiting <*key page from which you expect the user to respond to this CTA*>?	Percentage for each path of the total paths a user takes from this page during *xx* time period
What are people searching for when they arrive on your site?	Top *xx* search terms monthly
What pages are visited most frequently, and how do people get to them?	Top *xx* pages and percentages for each path users take to get to them
Where do people get stuck when completing <*description of task flow*>?	Abandonment rates of pages/ screens in the task flow

USER TESTING

 TIP
You don't have to do user tests with a jillion people. In fact, the law of diminishing returns suggests that you really need only five people.

Again, before sitting down with users, specify what you want to learn and how you'll get the answers from test participants. Examples of questions for which you might want answers are

- How does the content make the user feel? For example, is the user confident, at ease, overwhelmed?

- What words would the user use to describe your organization after reading your content?

- How well does the user comprehend your content?

- Is the user likely to take the action you want them to take after reading your content?

- Can the user find key information on your website?

- Do the results of onsite search terms meet the users' expectations?

- Do your users find your content relevant for their needs?

Using your list of questions (that correlate to your hypotheses), write a user test to walk through with your five participants.

I recommend trying it with a colleague or family member first to determine how long it takes and to practice explaining the tasks.

DON'T FORGET PEOPLE AND PROCESS

You probably think your content is a mess. You're reading or referencing this book because you want to fix it. What else do you need to know besides what specifically is wrong with your content? You need to acknowledge that your problems with content stem from problems involving people and the processes they use to do their work.

Keep in mind two important principles about people and processes. First, everyone—or almost everyone—has good intentions and is trying to do good work. The people involved in making content decisions and doing content work are doing the best they can with the skills they have and the guidance they get. Second, even the most pointless and cumbersome processes and tools were created to solve a problem at the time they were created. The problem is likely that the processes didn't evolve or they were never reexamined.

Why do I mention this? Well, mostly because I have to remind myself of those two things every time I start a new project. It's easy to mutter under my breath, "What in the world were they thinking?" or "Do they have any idea what they're doing?" But that doesn't help me or my client. Instead, I say, "Help me understand why they're doing things this way" or "Do you feel there are gaps in the skillsets necessary to create content better?"

OK, with that out of the way, here are some of the questions you should answer at this stage of the project:

- Who is involved in efforts to create content—including subject matter experts, legal/compliance reviewers, writers, editors, publishers, and so on?

- How much time do people spend contributing to content creation or publishing that content?

- How long does it take to publish new content from ideation/request to publishing?

- How much content do you publish daily/weekly/monthly/quarterly/annually?

- How do you decide what content to publish?

- What are the pain points and roadblocks related to your content that people complain about?

You likely don't want to spend a ton of time documenting processes and roles at this point in your quest, especially if you don't have funding or the go-ahead for a content strategy project yet. Do some walkabouts, talk with people in the breakroom, buy folks coffee, and make some assumptions based on your experiences. You can validate and vet all of what you learned later. For now, you want to describe how people and processes affect your content.

CONTENT STRATEGY TOOL 1.3

PEOPLE AND PROCESS MINI-ASSESSMENT

I've identified four characteristics for people and process optimization. Use the worksheet to jot down findings from your conversations and observations for each characteristic.

TIPS

- Right people with the right capabilities empowered to do the right work

- Documented processes with associated guidance and enablement

- Understanding of roles and responsibilities with mechanisms for accountability

- Collaboration and experimentation built into the way you work

TIPS

- What you find during this mini-assessment will help set you up for more detailed work to get the right resources and shore up your processes.

- Bring your observations to life with quotes from people working on content and concrete examples of challenges.

WHERE IT CAME FROM

Meghan Casey (www.dobettercontent.com) from work with some amazing clients and colleagues

TURN PROBLEMS INTO OPPORTUNITIES

Problems are depressing. Opportunities, you can work with. And opportunities are much easier to sell to your boss, your boss's boss, your coworkers, your clients, and even yourself. Fixing problems sounds hard. And seizing opportunities sounds like fun. Right?

This next bit of work will be the foundation of everything that follows. So take some time to connect the dots between what you learned about your content and your people and processes. Then, play around with positioning so that you can make a case for a content strategy project (more in Chapter 2).

Table 1.4 is an example of how you might summarize the problems and opportunities you've discovered so far. In this format, you can set up the larger problem and related implications you uncovered during the audit, analytics review, and user testing.

TABLE 1.4 **OPPORTUNITIES TO IMPROVE CONTENT**

PROBLEM	IMPLICATIONS	OPPORTUNITY
You are creating half as much content for your primary audience as you are for less important audiences.	▪ Misuse of writing resources ▪ Perception that you don't care about the primary audience ▪ Primary audience unable to find content that is relevant to them	Do user research to better understand users' needs along the customer journey so that you can spend your writing time and budget on fixing or creating the content most likely to lead to conversions.
Users say the results from their search don't include important information.	▪ Users feel we don't have what they need ▪ Time spent on irrelevant content ▪ Missed opportunities to demonstrate value	

TIP When writing opportunity statements, make sure they include the desired end result. In the examples in Table 1.4, the end results are more conversions. That's what your boss's boss and your boss's boss's boss care about most. If it makes sense, also include some context for how the result will make things run more smoothly or save the company money. For example, spending resources more wisely also directly contributes to the bottom line.

READY? LET'S GO

You know a lot about what's wrong. You've turned those problems into opportunities. Now you need to convince the people in charge that your organization needs content strategy. On to Chapter 2.

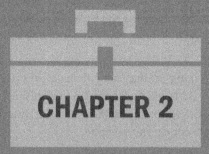

CHAPTER 2

CONVINCE LEADERS AND
GET THE RESOURCES

You've done the work to identify opportunities for making your organization's or client's content better. Next, you'll likely need to make the business case to get the time and resources to make it happen. Depending on how much convincing you need to do, keep in mind a few key things.

First, it may make sense to start with something small that doesn't require a ton of time or budget. Decision makers are less likely to say no to something with little risk... as long as you can demonstrate why it's worth prioritizing.

Second, consider pitching a project that, when successful, a lot of people will care about across your organization and will have tangible benefits—from executives/leadership to marketing to tech to subject matter experts to content creators to... I think you get it.

Third, remember that most people want to do what's right. Regarding getting time and money, your organization could spend its money on a lot of right things. Your project is just one of them.

THINK LIKE A BUSINESS PERSON

OK, so just admit it, you have at some point in your career muttered under your breath about some colleagues—likely decision makers—something like, "Elghhhh, they just don't get it." I have. And I'm not saying you were wrong. They probably didn't get it.

But here's the thing. In that same moment, they probably believed there was something *you* didn't get. And they were probably right too. That's why it behooves us content folk to think like businesspeople. Turn the "they don't get its" into opportunities to educate and inspire.

Businesspeople think in terms of return on investment (ROI) and risk and reward. They have to. Your case for content strategy absolutely must be presented in those terms. For example, how will your project increase efficiency, eliminate costs, or boost sales? Of course, none of those things are guaranteed, but we need to demonstrate how they could be affected by content and content operations improvements.

So make sure what you're proposing is a sound business decision. The people you must convince have been burned before by bright, shiny new sites and apps and big ideas that made no impact on sales... or client acquisition... or the brand... or revenue. Their budgets, their reputations, and sometimes even their jobs may be on the line. And they're just as worried that you don't get the business side as you are worried that they don't get content.

Pardon me for being a bit negative here. It's just really important. And I've found over the years that we sabotage ourselves when we aren't open to being a bit more humble.

QUANTIFY THE (MISSED) OPPORTUNITIES

And now for some math...

To make your case, spend some time on forecasting and projections (more business-ey terms) based on the opportunities you've identified. For inspiration, think about the word problems you had to solve in math class.

Here's an example of one I used to demonstrate the importance of doing some restructuring and making some nomenclature (how things are named and labeled) changes in a client's intranet site. It was based on real data:

> Corporate employees estimate that they spend an average of 30 minutes per week searching for something they need on the intranet. With 7,000 corporate employees with an average hourly wage of $40 per hour, that equates to $140,000 per week, or $7.28 million per year in staff time.

> 7,000 employees × 0.5 hours × $40 per hour × 52 weeks

> That's a lot of money, but there's more.

> Employees also estimate that once every three or four months, they have to call support for help with something that is available on the intranet but that they are unable to find. That equates to about 21,000 calls per year, each lasting an average of 4 minutes. The company pays approximately $1 per minute. That amounts to a cost of $84,000.

> 3 calls per year × 7,000 employees × 4 minutes × $1 per minute

> That amount doesn't include the staff time spent on the calls, which is about $56,000.

> 12 minutes per year × 7,000 employees × $40 per hour

> All told, problems finding information on the intranet cost the company about $7.42 million per year.

> If we can reduce the amount of time employees spend finding information on the intranet and the number of support calls by half, we would free up 92,400 staff hours over the course of a year and save the company $3.71 million.

Continuing with this example, the next step is to estimate what it will cost to fix the navigation and nomenclature. Be honest and inclusive with your estimate. **Table 2.1** shows some made-up costs for this example.

TABLE 2.1 **INTRANET INFORMATION ARCHITECTURE ESTIMATE**

ACTIVITY	COST
Review site analytics, call center reports, and user feedback. 20 hours × $48 (average hourly rate for team members involved)	$960
Conduct stakeholder interviews with business partners and user interviews with employees. Includes stakeholder interview time. 60 hours × $48	$2,880
Develop—and test with employees—new sitemap, page structure, and nomenclature. Includes analyzing interview data, reporting on user testing findings, and recommending revisions. 120 hours × $48	$7,680
Review and get approval from stakeholders. 12 hours × $48	$576
Technical implementation of the changes. Includes UAT (user acceptance testing). 200 hours × $48	$9,600
TOTAL	$21,696

Wow, $21,696 to potentially save the company over $3 million! Seems like a no-brainer.

CALCULATE THE RISKS

TIP

Risks aren't bad. Companies take risks all the time because they believe in the potential reward.

Now that you have a story to tell about the opportunity—saving the company millions of dollars, in this case—you can lay out the risk.

Fellow content strategy consultant Melissa Rach gave a presentation called "Content & Cash: The Value of Content (Cape Town Edition)" (www.slideshare.net/ melissarach/content-cash-the-value-of-content-capetown-edition). It has some great stuff in it, so look it up. A slide about estimating opportunity costs and losses is particularly relevant to helping decision makers evaluate your idea. According to Melissa, the inspiration came from the book *How to Measure Anything: Finding the Value of "Intangibles" in Business*, by Douglas W. Hubbard.

It involves more math. Here's the process:

1 List the maximum gain from the proposed project.

In this case, it's $3.71 million, which assumes you can cut calls to service and time spent looking for information by half.

2   List the maximum loss, which is your cost estimate to fix the content.

In the example, I estimated $21,696. I'm going to bump it up to $25,000.

3   Calculate the probability of success.

Of course, you can never be absolutely sure. But in this case, I think it's pretty high. So I'm gonna say 75 percent.

4   Calculate the risk associated with doing the work by multiplying the estimated cost of the project by the likelihood it will fail.

$25,000 × 25\% = \$6,250$

5   Calculate the risk associated with not doing the work by multiplying the estimated gain by the likelihood that it will succeed.

$3.71 million × 75\% = \$2.775$ million

Budget holders will find it pretty tough to say no to a project with a maximum risk of $6,250 and a potential gain of almost $3 million. Not all your projects will suggest such a large variance between the potential gain and loss, but it's still a good way to understand the value of what you're proposing and help budget-holders make an informed decision.

CONSIDER NON-MONETARY COSTS

Monetary costs will probably be the most important consideration when you're asking for budget and resources. It's also important, though, to mention the other costs—and benefits—your organization might incur.

In most projects I've worked on, the most substantial non-monetary cost is related to organizational change. The example detailed in this chapter doesn't necessitate much—if any—change in behavior. But often, implementing a content strategy requires a change in the way people think about and do their jobs. And although those changes eventually lead to efficiencies and content that's more likely to support business goals, the process of changing can be difficult and even costly.

You shouldn't avoid talking about these changes. Instead, be up front about them. Get agreement from decision makers that they will support the changes in behavior that are required to do content well.

HINT
Chapter 14 talks more about organizational change and designing the roles and processes to support your content strategy.

MAKE YOUR ARGUMENT

You make arguments for things you want or believe every day. When you think in terms of everyday decisions, it's pretty simple. For example, you may send your friend an email like this:

> I think we should go to *<awesome new restaurant for brunch>*. *<Trusted source>* says it has amazing cheesy hashbrowns. And *<friend>* went there last week and says it's her new favorite. I also read that it sources everything locally when possible. And it's on our way to *<awesome other thing you're going to do that day>*. The only drawback is that it doesn't take reservations, so we might have to wait a while. I think it will be worth it.

Bam, you made an argument. I hope your friend says yes. I love cheesy hashbrowns.

You probably took a class in high school or college about making an argument, and you can find lots of resources about the topic. One source I really like is Toulmin's Argument Model, which suggests six components to making an argument:

- **Claim**—The statement you are asking someone to accept
- **Grounds**—The data and facts that support your claim
- **Warrant**—How the data is relevant to your claim
- **Backing**—Information that supports your warrant
- **Qualifier**—The likelihood that the data supports the warrant
- **Rebuttal**—The response to anticipated challenges to your claim

Let's apply Toulmin's Argument Model to the example intranet project. Then, take a look at **Content Strategy Tool 2.1** to put together a presentation of your own.

The Toulmin
Model of
Argumentation ▶

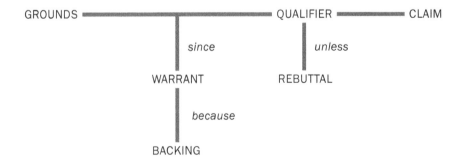

CONTENT STRATEGY TOOL 2.1

MAKING THE CASE PRESENTATION STARTER DECK

Use the presentation outline deck from the link below to provide some inspiration and get you started. I've even included a whole separate example there about why an organization should audit member communications content, structure it for reuse, and develop voice and tone guidelines to make it consistent, accessible, inclusive, and clear.

TIPS

- Every situation is different. Avoid a copy-and-paste solution. Use terms that will resonate with decision makers. You'll note that the template doesn't use a term like "warrant."

- Keep your audience and delivery method in mind. If you're presenting in person, you can use fewer words in your deck. But if it's something you'll send and not be able to defend, you'll need to provide more context.

- Be really clear about what you're asking for. If you're presenting in person, try to get a decision on the spot or ask how the decision will be made—be tenacious.

WHERE TO GET IT

Download the starter deck at www.peachpit.com/register.

WHERE IT CAME FROM

Meghan Casey (www.dobettercontent.com) and Brain Traffic (www.braintraffic.com)

CLAIM

In the intranet example, the statement you are asking someone to accept is that the organization should spend $20,000 on an information architecture project for the intranet.

GROUNDS

The data and facts that back up our claim include:

- Employees spend approximately 182,000 hours per year searching for information on the organization's intranet site. This equates to about $7.28 million in staff time per year.

- Each employee calls support for information they weren't able to find on the intranet about three times per year at about four minutes per call. This equates to $140,000 per year for call center costs and employee time spent on service calls.

WARRANT

The main reason why the data is relevant to the claim is that improvements in information architecture could save the organization:

- More than $3 million if the project results in a 50 percent decrease in staff time spent searching for information and on calls with support

- Approximately $42,000 in cost center expenditures

BACKING

Information that supports the warrant is based on analysis of employees' attitudes and behaviors in looking for information. This information was collected through an employee survey and by looking at site analytics. Key findings were that:

- 75 percent of employees reported being frustrated the last time they tried to find information on the intranet. Of those who reported frustration, 20 percent called support.

- Search log analytics suggest that employees do not use the same terms to describe topics/information as the intranet uses for navigation labels.

- Site-wide analytics suggest that employees click up to 10 times before they land on the page assumed to be the one containing the needed information, because their activity stops at that point.

QUALIFIER

You can suggest the likelihood that the data supports the warrant by referencing experts in the field and case studies of successful information architecture projects.

For example, Lisa Maria Marquis, in her book *Everyday Information Architecture* (A Book Apart, 2019), suggests user research and testing can help us identify the terms our employees use for common topics and mirror them back to our employees in our information architecture (IA). Improving the navigation labels will help employees find information and get back to work.

REBUTTAL

The likely challenge to the claim will be about budget. This is where you can lay out the budget and the risks of doing and not doing the work:

- The estimate is that it will cost about $20,000 in intranet team time to complete the IA project.

- The likelihood that the project could cut productivity and support costs by half ($3.71 million annual savings) is 75 percent.

- That means that the potential risk is only about $5,000 ($20,000 × 25%) and the potential gain is $2.755 million ($3.71 million × 75%) annually. That's a small one-time risk for a big monetary and employee satisfaction benefit that will likely last several years—even if you have to do some light rework from time to time.

THE ASK

Get specific about what you need. In this case, you're asking for a $20,000 staff resource commitment based on the estimate in **Table 2.1**:

- One IA resource for about 120 hours

- Stakeholder time of about 24 hours

Technical team for about 200 hours

READY FOR ACTION?

I think you're ready to build a case for your project. You might not convince them this time. Don't be discouraged. Change is difficult. Decision makers might not be ready to take a risk or challenge the status quo. Or other business priorities might rise to the top above your project.

But guess what? You can still make an impact by making some changes in the way you approach everyday content work. Or you can keep collecting evidence to bolster your claim and try again during the next budget cycle. Be opportunistic and sneak in content improvements wherever you can.

If you get the funding, hurray! Part II sets you up to run the project successfully.

SET UP FOR SUCCESS

For car insurance companies, the No. 1 indicator of a safe driver is how often they slam on the brakes. That's what those little thingies that Progressive puts in your car measure. For content strategy projects—well, most projects—I've learned that one of the primary indicators of success is getting the right stakeholders involved and engaging them in meaningful ways.

Ensuring that the right disciplines and departments are ready to jump in and collaborate from the beginning is equally important. The less throwing "finished" work over the wall to the next group to pick up, the better. And you know what's cool? Doing stakeholder engagement and cross-discipline collaboration well sets you up for future change.

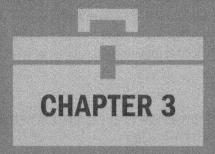

CHAPTER 3

GET STAKEHOLDERS
ON BOARD

Stakeholder involvement and alignment will make or break your project. This is true for pretty much any project an organization takes on. But it's especially true for content projects.

Why is stakeholder buy-in such a big deal for content? Because in some way almost everyone touches or shapes the content an organization creates and distributes—from setting the brand strategy, to writing technical product information and support content, to reviewing content for legal or regulatory compliance issues, to designing the documents and sites it lives in.

Content is very personal for many of your stakeholders, especially if they had a hand in creating what's out there. Changing what content to produce and how to create it sounds disruptive and scary.

The first key to getting stakeholders on board and aligned is to have empathy for where they are starting from. The second is to bring them along for the journey, rather than bestowing your expertise and recommendations upon them.

STAKEHOLDER ROLES AND TYPES

Every project has stakeholders, which I define as anyone who can affect or who is affected by your project. They aren't just decision makers and budget holders. They are people whose insights you need to craft your strategy and whose expertise and skills you need to implement the recommendations.

ROLES

Roles suggest how stakeholders are involved with the project. Let's break the roles into five types.

PROJECT OWNER

This is the person ultimately responsible for the success or failure of the project. It might be you or the person who brought you in to do the work. Usually, a project has only one project owner.

DECISION MAKERS

These are the people who have a problem your project can or should solve. They typically have a lot to say and can approve or veto your work. The budget people are sometimes part of this group. Other times, they approve the budget but don't stay involved with the work.

INFLUENCERS

These people have opinions and insights that should be considered, but they don't have approval or veto power. (Sometimes they think they do.)

CHAMPIONS

These people are your best friends. You can count on them to evangelize the importance of your project. Don't take them for granted just because they already get it. When stakeholder engagement goes well, you'll pick up a few more champions along the way!

DERAILERS

Derailers don't always have official veto power, but they can stop a project in its tracks. Sometimes, derailers are the stakeholders you didn't think to include whose insights are important or who might be affected downstream. Other times, they are the people most resistant to change… or who are skeptical of the project… or who fear that the project's priorities aren't aligned with work they are doing or want to do. (They usually aren't trying to be derailers. Empathy and compassion are important here.)

TYPES

Types are more about the opinions, insights, and information the stakeholder brings to the project. Let's break types into four categories.

STRATEGIC

Strategic stakeholders set the vision and goals for the business, operating area, or department.

EXPERT

These are the subject matter experts (SMEs) who have the detailed knowledge about an organization's products, services, offerings, and so on. Or they can be experts on a topic or in a discipline. Experts also include the people with specific knowledge of user experience, technology, and operations.

IMPLEMENTER

These are your other best friends. They are responsible for putting your strategy into action, from creating and publishing content to technology and CMS implementation.

USER PROXY

User proxies have knowledge or experience related to your target audience(s). Common examples are customer service representatives, customer experience staff, and site analytics folks.

YOUR STAKEHOLDERS

Now that you know the abstract definitions, you can focus on the real-life people who have a stake in your project.

LIST AND LABEL

With the roles and types in mind, it's time to make a list. Start by listing the departments, such as marketing, within your organization that will affect or be affected by your project. Then break them down into specific groups, such as digital marketing.

Figure out the person or people you should talk with, like Shannon Doubleday, director of content marketing, and Anthony Bauch, brand designer. If you're not sure who specifically to talk with, ask around or do some research from organizational charts or company directories.

Table 3.1 shows an example stakeholder and labels them with the roles and types they fulfill.

Once you have your list, start filling in the roles and types. I don't really like putting labels on people either, but I promise this is a helpful step. You can use the Stakeholder Matrix (see the **Content Strategy Tool 3.1**).

When you're finished, check for gaps. No derailers? Try harder. Missing expertise? Find it.

The worst-case scenario isn't talking to a few people you maybe didn't need to. It's failing to talk to ones you really, really did need to. And like I mentioned before, you might pick up some unlikely champions along the way.

TIP
One person can fit into more than one role and more than one type.

TABLE 3.1 **STAKEHOLDER ROLES AND TYPES**

Name and Title	ROLES					TYPES			
	Project Owner	Decision maker	Influencer	Champion	Derailer	Strategic	Expert	Implementer	User Proxy
Jane Doe Director, Digital Marketing		X		X		X			

CONTENT STRATEGY TOOL 3.1

STAKEHOLDER MATRIX

Download the stakeholder matrix to list and label your stakeholders, record how you'd like to get information from them, and make notes about topics, concerns, and your pitch. The matrix is also a place to note interview logistics and key takeaways from your discussions. P.S. An Airtable version is available too. Have I mentioned I love Airtable?

TIPS

- Start with a brainstorm. You can always whittle down your list if it gets too unruly.

- Avoid repeating the same topics and concerns for each person. Try to be as specific as possible for each stakeholder.

- If you're on the consultant side, use the matrix to document a conversation with your project contact about the stakeholders you'll encounter.

WHERE TO GET IT

Download the matrix at www.peachpit.com/register.

WHERE IT CAME FROM

Meghan Casey (www.dobettercontent.com) and Brain Traffic (www.braintraffic.com)

CRAFT YOUR APPROACH

Planning how you're going to work with stakeholders isn't just important for you. It's also super important for your stakeholders for a few reasons:

- You want them to see that you've taken the time to learn a bit about what they do and why it's important to the business.

- They want to know their time is being put to good use—your requests to talk or to gather information are one item on a laundry list of pressing tasks.

- Most people want to be understood and heard, and they appreciate the empathy that can come from thoughtful planning.

Chapter 6, "Understand Your Business Environment," talks more about creating a stakeholder interview guide and some best practices for conducting the interviews. At this initial step, figure out what topics you'll discuss with each stakeholder, what concerns they are likely to have about the project, and how you want to position the project to get their buy-in.

TABLE 3.2 **STAKEHOLDER DOSSIER DETAILS**

Name and Title	ROLES					TYPES				INTERVIEW METHOD		
	Project Owner	Decision maker	Influencer	Champion	Derailer	Strategic	Expert	Implementer	User Proxy	One-on-One	Interview	Workshop
Jane Doe Director, Digital Marketing		X		X		X						

Once you've thought through the details in the stakeholder matrix, think about how you'd like to engage with each stakeholder to get the information from their brain to yours. The two most common methods I use are in-person or phone interviews and workshops or working sessions.

Table 3.2 includes additional details—a *dossier* to be all fancy sounding—to help you plan for your discussions and working sessions and anticipate stakeholder concerns.

These methods are used in different ways throughout the project, and you'll dig into them more in future chapters. The following sections are a high-level summary of the interview and workshop/working session methods.

INTERVIEWS

I interview folks throughout a project for different reasons. The first interviews are more for discovery purposes to learn about the business and its offerings, business goals, pain points and challenges, and players.

Later in the project, I may need to fill in some gaps in knowledge. So I might go back to people I've talked with before or talk with some new people with specific insights or expertise.

Finally, if I'm actually creating content, I do some SME interviews to make sure I have a good handle on what I'm writing about. I like to do these interviews as a jumping-off point to creating content outlines, which I run by the experts before writing.

Topics	Concerns	Project Pitch
What topics should we cover?	*What will they be most concerned about?*	*What will sell them on the project?*
Expectations for this project: How will success be determined? *Past content efforts: What worked; what were the challenges?*	*Past efforts didn't yield the kind of results hoped for.* *How might the budget be affected next year if the project isn't successful?*	*We'll be able to focus our content efforts on fewer things that will have a bigger impact.* *We may be able to reduce headcount.*

WORKSHOPS/WORKING SESSIONS

As with interviews, you can conduct workshops and working sessions at various points in the project. Who you involve in a workshop depends on what you're trying to accomplish. The workshops and working sessions I do usually fall into one of these categories:

- Strategic—In these workshops, you're trying to understand the strategic vision of the company and how it relates to your project. The people involved are usually the decision makers on your stakeholder list.

- Content ecosystem analysis—In these workshops, you're seeking to understand such things as what the challenges and pain points that relate to the content are, who the content is for, what you want the audience to know and believe, what the audience wants to know about or expects from you, and how things will be better or different if the project is successful. Involving all stakeholder roles and types makes sense for this type of workshop.

- Tactical—Once you get into information architecture and content design, having working sessions with the people doing and implementing that work can be helpful. These sessions can help you collect the information you need in real time, get feedback on the spot, and complete the work more quickly (sometimes, but not always).

KEEPING STAKEHOLDERS IN THE LOOP

Stakeholder engagement isn't a one-time activity. If you want continued interest in and support of your project, communicate with your stakeholders regularly. I've seen what happens when you don't, and it's not pretty.

TIP   Just as your priorities shift, so do your stakeholders' priorities. You might have some who are really into your project in the beginning but seem to stop caring later on. Or you might have some who are difficult to wrangle right away but jump in later with lots of ideas and opinions.

The frequency and level of detail you communicate depend on the role the stakeholders play in your project and how much they'll be involved in completing the work. A stakeholder communications plan is a good way to keep you honest and let stakeholders know what to expect—both in terms of when they'll get updates and when you might need their input.

Think about the following for each stakeholder as you put together your communications plan (download the **Content Strategy Tool 3.2** for an example):

- On what schedule (daily, weekly, monthly, quarterly) should each stakeholder be updated?

- How often do you anticipate needing their input or feedback and at what points in the project?

- What's their appetite (or tolerance) for detail? What's the bare minimum they need to know?

- What communication vehicles are already in use that you could tap into?

- Will certain stakeholders prefer different methods of communication (email versus in-person meeting) or some focused attention to bring them along?

CONTENT STRATEGY TOOL 3.2

STAKEHOLDER COMMUNICATIONS PLAN AND TEMPLATES

Also in the Airtable samples, I've made tables for your stakeholders' communications planning and recording what you communicated when and to whom. If you are not on the Airtable train just yet, I made a Google Sheets version too.

TIPS

- Try not to over-engineer your communications plan. The last thing you want to do is add unnecessary work for you or your stakeholders.

- Communicate the most meaningful information as briefly as possible without sacrificing important details. Here's your outline:

  - What we did since the last time we updated you and why those things matter

  - What we are going to do between now and when we update you again and why that matters

  - What we anticipate needing from you between now and our next update

- Make sure you inform stakeholders how you'll communicate so they know what to expect (and even look forward to your updates).

WHERE TO GET IT

Download tables at www.peachpit.com/register.

WHERE IT CAME FROM

Meghan Casey (www.dobettercontent.com) and Jane Newman

ALL ABOARD

All right, you've identified your stakeholders and figured out how they'll be involved. You've put yourself in their shoes and started planning how you'll engage and communicate with them. Nicely done.

Next up, you'll learn how to assemble your cross-discipline team, align roles and responsibilities, and define how you'll work together. This is all-new material in this second edition of *The Content Strategy Toolkit*, and I'm so excited to share it with you. Ready?

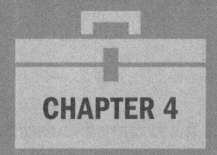

CHAPTER 4

ASSEMBLE YOUR CROSS-DISCIPLINE TEAM

Doing content well is a team effort, with expertise needed in a lot of different areas. You might have a big team of people with very specialized skills and expertise in particular disciplines. Or you might have a smaller team of people who have skills and expertise in multiple areas. Your team could be made up of all "internal" folks, or you might bring in outside experts (like me!) to round out your team.

How your team is composed is less important than making sure you have the skills and experience necessary to set and execute your strategy. In this chapter, we'll walk you through the areas of expertise you might need on your content project and how to kick off your project by aligning on who does what when and co-creating guidelines for how you'll work together.

PICK YOUR TEAM

I'm having flashbacks to elementary school gym class. Not an athletic child, I was always the last person picked when choosing teams. I didn't have the skills the captains were looking for to give them a chance to win.

But if content strategy were a sports skill, I would be picked early! Like in sports, you need to think about what skills and knowledge are needed before picking your team.

DETERMINE THE EXPERTISE YOU NEED

Not every project needs involvement from every discipline. The first step is to figure out what disciplines should be represented.

Sometimes, making this determination will be simple and straightforward. Other times, it might take a little thinking.

Table 4.1 is a list of disciplines (in no particular order) with a high-level description of what each brings to your content project and some questions to ask yourself to determine if the discipline is required for your project.

HINT *If you're working on a new website or applica-tion or fully redesigning an existing one, assume you need all the disciplines represented.*

TABLE 4.1 **DISCIPLINES**

DISCIPLINE	CONSIDERATIONS
CONTENT STRATEGY Defines why you need content in the first place.	▪ Do you know what organizational goals the content should enable you to achieve? ▪ Do you know which audiences the content is for? ▪ Do you know what content the audiences need and why they need it?
CONTENT DESIGN Specifies how the content is organized, labeled, prioritized, and displayed so it is findable, useful, and usable for the people who need it.	▪ Do you anticipate changing the way the website or a section of the website is organized? ▪ Do you need to define content requirements to guide writers and subject matter experts in creating content? ▪ Do you need to define taxonomies to relate content to other content?
BRAND Owns and articulates the look, feel, and voice of the organization.	▪ Does your brand team require you to get their approval for content, design, and so on before it's finalized? ▪ Have there been updates to your brand recently?
EDITORIAL AND AUDIO/VISUAL PRODUCTION Creates compelling, relevant written, audio, and visual content.	▪ Will you need to create, or revise, written, audio, or visual content? ▪ (This one is obvious.)
ACCESSIBILITY Ensures content follows best practices for making content usable for people experiencing situational (for example, using your website while in a loud environment that makes it difficult to hear a video) or short-/long-term (for example, hearing loss) disability.	▪ Are there known issues with accessibility you need to address with this project? ▪ What level of knowledge of accessibility best practices do you have as an organization?
USER RESEARCH AND TESTING Plans, conducts, and reports on research designed to understand users' needs and preferences.	▪ How well do you understand what your users need and want from you? ▪ Do you plan to test with real users throughout the project?

continued

DISCIPLINE	CONSIDERATIONS
USER EXPERIENCE Defines users' journeys to solve a problem or complete a task inside and outside a website, application, device, and so on.	▪ Are the user journeys on and off the site, application, device, or other product well defined? ▪ Do you have questions about how people use the website or application and how it fits into the user journey?
USER INTERFACE DESIGN Specifies how users interact with a digital product or service, including screen flows, components, navigation, buttons, gestures, links, and more.	▪ Do you anticipate or do you understand whether you will need new page types or content components or need to revise existing ones for this project? ▪ Do you plan to update the content entry forms in the CMS as part of this project?
ANALYTICS AND INSTRUMENTATION Defines mechanisms for monitoring the performance of digital product or service and provides data to inform strategy and implementation.	▪ Do you want existing data and insights about current content on the website or application? ▪ Do you want to collect data to inform insights and recommendations after launching your project?
BUSINESS ANALYSIS Collects and documents business goals and requirements.	▪ Do you have a solid understanding of the business goals that content for this project should support? ▪ Are there open questions about things like how often content is created and updated or what content is required to be published?
SEARCH INTENT AND OPTIMIZATION Analyzes search data to determine user needs, identifies user-focused language to include in content, and consults on best practices for making content findable through search engines.	▪ Do you understand what people are looking for when they search for terms related to your products or services? ▪ Do you know what words and phrases your audiences use to describe or find what you offer? ▪ Do you need direction for making your content findable by search engines?
VISUAL DESIGN Defines and documents the aesthetic (including colors, typography, imagery, link and button styles, and so on) of the website, application, device, or other product.	▪ Has your brand identity been updated recently, requiring changes to the look and feel of the website or application? ▪ Is your current visual design dated? ▪ Do you need visual design applied to new page types or components?

continued

DISCIPLINE	CONSIDERATIONS
BACK-END DEVELOPMENT Builds and connects the behind-the-scenes databases, data feeds, content entry forms, taxonomies, and so on that enable the digital product.	▪ Will you need to set up new data feeds to pull in content or information? ▪ Do you need to implement taxonomies to pull in relevant content? ▪ Do you plan to update the content entry forms in the CMS as part of this project?
FRONT-END DEVELOPMENT Programs the user interface and visual design of the website, application, device, or other product so that people can use it.	▪ Has your brand identity been updated recently, requiring changes to the look and feel of the website or application? ▪ Do you need visual design applied to new page types or components?
PROJECT MANAGEMENT Ensures the project runs as efficiently as possible and keeps the team and stakeholders informed about status, budget, risks, requests, and so on.	▪ Will there be a lot of moving pieces to manage? ▪ Is there a must-launch-by date? ▪ Are there a lot of new team members? ▪ Will you likely need to hire outside resources?
PRODUCT MANAGEMENT Owns the implementation of the website, application, or other digital product strategy, including deciding what projects happen when.	▪ Do you need the product manager's approval to implement the project? ▪ Does the product manager need to schedule resources for implementation?
CONTENT DISTRIBUTION Publishes content to the CMS, social media channels, email newsletters, and so on.	▪ Will there be changes to any of the channels used to distribute content? ▪ Do you understand what challenges people who distribute content experience today?
CHANGE MANAGEMENT Equips teams with the information and skills needed to adopt new processes, tools, technologies, and so on.	▪ Does this process represent a shift in organizational culture or understanding of content as a business asset? ▪ Will this project result in implementing new processes or technology?

MATCH EXPERTISE WITH PEOPLE

Now that you've identified the disciplines you need, you can figure out who in your organization has the relevant expertise. Sometimes you'll need help from leaders of various departments to map this out.

You're probably thinking, "Wowza, that's going to be a big team!" And you might be right, but keep in mind that there is likely some overlap between disciplines, so your content strategist may also be the user researcher and content designer. Similarly, people representing certain disciplines may collaborate with other people on your team.

In the example in **Table 4.2** (which uses one piece of **Content Strategy Tool 4.1, Roster and Responsibilities Templates**), I'm showing a few of the disciplines with people mapped to them.

TABLE 4.2 **EXAMPLE OF DISCIPLINES MAPPED TO TEAM MEMBERS**

DISCIPLINE	NEEDED?	TEAM MEMBER(S)	INTERNAL OR EXTERNAL
Content strategy	Yes	Natalie Dunbar	Internal
Content design	Yes	Natalie Dunbar (Content requirements)	Internal
		Lisa Maria Marquis (IA and taxonomy)	External
User interface design	Yes	Natalie Dunbar (content entry forms)	Internal
User research	Yes	Natalie Dunbar	Internal
Search intent and optimization	Yes	Onward	External
Editorial and audio/ visual production	Yes	Cameron Siewert (editor and writer)	Internal
		Carla Januska (graphics)	External
Back-end development	Yes	Kev Walsh	Internal
Product management	Yes	Sean Tubridy	Internal

As you can see from the example, Natalie Dunbar has expertise in multiple needed disciplines. I intentionally chose my friend Natalie because she's the author of *From Solo to Scaled: Building a Sustainable Content Strategy Practice* (Rosenfeld) and does all things content related.

Once you've identified who represents what disciplines (and where you may have gaps), you can start to flesh out project roles. To use Natalie as an example again, **Table 4.3** shows an example of an entry in a team roster (also part of **Content Strategy Tool 4.1**).

TABLE 4.3 **TEAM ROSTER EXAMPLE**

TEAM MEMBER	DESCRIPTION OF ROLE	CONTACT INFORMATION	TIME ZONE
Natalie Dunbar	▪ Define the content strategy based on internal and user research ▪ Create content requirements documents ▪ Wireframe content entry forms ▪ Manage partner relationships for content design and search	natalie@awesomeco.com + 1 123-456-7890 Slack: @natalie	PST

CONTENT STRATEGY TOOL 4.1
ROSTER AND RESPONSIBILITIES TEMPLATE

Download the template or check out the Airtable database to document your team roster, roles, responsibilities, and activities.

TIPS

▪ Modify the roster template as needed to work for your team. For example, you can include additional information in the roster about things like communication method preference and working hours.

▪ You won't be able to fill out everything right away. A lot of what will end up in your Roster and Responsibilities documentation is stuff you'll work through during your kickoff and over the course of your project.

WHERE TO GET IT

Download the audit template with instructions included at www.peachpit.com/register.

WHERE IT CAME FROM

Meghan Casey (www.dobettercontent.com)

KICK OFF YOUR PROJECT

Are you excited? I'm excited for you! It's time to pull your people together and get set up to do amazing work together. But first, you need to tell the team about the project and invite them to be awesome with you.

TIP *It's almost always better to invite someone whose expertise might not be needed than to not include them and figure out you have a big gap later. Folks tend to be quick to let you know if they don't feel their involvement will be valuable.*

I usually recommend that my clients send an email that includes the following elements as an invitation to participate in a kickoff working session:

- **Introduction.** Even if you think the invitees know who you are, it's a good idea to say what your role is in the organization. If you're a consultant leading the kickoff, work with your client to write the email and introduce you to the team.

- **Project overview.** Explain this in terms of the opportunity to solve a problem.

- **Why you need them.** Tell each person why you specifically want them involved. People want to feel important and valued.

- **Expectations.** Tell them a bit about the meeting and the kinds of ideas and input they'll be asked to contribute.

- **A big thank-you.** Recognize that this is a commitment and that you realize they are taking time away from other pressing projects and tasks. They'll appreciate it.

HINT *Consider copying each internal team member's leader on your emails so they are reminded of the ask (you've probably already communicated with them) and your colleagues can be confident what you're asking for is a-OK with their leaders.*

Here's an example of what your email might say:

Hi, Tiffany,

I'm Meghan Casey, the new product owner for www.awesomeco.com. I'm working on a project to redesign the website, including all its content.

You've been identified as the lead back-end developer for the project. Your expertise and partnership will be invaluable because you understand how the CMS was built and can provide guidance for how we might implement some improvements in the forms and workflows.

Project Overview

The purpose of the project is to make our content easier to find and easier to understand and act upon for the people who need it. Analytics over the last year suggest that people looking to buy from us aren't finding the information they need to choose a product. That's making it hard for us to meet our sales goals.

Kickoff

To get going on the project, I'm inviting everyone who will be involved to a kickoff working session. The outcome of that working session will be to align on process, roles and responsibilities, communication, and collaboration. We want your input.

I'll send an invitation separately—you can expect the meeting to be approximately three hours with a couple breaks. Thank you in advance for prioritizing this session; I know it's not the only thing on your plate. If you have questions or concerns that I can address before the meeting, let me know or contact your leader.

Best,

Meghan

PLAN YOUR KICKOFF MEETING

You've given everyone a heads-up about the project. Time to plan the kickoff! Setting the agenda comes next, but first make sure you're clear on the expected outcomes for the meeting.

Examples of outcomes include the following:

- Ensure everyone understands the project and why we're doing it.

- Align on terminology to ensure everyone is using the same words for the same things.

- Understand each person's/discipline's high-level process and milestones and where they intersect

- Co-define how we want to work together as a team.

What you include on the agenda depends on your outcomes and few other factors, such as:

- How accustomed to working together the team is

- How much time you have

- How much potential overlap in or misalignment about roles you foresee (because that can get a little sticky)

For the purposes of this book, we're going to assume that it's a team that hasn't worked together before and that you magically have three hours to kick off the project.

I recommend including the desired outcomes and a high-level agenda in your meeting invitation. (If your agenda is not ready when you send out the invitation, add it later.) The sample agenda in **Table 4.4** suggests the level of detail you might provide to participants.

TABLE 4.4 **SAMPLE KICKOFF MEETING AGENDA**

ACTIVITY	DURATION
GETTING SETTLED AND GROUND RULES We'll agree to some ground rules for the meeting to help make it as productive and efficient as possible.	10 minutes
PROJECT OVERVIEW I will provide some project background, including what problems we're trying to solve, our high-level timeline, and what we'll deliver as the result of our work.	15 minutes
INTRODUCTIONS We'll each share our name, title, and area of expertise.	30 minutes
TERMINOLOGY ALIGNMENT We'll align on definitions of concepts, disciplines, and so on. This may happen throughout the meeting as well.	20 minutes

ACTIVITY	DURATION
5-MINUTE BREAK	
PROCESS POST-UP We will map out our processes, including activities, inputs, and deliverables to identify opportunities for collaboration and handoffs between disciplines/roles.	45 minutes with a 10-minute break halfway through
10-MINUTE BREAK	
PROJECT NORMS We will do some brainstorming to co-define our ways of working.	30 minutes
WRAP UP AND NEXT STEPS We'll note any unfinished business and agree on next steps for the project.	15 minutes

The **Content Strategy Tool 4.2: Kickoff Agenda and Exercises** contains an agenda template and working session activities in collaboration tools Mural and Miro with facilitation notes to help you run your workshop. Let's walk through a few examples of the exercises to get you prepared!

CONTENT STRATEGY TOOL 4.2
KICKOFF AGENDA AND EXERCISES

Use the agenda template to summarize your working session plan and share it with your team. You may not yet have all the details of how you'll run the meeting. That's where the Miro or Mural templates come in to help.

TIPS

- Tailor your agenda to the team. For example, if your team has worked together before, you might not need to do the process post-up. Instead, you might show the process from a previous project and talk about ways you might change or improve it.

- It can be a good idea to do a smaller version of the project post-up to start each phase versus trying to do it all at once.

- Check in periodically on your team norms to provide an opportunity to recalibrate if anything has gone awry.

WHERE TO GET IT

Download the audit template with instructions included at www.peachpit.com/register.

WHERE IT CAME FROM

Meghan Casey (www.dobettercontent.com)

SPOTLIGHT ON TERMINOLOGY ALIGNMENT

Back in 2017, I wrote an article for the Brain Traffic blog (www.braintraffic.com/insights) called "Words Matter: Why Your Project Team Should be Aligned on Definitions." The introduction went like this:

> Client's design vendor: "Who is doing the information architecture?"
>
> Me: "We are."
>
> Client: "You are? I thought you didn't do CMS development."
>
> Me: "We don't. I meant the sitemap and content model framework. What do you mean by information architecture?"

Have you ever had a conversation like this? Yeah, me neither. That was totally made up.

Ahem.

We can save ourselves a lot of conflict and wheel spinning if we align on terms up front. Sometimes, this simply means coming to your kickoff session with a couple slides containing your working definitions of terms. Then, you can facilitate a discussion to align on the definitions you'll use on your project.

Other times, you might need to spend some time digging into a particular definition. On one of my recent projects, my colleague and I were tasked with doing some discovery on content operations for a large health-care company, identifying their biggest challenges and opportunities and making recommendations for how to address those challenges and opportunities.

It became clear early in the project that everyone had different definitions for *content operations*, from the vice presidents to the people who publish content. So we did an exercise to co-create a definition for the organization. (The template for this exercise is in **Content Strategy Tool 4.2.**)

To do the exercise shown in the example, follow these steps:

1 Break people into smaller groups.

   In this case, I had four groups of two people each.

2 Have each group work together to draft a definition for the term.

3 Bring everyone together and have each group share their definition and allow for discussion.

4   Combine the first two groups into one group and the second two groups into another and have those new groups work out a combined definition.

5   Bring everyone back together again to share definitions and discuss.

6   Assign one person to write a definition based on the discussion if you have time. If you don't have time, your homework will be to craft a definition to share with the group later.

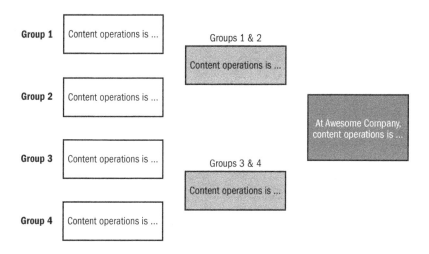

SPOTLIGHT ON PROCESS DEFINITION

On many projects, I'm brought in to work as part of a team that has different disciplines, often working in silos with little collaboration. This leads to multiple people doing the same work, stakeholders being asked to participate in multiple interviews for the same project, missed opportunities to bring together expertise to solve a problem more holistically, and team members not getting the information they need to do their work in the ways they need it.

The following exercise can help prevent those things from occurring by providing a holistic view of how people approach their work, what they need to do their work, and what is produced by the work they do. Here's an example of how this exercise helps identify how disciplines might collaborate:

Define

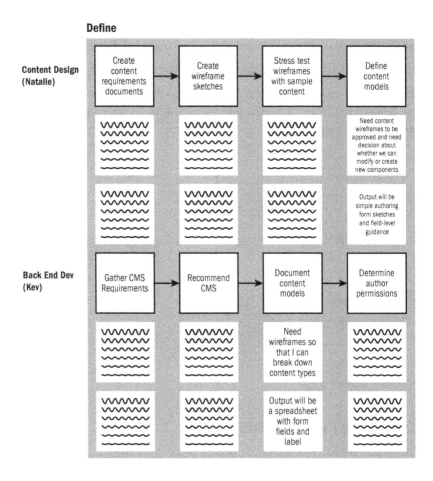

You'll note in the example that both the back-end developer and the content designer have content modeling in their process. Each has provided the following information for their "swim lane":

- *When* in the process they do content modeling

- *What* inputs they need to do content modeling

- *What* the output or artifact is that they produce when they model content

From this (simplified) example, you can see an opportunity to make this process more efficient by having the content designer and the back-end developer schedule a working session to document the content models based on the content requirements templates. Since this is a simplified example, I haven't accounted for the other disciplines that could be included in the content modeling work—namely the user interface and visual designer and the front-end developer.

This exercise helps the project manager build a realistic set of activities, milestones, and dependencies. And it helps to continue to flesh out your roles and responsibilities matrix. **Table 4.5** is an example of what that might look like based on our process post-up example.

TABLE 4.5 **ACTIVITY MATRIX SAMPLE**

ACTIVITY	O	C	U	A
Authoring form definition	NB	CS	KW	KW
Field-level authoring guidance	NB	CS	KW	CS
Content model documentation	KW	NB	KW	ST

You might notice in this example that instead of the more familiar RACI (responsible, accountable, consulted, and informed) matrix (which I find to be a bit confusing), I've replaced the letters with OCUA, something I made up because it made more sense to me. Here's what those mean:

- **O**wns—The person responsible for making the activity and associated artifacts/deliverables happen
- **C**ollaborates—The person or people who work with the owner or provide inputs into the artifacts/deliverables
- **U**ses—The person or people who rely on the artifacts/deliverables to do their work
- **A**pproves—The person who determines if the artifacts/deliverables are acceptable and done

SPOTLIGHT ON TEAM NORMS

Culture and communication have a lot to do with how well a project runs and how successful it is. I've found it extremely helpful to give people an opportunity to co-define ways of working that set up everyone for success.

The result of defining ways to work can take a few forms. Common categories of norms include communication, meetings, and principles.

Communication covers how you communicate and what kinds of things you communicate. For example:

- We use Slack for impromptu small-group collaboration or questions.
- We use Confluence to record project decisions.

- We manage tasks and deliverables in Asana.
- We use email only when we need to loop in or get feedback from a senior leader on a conversation or decision.
- We report progress monthly to the leadership team and weekly to the project team.

Meetings refers to when and why you meet throughout the project. For example:

- We kick off each phase with an in-person or remote meeting.
- We invite senior leaders to monthly demos of work in progress or completed.
- We have standups every other day. When people are unable to attend a standup, they post their progress and blockers in the standup Slack channel.

Principles define the philosophical and practical guidelines for how we work together. Examples from my previous projects include:

- **We believe that connected teams lead to connected content.**

  This means that we model collaboration, prioritize transparency, tear down silos, embrace conflict, and keep everyone in the loop.

- **We are humble experts.**

  This means we acknowledge that each of us are experts in our own right and that we are at our best when we leave our egos at the door. We embrace that smart ideas can come from anywhere and that there will never not be something to learn.

- **We consider feedback a gift.**

  This means that we provide regular opportunities to ask for and give feedback. When giving feedback, it is constructive and actionable. When receiving feedback, we are curious and prepared to contextualize the decisions that informed our work.

TIP
Michael Metts and Andy Welfle in their book Writing Is Designing: Words and the User Experience *(Rosenfeld) offer some great guidance on running critique sessions. Grab their book and check out pages 156–158.*

To arrive at team norms, I typically borrow from the well-known agile methodology concept of a retrospective. In retrospectives, teams have an opportunity to identify what worked well, what didn't work so well, and what they'd like to see happen in future sprints. Although everyone in your kickoff might not have worked together before, each person has thoughts about how projects they worked on in the past went.

This exercise can run in a few different ways. I like to keep it simple. On a digital whiteboard, I set up three columns filled with blank sticky notes:

- Things that went well on previous projects
- Things that did not go well on previous projects
- Things I'd like to see happen on this project

Fill each column with blank sticky notes—one color per column. During your kickoff, ask everyone to populate the columns with their thoughts and experiences. Then, work to group the sticky notes into themes. These themes will help you document your team norms.

As you may have guessed, there's a template for this exercise in **Content Strategy Tool 4.2**. Here's an example of an in-progress team norms exercise:

What Went Well	What Went Wrong	What I'd Like
Collaboration between visual design and UX design	Didn't have a documented content purpose	Include content strategy in UX and visual design working sessions
Comprehensive discovery phase	Didn't consider what was realistic to implement	Developers brought in earlier
Getting actionable feedback	Feedback coming from leaders at the 11th hour	Content strategist and developer collaboration on content models / Pair writing with SMEs
Had documented user journeys to guide decisions	User personas weren't helpful	Regular crits with all disciplines
Pair writing with SMEs saved time	Poorly planned sprints	

KICK OFF FOR CLARITY

When you're kicking off a content strategy project, think of yourself as a consultant (even if you're internal to the organization). One of a consultant's primary jobs is to create clarity. That's what this team kickoff session is all about.

With that in mind, it's important to think about whether you can be both the consultant or facilitator and an active participant. Most experienced facilitators will suggest that you bring someone from the outside (not necessarily outside the organization, but outside the project) in to facilitate one of these clarity-getting conversations.

It's up to you. If you feel like you will have a hard time facilitating conversation because you'll be worried that your viewpoints won't be heard and included, ask a colleague to help. If you're working with a consultant, it's probably best that they lead the meeting.

Now that we have that out of the way, you can dig into some facilitation best practices and tips. Almost everything in this section is influenced by the book *Facilitator's Guide to Participatory Decision-Making* by Sam Kaner (Jossey-Bass, 2014) or the online training "Facilitate for Freedom" from the Anti-Oppression Resource and Training Alliance (www.aorta.coop).

GROUP DECISION-MAKING

It's important to understand how group decision-making works so that you don't get discouraged when it seems as if things are falling apart—and *there will be* a time in your meeting that it seems like things are falling apart. That usually happens before a big breakthrough.

Kaner and his team coined the phrase *Diamond of Participatory Decision-Making* to explain this phenomenon (see image). It's a useful reminder of how your meeting is likely to go.

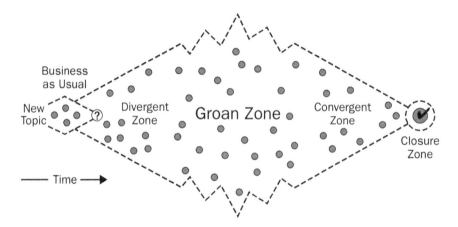

In a nutshell, this process suggests that everything will seem very messy at first. Then, you'll reach a point where there's a lot of discussion and even disagreement. At this point, it often seems as if you won't get anywhere, and that might feel frustrating. But then, the ideas will converge if you trust the process.

GROUND RULES

You might remember that I included ground rules in the example agenda. Although they may seem obvious, I find it beneficial to remind people of some simple ground rules before you get started. We wouldn't need them if they were never broken, intentionally or unintentionally. I typically start with these:

- No laptops, no phones (unless you need them to participate).

- Avoid interrupting.

- There are no bad ideas when brainstorming.

- Ask for clarification when you don't understand—it's helpful for everyone.

- Everyone talks and everyone listens.

- Avoid side conversations.

You know your culture better than I do, so you might not need all the rules on this list, and you may need others that aren't listed. You can add ground rules as you go if you notice things going awry.

> **TIP**
>
> *Let people know you will be taking breaks to ease their concerns about pressing emails or tasks that may require their immediate attention.*

FACILITATIVE LISTENING

The person facilitating the discussion is a bit like connective tissue. They are employing techniques to spur discussion, connect the dots, build on ideas, and identify agreement and disagreement.

Here are just a few of those techniques.

PARAPHRASING

Paraphrasing is all about letting the participants know that you're listening and to help reiterate their thoughts to the larger group. Paraphrase to get clarity and to ensure everyone understands what was said. Use phrases like, "I think what you're saying is . . . Is that what you meant?"

DRAWING PEOPLE OUT

Sometimes a stakeholder will have a hard time articulating their idea, which can cause them to stop trying to explain it and withdraw. The facilitator can—and should—help in these situations. Start by paraphrasing what you think they meant and then follow up with "Can you think of an example of when that happened?" or "Tell me a little more about that." It's also important to consider why someone might not feel safe to share their thoughts out loud and offer alternatives such as typing in the chat.

CONVERSATION TRACKING

We've all been in a meeting where two or more conversations are happening at the same time. Sometimes it's side conversations (which are against our ground rules!). But sometimes it's just that people are focused on different aspects of a question. All those aspects are likely important. As a facilitator, you want to listen for the various tracks and lead conversations around them. When you notice multiple conversations, you can say, "It seems we're discussing a few different things here. Let's talk about one at a time so that we don't lose anything."

PRINCIPLED DISAGREEMENT

Disagreement should be expected, not avoided. But it takes some skilled facilitation for disagreement to culminate in a positive result. To encourage principled disagreement and facilitate understanding, you can make room for conflicting perspectives without dismissing either or shutting down the conversation. Sometimes it might be more important to the success of the project to follow the conversation to a conclusion even if it means you don't get to other items on your agenda.

SILENCE

If you're like me, this silence thing is hard. It's also effective. You can use it a few ways. One is to give people a chance to collect their thoughts. Don't jump to fill the silence. Another is to slow down the conversation when something exceptional has happened—someone shares an idea that seems to blow everyone away or agreement was reached when you never thought it would be. And sometimes, people need a break. It's OK to say, "Let's sit for a minute and process what we've just discussed."

READY TO WORK

It is very unlikely you will get all the way to fully fleshed-out outcomes in your working session. Even if you don't, you'll have most of the ideas and insights you need to document roles and responsibilities, put together a project plan, and summarize how you'll work together.

Next up, we'll talk about how content strategy projects often lead to larger organizational transformations in the way organizations think about content and do content work. It can get spicy. But it's worth it!

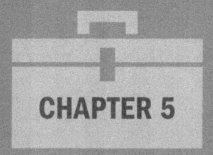

CHAPTER 5

PREPARE FOR CHANGE

Let's face it. Change can be unsettling for so many reasons. And content can be emotional and political in the healthiest of companies and organizations.

That's why it's so important to consider how to communicate and facilitate change early on in your project. Although you may not know exactly what change you'll need to manage, change is guaranteed. And the effectiveness of all your and your team's hard work hinges on successfully moving through change.

In this short yet significant chapter, we'll talk about some of the reasons why change is so difficult and an approach I've developed to plan for communicating about content transformation.

WHAT MAKES CHANGE SO HARD?

Long ago, an organization I worked for (let's call it Brain Traffic... because it was Brain Traffic) brought in a coach to teach us introverts how to sell. One thing she said that has always stuck with me is that objections to price or approach are typically needs a potential client hasn't yet named.

In my experience, objections or resistance to change can usually be tracked to unrecognized or unnamed fears. It makes sense, doesn't it? With change comes a lot of uncertainty. And uncertainty can be scary. Let's talk about the kinds of fears that might be on people's minds. (We won't be talking about mitigating these fears, but rather describing examples so that you can recognize them.)

FEAR ABOUT PRODUCTIVITY AND PERFORMANCE

Very often, but not always, content strategy and the resulting transformation means that an organization will create less content. In a world where the sheer number of things produced is a metric of success (read: capitalist), we are often measured on quantity versus impact.

As an example, teams are often asked to produce a laundry list of content assets when a new product launches. A good portion of these things are *never* used by the intended audience. But they are on the list, and the teams are evaluated on whether the things were made... not whether they were relevant or valuable.

So imagine if that's how your worth is defined and you are no longer required to make those things. Two thoughts likely go through your mind:

- "Phew, that was such a waste of time."
- "Will my role or the roles of my colleagues become obsolete?"

Very often, the results of a content strategy project offer opportunities to work on more meaningful things. That said, getting more strategic with content can result in organizational changes. And organizational changes can mean reductions in resources.

And sometimes those opportunities necessitate learning new skills and technologies or sharpening skills people haven't had a chance to use. That can also be scary.

FEAR OF BEING IGNORED

On most every project, I talk with at least one stakeholder who mentions feeling like their individual, team's, department's, or discipline's perspectives have not been considered or incorporated in a previous project. That's super frustrating.

I'd venture to say that most of us don't love to be expected to make major changes to the way we work when we don't feel like whoever is requiring these changes understands our role, our skills, our challenges, and so on. And no one I know is fond of being blindsided by changes that seem disruptive with no context or consideration.

FEAR OF UNNECESSARY UPHEAVAL

Some fears related to disrupting the status quo are absolutely valid. Some, however, should be challenged... with kindness and care.

A common issue I've seen—and frankly have probably contributed to—is over-engineering content processes. The intent is usually good, but all too often one of two things is true:

- We try to solve problems that don't exist, such as fixing things that aren't broken.

- We assume that our ideal solution will work for every team, department, distribution channel, and so on if only people would get on board.

When issues happen over and over, *change fatigue* sets in. When that happens, people are likely to find ways to subvert the solution so that they can get on with their work.

So, it's important to be mindful of the difference between resistance that is based on past experiences that didn't go so well and resistance of the "but we've always done it this way, and doing it differently sounds too hard" variety. Regardless of which end of the spectrum the resistance comes from, the fears must be acknowledged and addressed.

HINT
In Chapter 6, "Understand Your Business Environment," we will talk about ways to gather perspectives and insights from stakeholders. Asking the right questions during the discovery process will go a long way in alleviating these fears.

FEAR OF LOSING CONTROL OR BEING "FOUND OUT"

Often content transformation means establishment or rebalancing of decision-making purview. This can take a few forms.

The most common situations I've encountered for which I've made recommendations are:

- Establishing decision-making authority when previously there was none. In this situation, the current state is typically everyone doing anything and everything they want to do regarding content with no centralized strategy or oversight.

- Shifting who has decision-making authority. I've observed that ownership over content tends to ping-pong between technology and communications or marketing. Depending on which teams currently "own" content decision-making, execution priorities shift. For example, when technology owns decision-making, priorities are often about technology improvements for managing content. However, when communications or marketing "own" content decision-making, priorities seem to be more about substance and voice.

Whether new authority is established or current authority is shifted, people often fear losing autonomy to do the things they want or have been asked to do. And often those fears are related to having to tell their leaders "no" when they are asked to work on something that doesn't fit the strategy.

Another fear I've seen play out is when someone in a leadership position doesn't have the expertise or skills needed to be successful in their current or proposed role. In those cases, they may fear that the mismatch in skills will be discovered as content transformation transpires. This is certainly not a good feeling and can lead to active resistance of change.

FEAR THAT THE PROPOSED CHANGE IS UNREALISTIC OR IMPOSSIBLE

Any of this sound familiar?

"We have tried this. It does not work."

"We are too <unique, complex, large, siloed, and so on> to standardize how we approach content."

"No matter what we put on paper, people will go around the strategy to get what they want."

HINT
In Chapter 16, "Define How You'll Govern Your Content," we will talk through various approaches to strategic and implementation authority to help you decide which to consider for your organization.

"We have seven content transformation recommendation decks from seven different consulting firms in our files, and none of them have been implemented."

"We want to do things differently, but we just don't have the <technology, support, bandwidth, and so on> to make it happen."

I'm guessing you are nodding your head. These are super genuine concerns. And quite often, they relate to problems that cannot be solved.

I'm interviewing C-suite stakeholders right now for a large health-care company. While they are very supportive of defining what enterprise content strategy might look like, almost every leader has said that it's practically impossible to do. And almost every implementer agrees. The desire is there, though, so we're going to keep pushing to identify a few opportunities for transformation that will make a meaningful difference for the organization and its audiences.

AN APPROACH TO PREPARING FOR CHANGE

A couple years ago, I gave a talk at Confab: The Content Strategy Conference about having difficult conversations with colleagues. I put together a framework to help folks plan for and have those tough talks that I called the DAISY Framework (after my dog Daisy, RIP):

- Define
- Anticipate
- Introspect
- Speak
- Yield

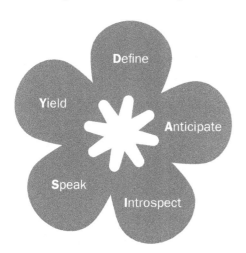

> **HINT**
> *If you're interested in my "Tough Talks and How to Have Them" presentation, you can purchase the video, slide deck, and worksheet at www.dobettercontent.com/presentations/tough-talks.*

As I was working on this chapter, it occurred to me that the approach I outlined is applicable to content transformation, too, with a few tweaks.

Let's walk through the framework and how you can use it to plan for content transformation. You may want to download **Content Strategy Tool 5.1: The DAISY Framework for Content Transformation** for a handy worksheet to record change planning details.

D IS FOR DEFINE

TIP   You can use the Iceberg Model in a variety of contexts. I reference it again in Chapter 10, "Align on a Strategic Foundation."

The first step of applying this framework is to define what's going to change. I use the concept from the webpage "Iceberg Model: Learn about the Theory and Practice of Systems Thinking" (https://ecochallenge.org/iceberg-model) to do this.

This approach helps me think through and communicate what kinds of changes are going to be happening "above the surface" that will be recognizable and actionable to the people whose ways of thinking and ways of doing will change.

Questions you'll want to answer include:

▪ What is changing?

▪ Who is affected by this change?

▪ What will team members need to do differently?

The approach also helps me formulate a narrative around the "below the surface" factors associated with the change.

Questions to think about include:

▪ Why are we making this change?

▪ How will we remove barriers to effectively making this change?

▪ What cultural shifts are needed to do things differently?

▪ What will be necessary to enable this change (for example, technology, guidelines, leadership support)?

A IS FOR ANTICIPATE

The next part of the framework is to anticipate all the things team members may be thinking, feeling, doing, or seeing related to how they work today and how that will change. I borrow from user experience design and use an empathy map to record what I know or assume.

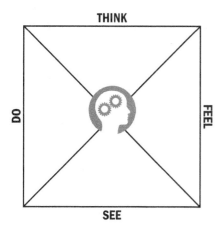

HINT

You know all those fears we talked about earlier in the chapter? Those are the kinds of things you'll want to antici- pate here.

I IS FOR INTROSPECT

I find it important to check in with myself about my attitudes and expectations related to proposed changes. That's because I know that I become frustrated about resistance or feel as though people are not listening to my opinions or expertise. That's valid.

But if we are to be effective at leading through transformation, we need to let go of our egos. So, I'll reflect on questions like these:

- What am I worried about related to this change?

- What can I do to help alleviate fears and resistance?

- Am I sure this change is needed, or do I just think things could be done differently?

- What am I prepared to change to make this successful?

S IS FOR SPEAK

I probably should change the spelling of DAISY to DAICY because *speak* refers to *communicating* the change. You should keep a few things in mind related to communicating the change.

The first is to figure out the best methods of communication, which could be different depending on the audience. For anyone who is expected to do something differently or drastically change the way they think about content work, I always recommend face-to-face (in-person or remote) meetings with teams (and sometimes with individuals). For some folks, the change is more of an FYI, and an email, Slack message, or other form of communication suffices. Video can also be a way to communicate change when you don't anticipate a lot of questions or discussion.

Once I decide how to communicate, I put together a little brief to help me prepare. The brief contains the following information that I've thought through in the previous parts of the DAISY framework:

- Meeting or communication purpose

- My mindset going into the meeting or preparing the communication

- The mindset(s) I anticipate team members to have going into the meeting or receiving the communication

- Key messages to communicate

- Desired outcomes after holding the meeting or sending the communication

- An agenda for the meeting or outline of the communication

Y IS FOR YIELD

The final piece of the framework is Yield. Yield refers to what you and your team expect as you're moving through content transformation.

There are a few ways to put this part into practice to help ensure that everyone gets what they need. I like using some sentence starters to facilitate a conversation. Example sentence starters include:

I acknowledge...

This sentence starter is a great way for you to name things you heard related to challenges and opportunities and other team members to name what might be tripping them up about the change.

For example, you as the "instigator" of change might say: *I acknowledge that making this change could put you at odds with your partners who are used to you doing what they ask.*

Or a member of your team might say: *I acknowledge that my past experiences with attempting something like this make me question whether the change will make a difference.*

I commit to...

This sentence starter can help you formulate a list of agreements to help facilitate successful implementation of proposed changes.

For example, you might say: *I commit to listening to your feedback on how this change is affecting your work and collaborating on solutions when challenges arise.*

Or a member of your team might say: *I commit to approaching this change with an open mind and sharing feedback in a constructive fashion.*

And there you have it. Did I mention that I wrote a short song about the DAISY framework to play on the ukulele?

     C   **G**
The Daisy Framework for content change...

F   **G7**
It's a great tool, though it may seem strange.

         C   **G**
You gotta define the situation, anticipate the needs,

     F   **G7**
and look inside before you fix your mouth to speak.

C   **G**
While I can't make any guarantees,

        F   **G7 G C**
you'll yield good results. Just you wait and see!

G7 C
DAI-SY!

CONTENT STRATEGY TOOL 5.1

THE DAISY FRAMEWORK FOR CONTENT TRANSFORMATION

Download the worksheet to help you think through how to communicate about change.

TIPS

- While you won't know just yet what exactly the changes will be, it's smart to start thinking about them now.

- You can fill out as many worksheets as you need... you might do one per change or any other configuration that makes sense.

WHERE TO GET IT

Download the templates at www.peachpit.com/register.

WHERE IT CAME FROM

Meghan Casey (www.dobettercontent.com)

YOU CAN'T MANAGE CHANGE

(I was singing *You Can't Hurry Love* by the Supremes when I wrote that heading.) I am not a fan of the term *change management*. Our job when transformation is required is really more like stewardship. Although you may not know all the change that will be required just yet, you're now prepared to take on the important responsibility of stewarding transformation.

Next up, we'll excavate the internal and external factors that affect your content, your audiences and what they need from you, and the current state of your content and the processes you use to make it. Let's dig in!

PART III

DIG IN AND GET THE DIRT

A successful content strategy project is rooted firmly in business goals, user needs, and realistic expectations. That's why this discovery and diagnosis phase is so important to articulate your content strategy, determine how you'll measure success, and execute it all as efficiently and effectively as possible.

You'll start by exploring the business environment and how your project fits into it. Then, you'll learn what you can about the audiences you're trying to reach. With a solid understanding of business goals and user needs, you can start to identify opportunities and gaps in your current content and processes.

All of this sets you up to align stakeholders on a strategic approach to content and set the compass to guide your work.

CHAPTER 6

UNDERSTAND YOUR BUSINESS ENVIRONMENT

I'm wrapping up a project with a client that has a very complex product architecture, especially compared with their competitors. Things that are features of competitors' products are products unto themselves with separate subscriptions. It's really confusing. And my colleague and I have asked a lot of questions to make sense of it all.

Some of the stakeholders don't understand why the folks working on the content would care . . . we have to figure out how to organize and write about the products, right? Turns out, it matters quite a lot. Oftentimes, those of us who create content or build the experiences in which content is the central focus don't get the opportunity to ask such questions. And that missed opportunity is part of the reason our websites, applications, and so on are in such rough shape.

To make strategic recommendations about content, you must understand the business. If you don't, you're more likely to recommend solutions that don't help the company achieve its business goals.

I'm not saying you need to run out and get an MBA. I am saying you need to understand (among other things) how companies or clients make and spend money; what guides those decisions; who they are trying to reach with their product, services, or offerings; how their products, services, or offerings have evolved; what requirements or constraints influence their operations; how they are perceived in the marketplace; how they are different or better than their competitors; and what outside influences have an effect on their business decisions.

Let's dig in to how you can gather, synthesize, and analyze all these things!

DEFINE THE INQUEST

So yeah, it's a little bit like an inquest or investigation. And that sounds complex and complicated and tedious. It can be. If you're on the inside, however, you're already well informed, but you need to validate and fill gaps in knowledge. If you're a consultant coming in, your learning curve is probably steeper. Either way, what fun!

I separate what I want to learn about the business into two categories: internal factors and external factors. You don't have to think of it that way, but that's how these next sections are organized. Another useful model I've found is the Business Model Canvas from Strategyzer (formerly the Business Model Generation)—see the **Content Strategy Tool 6.1** for more details.

INTERNAL FACTORS

Internal factors are what a business can realistically control. The business's decisions and actions may be influenced by something outside its control, but it ultimately has a choice in how to respond to those outside influences.

I organize internal factors into five groups: direction, offerings, customers, revenue, and expenditures. You might think about these factors differently, and that's OK. The point is to make sure you gather enough information about the business to feel confident in your content strategy recommendations.

CONTENT STRATEGY TOOL 6.1

THE BUSINESS MODEL CANVAS

Download my content-focused version of The Business Model Canvas to start pulling together information about how your company makes and spends money.

TIPS

- Stick the canvas in Miro, Mural, or a digital whiteboard tool of your choice to start gathering information as you uncover it.

- Make the template canvas your own by including additional or different information that makes sense for your project.

- Pass it around to your team and other stakeholders to fill out, and then analyze whether everyone has the same understanding of your business model.

WHERE TO GET IT

Download the canvas at www.peachpit.com/register, or download it directly from http://strategyzer.com.

WHERE IT CAME FROM

Strategyzer (http://strategyzer.com) for the base template; Meghan Casey (www.dobettercontent.com) for the content edition

DIRECTION

The Direction category is all about what the company or organization is prioritizing currently. This category has a lot of overlap with the other categories. I'm including it in the second edition because I kept adding direction as a separate category while synthesizing all my insights on projects.

- Why does the company or organization exist?

- What are the company's or organization's short- and long-term goals?

- What strategies have been defined to achieve them?

- Is there clarity about the desired objectives or outcomes for those goals and strategies?

- What projects and larger efforts are underway to help achieve short- and long-term goals?

- Does the project you're working on tie in with other projects and efforts?

- Where is the company or organization investing in hiring and capabilities?

- Does the company's budget reflect the stated strategies, goals, and desired outcomes?

TIP *For a great, easy-to-understand primer on vision, mission, goals, strategy, and objectives, head over to www.braintraffic.com/insights/what-is-strategy-and-why-should-you-care and read Kristina Halvorson's article "What Is Strategy (and Why Should You Care)?"*

OFFERINGS

The Offerings category refers to the products, services, or other commodities (such as news for a media outlet) that the company or organization offers to its customers or clients. To clarify, customers or clients include people who receive offerings at no cost or a reduced cost from a nonprofit or government organization.

- What products, services, or other commodities do you offer?

- What's the history behind each offering (for example, how long has it been available, and why did you choose to offer it)?

- What is the offering life cycle like (for example, how long is an offering available, and what determines whether to continue it)?

- What marketplace need do your offerings fill?

- How would you describe the value proposition for each of your offerings?

- How often do you create new offerings?

- How do you decide what new offerings to provide?

- What's the typical time to market (for example, how long does it take for an idea to become a reality) for your offerings?

- What goals have you set around your offerings for the next year?

CUSTOMERS

The Customers category includes people who currently use the products, services, and other commodities you offer and people who you'd like to use your offerings. Customers fall under internal and external factors (more on this later). As an internal factor, this is about who the company or organization has chosen as its target customer.

- How do you describe your target customer?
- What segments (which are typically based on demographics or other data, such as income level, geography, gender, education, dollars spent, frequency of using your service, ethnicity, and so on) do your customers fall into?
- How big are your current and prospective customer bases?
- How would you prioritize your customer segments?
- What customer problems do your offerings solve?
- How do you interact with and provide information to your current and prospective customers?
- What goals have you set for customer acquisition and retention for the next year?

REVENUE

For businesses and some nonprofit organizations, revenue comes from selling their offerings. Other nonprofits and organizations get revenue through donations, grants, association fees (which usually come with some offerings), and so on.

- How do you sell your offerings (direct to consumer, business to business, and so on)?
- Through what channels do you sell your offerings (point of purchase or service, online, telemarketing, and so on)?
- In what markets do you sell your offerings, and how do you prioritize them?
- If you sell through multiple channels, which are the most successful and which are your priority (for example, do you attract more visitors to your website versus a social media account, or is your target audience more likely to use your mobile app versus your .com site)?
- How do you prepare sales staff, associates, and so on to talk about your products?
- Do you get any post-sale revenue (royalties, service contracts, and so on)?

- What is the sales cycle like for your offerings (for example, how long does it typically take, and what steps are involved from lead to sale)?

- What do you know about why prospective customers choose (or don't choose) your offerings?

- What ratio of leads converts to a sale?

- What are your revenue goals in each sales channel for the next year?

EXPENDITURES

You must spend money to make money—or so the saying goes. That's what I'm talking about here—what investments does a company make or what costs does it incur to support selling its offerings (or to support getting funding to offer them)?

- What investments in technology, including your website, do you have planned?

- How do you make decisions about technology investments or enhancements, such as switching platforms or content management systems?

- Do you want the content strategy recommendations to fit within any technology restraints, or are you open to recommendations that might require a change in technology?

- How are sales professionals compensated?

- What are your expenditures for providing customer support (for example, do you use a call center vendor; do you maintain a knowledge center)?

- On average, how much do you spend on each customer to get the sale and provide support?

- Have you set any business goals related to expenditures for the next year?

EXTERNAL FACTORS

External factors affect the business in ways that are, for the most part, out of its control. In some cases, businesses or organizations influence these factors, just as these factors influence the business. I put them in four categories: competitors; legal, compliance, and regulations; trends and current events; and customers.

COMPETITORS

A company or organization has competitors whether they think so or not. I've had some clients tell me they are the only ones who do what they do, so they have no competition. The truth is that even if your company is truly the only one in its class, you are still competing—with companies who do similar things or for a spot at the top of a customer's go-to source of information on *topic x*.

- Who do you see as your direct competitors for your products and services?

- How are your direct competitors better or different than you?

- Why do you think your prospective customers choose your competitors over you?

- How do your competitors' talk about their products, services, and other offerings?

- What's the state of their content?

- Who is seen as an expert source of information about your industry and offerings?

- **Content Strategy Tool 6.2: Competitive Content Analysis Guidance and Template** is a new tool in this edition that gives you guidance and a template for conducting an analysis of competitors' content.

CONTENT STRATEGY TOOL 6.2

COMPETITIVE CONTENT ANALYSIS GUIDANCE AND TEMPLATE

Download the instructions and templates for recording your observations (yep, there's an Airtable version) and reporting your findings.

TIPS

- There's value in looking at direct competitors and businesses/organizations whose approach to content you admire even if they don't do what you do.

- Be clear up-front about what you will look at: their website, their social channels, their blog, or some or all of the above.

- Always include a set of opportunities or further inquiries you recommend when you report your findings.

WHERE TO GET IT

Download the interview guide at www.peachpit.com/register.

WHERE IT CAME FROM

Lots of people: Adrienne Smith (www.adrienneksmith.com), Meghan Casey (www.dobettercontent.com) with Airtable support from Jane Newman

LEGAL, COMPLIANCE, AND REGULATIONS

Most companies must follow some rules about what they can and cannot say or about what they must provide to customers. Learn about these rules up-front to avoid serious problems down the line. And building a relationship with the internal legal and compliance folks early in your project is really helpful—you'll need them later.

- What are the high-level rules about what you can and cannot say in your content?
- What accessibility, readability, or other online standards must you adhere to?
- What government laws or regulations affect what you offer and how you talk about it?
- What's the process for making sure your content is compliant with any legal or regulatory requirements?
- Are laws or policies being discussed currently by lawmakers or government agencies that could affect your current or future content?
- What trademarks, service marks, copyrights, and so on do you have, and are there guidelines for referencing them in your content?

TRENDS AND CURRENT EVENTS

Trends refer to external factors such as technological advancements, global markets, and new occurrences that affect what you offer and why people need it. A good example is that increases in digital hacking have led to the need for more secure data servers. Current events are, well, current events, such as natural disasters and elections, that affect customers' attitudes and behaviors.

- What's going on in the industry that affects or might affect your business?
- What changes in the business environment are you aware of that might affect what you offer or how you position what you offer?
- In what ways have current events, such as natural disasters, elections, celebrity news, high-profile crimes, and so on, affected your business in the past?
- What's your process for updating positioning, content, and so on if a trend or current event necessitates it?

CUSTOMERS

When you think about customers as an internal factor, you're talking about what the company or organization knows or believes about its target customer. Sometimes, that's all you'll have to go on. But if you're able, you can validate the information with user research about users' actual attitudes and behaviors. Those are the external factors that affect your project. You'll learn more about user research in Chapter 7.

- How do your prospective customers shop for or make decisions about your products and services?

- What or who influences your prospective customers' decisions about the products and services you offer?

- What do your prospective and current customers care most about in the products or services you offer?

- How do your prospective and current customers want to interact with you?

- What kind of content do your prospective and current customers expect from you?

- What is a typical customer life cycle like?

GET THE GOODS

OK, you know what information you want to learn. Now what? The two main ways to get that information are stakeholder interviews and documentation review.

INTERVIEWING STAKEHOLDERS

Use your stakeholder matrix and start setting up 30-minute to one-hour meetings with each of your stakeholders. You may be tempted to interview some people in groups to save time. I usually recommend against that approach because you may not get the most straightforward answers. Use your best judgment. You can always follow up with people later if you think they held back.

PLANNING THE INTERVIEWS

TIP

The only preparation I ever ask stakeholders to do is to make a list of any documentation they think I'd find helpful. And I never send full interview questions in advance. I don't want them to just fill them out like a survey, and I don't want them to come in with canned responses.

If you filled out your stakeholder matrix, you've made some good notes concerning what topics to talk about with each stakeholder. With those notes as a reference, send each stakeholder an email detailing what you hope to learn (at a high level) and what they should do to prepare (which is usually nothing).

The stakeholder matrix is also a great starting point for putting together a stakeholder discussion guide or checklist. I usually create a master interview guide with questions on all the topics and then chop it up for each stakeholder, depending on what makes the most sense to ask them. **Content Strategy Tool 6.3** is an example discussion guide from Kim Goodwin, author of *Designing for the Digital* Age (Wiley, 2009).

Before you jump in, consider how you want to structure the interview. The order in which you ask your questions can make a huge difference.

CONTENT STRATEGY TOOL 6.3
STAKEHOLDER INTERVIEW GUIDE

Download the interview guide as a starting point for creating your own.

TIPS

- Create a master stakeholder guide to ensure you've got all the topics and questions covered. Then, break it up for each stakeholder or groups of similar stakeholders.

- Include the goals of the interviews on all versions as a reminder for yourself and as talking points when you kick off each interview.

- Make the interview guide your own by breaking it into topics or sections, adding or subtracting questions, making notes that prompt you, or including the details about each interviewee (whatever you need for it to be useful).

WHERE TO GET IT

Download the interview guide at www.peachpit.com/register.

WHERE IT CAME FROM

Kim Goodwin, *Designing for the Digital Age* (Wiley, 2009)

STRUCTURING THE INTERVIEW

In its facilitation course, "Technology of Participation (ToP) Facilitation Methods," the Institute of Cultural Affairs recommends a technique known as the *focused conversation*. The approach helps people facilitate group conversations.

I've also found the approach helpful in planning stakeholder interviews. It's composed of four types of questions: objective, reflective, interpretive, and decisional. The first three apply more directly to stakeholder interviews. I won't cover the decisional type.

OBJECTIVE QUESTIONS

Objective questions are about revealing the facts and warming people up. They should be questions that are easy to answer. Examples include:

- What's your role at *company*?
- What do you know about this project?
- What are your team's top goals and objectives for this year?

REFLECTIVE QUESTIONS

Reflective questions are meant to elicit a more personal or emotional response from the stakeholder. They add meaning and context to the facts. Examples include:

- What's the hardest part of your job?
- What is the most important thing this project can do related to your work and the work of your team?
- What do you like and dislike about the content on the current website?

INTERPRETIVE QUESTIONS

Use interpretive questions that reveal the stakeholder's view of issues outside their role or team, such as the company at large, the industry, or the customers. Examples include:

- What do you think your customers expect from your website?
- What will this project's success mean for the company?
- What do you think will be the biggest challenges for the company related to this project?

CONDUCTING THE INTERVIEWS

I won't spend a ton of time here, but there are a few items I keep in mind or do as part of the stakeholder interview process.

First, focus on listening. Avoid trying to fill silences. Resist the urge to jump in with your own insight because you think it will make you sound smart. (I do that. Don't do that.) And avoid scurrying past a topic because at first it seems the stakeholder doesn't have much to say. Let the interviewee think. Some of the best insights come after a long silence.

Second, whenever possible, have someone along who can take fairly verbatim notes for you. Or record the conversation with a tool that provides transcripts. That's not to say you shouldn't take any of your own notes. I almost always jot down a few things that stood out to me. But it's easier to have an authentic conversation if you're not trying to write down every word and facilitate the discussion.

And finally, pay close attention when stakeholders mention something or someone you have not heard of before. I'll often hear a name mentioned repeatedly, and I immediately think *hidden stakeholder*! Or someone mentions a project that I don't think my client has any idea is happening and has a direct impact on the work I'm doing. And sometimes, someone will mention something like the 2015 digital roadmap that I have not seen or heard about.

 **TIP** *As soon as possible after each interview, write up three to five key takeaways.*

REVIEWING DOCUMENTATION

Reviewing documentation, such as strategy presentations, site analytics data, creative briefs, organizational charts, brand guidelines, or user research reports, often can seem quite aimless. Following the two-step process I've outlined can help add some structure and order to your documentation review. **Content Strategy Tool 6.4** is an Airtable database (and spreadsheet) dubbed "Insights Engine" that you can use to inventory the documents and record your insights.

CONTENT STRATEGY TOOL 6.4

INSIGHTS ENGINE

Use the Insights Engine Airtable tables or spreadsheet to document insights gathered from interviews and documentation.

TIPS

- You can set up whatever topics you want. And you may want to have two topic columns in cases where you need a subtopic for better classification.

- Write in a professional manner so that you can share the document with your client if needed or even lift notes verbatim for your deliverables.

- Make sure you call the source documents what your clients call them or refer to them by filename to avoid confusion regarding the source of an insight.

WHERE TO GET IT

Get the Airtable version or spreadsheet version at www.peachpit.com/register.

WHERE IT CAME FROM

Meghan Casey, Brain Traffic (www.braintraffic.com)

INVENTORY THE DOCUMENTS

I usually start by making a list of the documents I've received from my client and categorizing them by type. The types may vary by project but usually include these standard ones:

 TIP
I always ask my clients to send me everything they think might be relevant. I'd rather look at something and decide I don't need it rather than find out later I missed something important.

- **Strategy**—Often these are presentations that outline what the company or a department within the company is trying to achieve and the actions or projects it's pursuing to do so.

- **User information**—This includes items such as user or market research reports, usability testing data, personas, and customer demographic information.

- **Analytics**—Mostly, analytics relate to conversion rates, site visits, page views, user paths on a website or application, and so on. Additional examples include call center data and data around cost per sale.

- **People and process**—Documents I might review in this category include organizational charts and process maps for content planning, sourcing, creating, and publishing.

With those categories in mind, I have a better idea of what kind of information I can expect to glean from each document. It's also a good way to validate with your client or business partner that you have all the relevant information; seeing the spreadsheet might spark additional ideas for things you should review.

REVIEW AND RECORD

You can complete this process any way that works for you, such as creating printouts and highlighting key information. Maybe even color-code your highlights. A method I've started using is one I learned from my former colleague Emily Schmittler.

I create a spreadsheet (now usually an Airtable) with the following columns:

- **Insight**—What did I learn that was important?

- **Topic**—What is the note about? (I tend to use the categories of information described earlier in the "Define the Inquest" section.)

- **Source**—What document did I get this insight from in the inventory?

- **Source category**—What category (strategy, user information, analytics, people, or process) is the source document from?

Then, I start going through my documents, usually a category at a time, and record my insights as I go. I like this approach for a few reasons.

First, I don't have to go back to a stack of scribbled, highlighted papers to find that one bit of information I think I remember seeing. Second, I can share this document in a way that's easy for others working on the project to understand. And third, if I make an assertion in a deliverable and my client asks me where I got that information, I can find it on my spreadsheet.

Trust me, the Insights Engine will come in super handy when you're putting all you've learned and analyzed together to set up for strategic alignment. You'll be able to filter your insights to discover patterns. It'll be awesome.

OPEN FOR BUSINESS

Wow. You've learned a lot about the business—so much that your head is probably spinning. Do what you need to do to get your brain in gear for the next part of your discovery process. Sometimes, I need to walk away for a day. Sometimes, I need to immediately type up all my notes so I feel completely immersed. It's up to you.

Next, you'll find ways to learn all about the people who use the content you're strategizing about. That includes digging deeper into the insights your stakeholders already have and validating (or invalidating) what they think they know.

TIP
You can use the Insights Engine for interview takeaways and insights, especially if you plan to type them anyway. Your source is just the person you talked with. If you use the Insights Engine for recording, include another column for Source Type so you can easily separate interviews from documents if you need to.

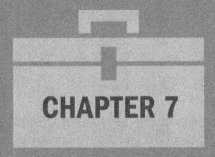

CHAPTER 7

LEARN ABOUT YOUR AUDIENCE AND USERS

So, this is cool... in the first edition of this book, I opened this chapter with:

A user-experience (UX) designer friend posted on Facebook as I was writing the intro to this chapter. She was elated because every single one of her current projects included a budget for user research. I was so jealous.

That has changed! I get to do some work to understand the users of what I'm working on these days. Maybe my clients read the book? More likely, user-centered approaches to content and design have become the standard (philosophically, anyway).

That said, it is often difficult to convince businesses and organizations to spend money on audience and user research. Sometimes, they have already made an investment in content strategy and can't find additional budget.

More commonly, the budget holders don't think it's necessary or valuable. They believe the company or organization already knows everything about their audiences and users. Or they don't think knowing more than they already do is important. (And they are usually very, very wrong.)

So this chapter is all about how to get the user insights you need with the budget you have—or more if you can make the case. It starts with documenting and communicating what you want to learn. Then you develop your approach for getting the information in as scrappy a way as needed.

WHAT YOU WANT TO KNOW AND UNDERSTAND

Documenting what you want to know and understand about the content users can help you identify the documentation and insight gaps the organization already believes it has. In addition, it gives you the foundation for developing a user-research plan that satisfies you and your client or stakeholders.

MARKET RESEARCH VS. USER RESEARCH

Make sure everyone understands the difference between user research and market research. Most organizations have some amount of market research—which is super important—but its focuses are different from user research.

MARKET RESEARCH

Market research tells you whether people in the world or country or state or city or neighborhood want to buy or need your current (or planned) products and services. It answers the questions, *"Is there a market for our product or service, and how much would people pay for it?"* Or in the case of a nonprofit organization, *"Do people need and are they interested in a service that..."*

It also gives you some demographic details—such as gender, income, family size, and ethnicity—that help companies segment their audience. For example, they may decide based on market data that single mothers making a certain income are most likely to buy what the company is selling.

All good stuff. But it's important to consider the following:

- Market research provides a macro, quantitative view derived from a large survey sample representing the entire market. Not all those people who say they might buy what you're selling are or will be users of your content (or your offering, for that matter).

- Because market research tends to come from quantitative methods, it's more focused on what people say and less on what they actually do or believe.

- Market research doesn't usually give you insights about the content you have or might create in the future as a way to persuade, convince, or otherwise influence your audience.

All these considerations are where user research comes in.

USER RESEARCH

User research is the exploration of the attitudes and beliefs, concerns, experiences, behaviors, and motivations of people who interact with your content or who you would like to interact with your content. (We'll use the word "users" as shorthand, but I've come to not like that word very much because it depersonalizes really important people.) Let's dig into each of these in more detail by examining a real-life example: finding a new dentist.

So let's say you are creating a content strategy for a recently board-certified dentist who has just opened a private practice and wants to launch a website to attract new customers (that's the business goal). The dentist is a pediatric and family dentist who picked their location after doing some market research to determine the number of families with children younger than 12 in a 10-mile radius and the number of pediatric and family dentists already practicing in the same area.

Great. A market exists for pediatric and family dentistry in their area. What about potential customers' attitudes and beliefs, concerns, experiences, behaviors, and motivations related to choosing a dentist?

ATTITUDES AND BELIEFS

Attitudes refer to what people think and feel about the offering and the people who provide it. Do parents of young and preteen children believe that their children should go to a pediatric dentist? Why or why not? Are potential customers afraid of going to the dentist? If so, why? Do the parents feel strongly about everyone in the household going to the same dentist? Why or why not?

CONCERNS

Concerns related to the provider, product, or service can cause a potential customer to worry or feel unsure. What concerns do potential customers have about dental care for themselves and their families? Do they have concerns about paying for dental care? Do they have specific dental care conditions or needs they want to make sure the dentist they choose has dealt with? Would they be concerned about going to a dentist with fewer than five years of experience? Why?

EXPERIENCES

Experiences are the interactions someone has had (or not had) with a similar provider, product, or service in the past. What positive or negative experiences have potential customers had with going to the dentist? Have they been to a dentist, or was a dentist in the past unable to address specific dental conditions or needs? How do those experiences influence what they are looking for in a new dentist? Have they taken their children to the dentist before? What were their experiences like?

BEHAVIORS

Behaviors are what people do that are related to the products and services an organization offers or plans to offer. How do potential customers typically research when looking for a new dentist? Who do they talk with before choosing a new dentist for their children? Have they switched dentists in the past because of a bad experience or other factor?

MOTIVATIONS

Motivations refer to the internal or external factors that trigger someone to seek a provider, product, or service. Are people likely to find a dentist for their family before they actually need one? Do they look for a dentist when something urgent happens, or do they already have a dentist they can call on? For what reasons do people switch dentists?

QUESTIONS AND GAPS

With the differences between market research and user research in mind, you should document what information you want to know about the audience and users. **Table 7.1** describes the components you might include in your documentation.

TABLE 7.1 **USER UNDERSTANDING MATRIX**

WE WONDER...	WE CARE BECAUSE...	WE ASSUME...
What concerns do potential customers have about dental care for themselves and their families?	We want to address these concerns effectively on the website.	Parents want to get everyone in at the same time and are worried we can't accommodate their schedules.
Are people likely to find a dentist for their family before they actually need one?	It affects whether we prioritize positioning about our philosophy and credentials versus information about getting an appointment in an emergency or on short notice.	A lot of people aren't proactive about finding a dentist.

And **Content Strategy Tool 7.1** is a version of the matrix you can download so you don't have to start from scratch. If you have a version from the first edition of the book, you should download the new one—I've added some columns since 2015.

Read on for a step-by-step approach for how to use it:

1   Start by filling out the first two columns:

In the **We wonder...** column, list the questions you'd like to answer through user research activities (which you'll propose later).

Under **We care because...**, describe why this information is important to learn or how you'll use it.

2   Call a meeting of the key stakeholders and colleagues who would have the most knowledge of what is known about users today. With them, fill out the next three columns using a rapid response, first-thoughts-that-come-to-mind approach:

In the **We assume...** column, you and your stakeholders can list their assumptions (which haven't been validated) that answer the related research question.

In the **We know...** column, you and your stakeholders should list anything that has been validated about your research question.

For the **Confidence level** column, facilitate a discussion to align on how confident you and your stakeholders or colleagues are that any assumptions you are making are true.

3   Set a meeting with anyone who needs to be convinced that conducting some user research is necessary or who makes the final decision about whether to do additional research.

We'll talk about filling out the last two columns next.

WE KNOW...	CONFIDENCE LEVEL	RISK LEVEL	RISK TOLERANCE
	Medium	Low	High
Ten people have called for emergency appointments in the first month we were open after finding us in their insurance providers' online directory.	High	Medium	Low

CONTENT STRATEGY TOOL 7.1

USER UNDERSTANDING MATRIX

Download the matrix and use it to record your user research questions and rationale for answering them so you can start a conversation with your stakeholders.

TIPS

- Approach this exercise like a brainstorming session. The questions don't have to be perfectly articulated or structured.

- I've included, with the matrix this time around, an amazing new diagram from Erika Hall that outlines the different types of user research questions, purposes, methods, and how they can inform your work every step of the way from initial ideation to ongoing improvements. It blew my mind.

- In accordance with the rules of brainstorming, avoid questioning what stakeholders assume or know.

- Continue to add information to this document as you come up with additional questions, assumptions, and knowledge.

WHERE TO GET IT

Download the matrix at www.peachpit.com/register.

WHERE IT CAME FROM

Brain Traffic (www.braintraffic.com)

As the matrix takes shape, gaps in user understanding will become apparent, which is important because you involved stakeholders in identifying the gaps instead of just telling them what is lacking. It's also your starting point for planning how you'll approach learning about the audience and users on this project. We'll get into that next.

YOUR APPROACH TO USER RESEARCH

Tough-love time. Let's face it: Most of us who do content strategy or user experience work aren't satisfied unless we get to do user research with actual users. At least, that's how I feel.

That is the best-case scenario, of course. But right now is when you need to get yourself mentally prepared to do the best you can with the budget and appetite afforded on your project.

ASSESSING APPETITE

Your client's or stakeholders' appetite for user research comes down to an assessment of their level of confidence in what they assume or know and their tolerance for risk. That's where the final two columns of the User Understanding Matrix come in.

In your meeting, pull out the User Understanding Matrix and walk through what you've documented, including the confidence level you arrived at in the previous meeting. Facilitate a discussion about the risks associated with not validating what you think you know and the tolerance for taking those risks.

Ask your clients or stakeholders if they agree with the level of confidence assessment in your matrix of the rest of the team about what they assume or think they know. Then, let them know your point of view on the level of risk related to not validating the assumptions or seeking answers to questions. And finally, probe into how comfortable they are with the consequences of those assumptions being wrong. Give them time to discuss and process on their own without interjecting. There will be some silence. And there may be some heated discussions. That's good.

When the discussion has died down, ask them to identify where they best fit in the risk tolerance/confidence level matrix for each item in your matrix. I recommend starting with the highest-risk items as shown in the image on the next page.

From there, you can put together a user understanding approach that meets their needs. The options or combinations of options in that approach include reviewing what they already have (for example, market research and site analytics), pulling opinions and insights out of the stakeholders' brains, and talking with or observing actual users "in the wild."

<table>
<tr><td>I AM NOT VERY CONFIDENT IN OUR USER KNOWLEDGE, AND I'M NOT THAT WORRIED ABOUT WHAT WE DON'T KNOW.</td><td>I AM PRETTY CONFIDENT IN WHAT WE KNOW ABOUT USERS, AND I DON'T THINK THE GAPS ARE A BIG DEAL.</td></tr>
<tr><td>I'M NOT SURE WHETHER WE KNOW VERY MUCH ABOUT OUR USERS, AND I'M UNCOMFORTABLE NOT KNOWING MORE.</td><td>I FEEL PRETTY GOOD ABOUT WHAT WE KNOW ABOUT OUR USERS, BUT I'D FEEL BETTER IF WE VALIDATED IT.</td></tr>
</table>

RISK TOLERANCE

CONFIDENCE LEVEL

PROPOSING AN APPROACH

Start to build your recommended approach based on their assessment of confidence and risk, the gaps in knowledge you've identified as a group, and your perception of how much time and money they are willing to spend.

Generally, I propose at least a documentation review of current market or user research and a stakeholder workshop targeted toward understanding internal perspectives on users' context and content needs. In cases where risk tolerance and level of confidence are low, I always recommend you research with actual users.

If risk tolerance is low and confidence is high, or risk tolerance is high and confidence is low, I go with my instincts about budget, gaps, and my confidence in making good recommendations with or without research with actual users. There's no one right solution except that you should answer as many of your outlined questions as completely as you can.

Have a conversation about your approach before putting anything in writing (if something in writing is necessary). Start with the best-case scenario but have a scaled version in mind. Avoid the temptation to offer the scaled version at the first sign of resistance. Because you've worked with them to figure out how they feel about their assumptions and risk-aversion level, your approach should be pretty spot on.

> **TIP** *Gauging what you'll need for user research is difficult until you dig into the discovery phase. I always include a bucket of time/money in my original proposal. And then I revisit it at this phase so that I can have a conversation about how I'll use the hours/funds and whether I want to ask for more.*

Once you've agreed on the approach—whether it was your original proposal or a negotiated scaled version—you can document it formally if you need to. Usually, I've been able to use an outline similar to the one in **Table 7.2** via email or in a proposal or change order.

TABLE 7.2 **SAMPLE USER RESEARCH PROPOSAL**

ACTIVITY	EFFORT/COST
Call center data review: We will review one year's worth of call center logs to understand common customer service needs.	$### (# hours × $rate)
Stakeholder workshop: We will facilitate a half-day user-focused workshop session to document current knowledge and assumptions about users and map content to the customer life cycle.	$flat_fee
User interviews: We will conduct user interviews with up to six users to validate assumptions documented through the market research review and stakeholder workshop.	$### (# hours × $rate)

DOING THE RESEARCH

The methods you're able to use for your project depend on your client's or stakeholders' appetite for user research activities and user research costs (in hours and budget). You can learn valuable information and get some useful insights without talking to real users.

Just make sure your client or stakeholders know that your informed assumptions will have to do. Don't forget to explain that making assumptions also poses a risk that your content won't meet users' needs. And content that doesn't meet users' needs is less likely to positively affect the bottom line.

For example, you might assume that the most important issue a potential customer considers is your product's price. So, you'd likely prioritize messaging about price in your content. If, in fact, convenience is more important to your audience, you might miss an opportunity to provide content focused on what your users care about most.

DOCUMENTATION AND ANALYTICS REVIEW

Get out or pull up your Insights Engine (Content Strategy Tool 6.4) for this task. The tool contains columns for insights, topics, sources, and source categories. I've applied those more specifically to users here:

- **Insight**—What important thing did I learn about users?

- **Topic**—What topic is the insight about? I use the categories discussed earlier in this chapter (attitudes and beliefs, concerns, experiences, behaviors, and motivations). You'll probably want a general one for demographic information as well.

- **Source**—What document or other source did I get this insight from in the inventory? Examples here might include market research report, audience segmentation strategy, user research summary (if they've done some before), personas, user scenarios, or site analytics.

- **Source category**—What category (strategy, user information, analytics, people, or process) is the source document from?

I usually create a separate sheet for reviewing user research-related documentation and include a few more items. First, I add a column for research questions (for example, which of my questions about users does this insight answer or inform?).

Then, I add two columns I can mark with an X for whether I feel my insight is an assumption or knowledge. For example, I might learn from site analytics that most people who visit a dentist's website click the About Us tab within a few seconds. I might assume from that bit of data that people are very interested in information about the dentist. (We'll come back to that.)

Once you've gone through the documentation, you have a great starting point for setting up your research with real users—if your budget allows it. And your list of assumptions and actual knowledge might just be what you need to convince your client or stakeholders that more user research is needed.

STAKEHOLDER WORKSHOP

You can use some collaborative activities to understand what your stakeholders know and assume about their audience and users. When you hold one of these sessions, get your participants warmed up and ready to participate.

One of the ways I like to do that is to ask everyone to share a recent experience using a website and talk about ways they were frustrated, just satisfied, or delighted. Then, you can jump in to some other activities that require that they put themselves in their users' shoes... or minds.

I plan these activities to build upon each other, which creates some continuity in the session so that participants don't feel they are doing a series of random things. A typical set of activities includes the following:

Trigger brainstorm—Ask stakeholders to spend a couple minutes brainstorming by themselves all the reasons a user might visit their website, use their app, or interact with their content in some other way. Each person writes their ideas on a note. Then, one at a time, they read their notes and put them on the wall. As each person takes a turn, I ask them to start grouping the triggers into categories.

Name the user—Here, we're trying to put a human face on the categories of triggers. First, I ask them to stand up and make sure they feel comfortable with the categories they've formed. Next, I ask them to come up with a label for the category, like *loyal customer* or *casual visitor*, and give that person a name. So, they end up with something like Casual Visitor Veronica. Finally, I ask them to collectively put the labeled and named users in order by priority to the business.

HINT *The stakeholder workshop serves a dual purpose. Once you've created the user stories, you'll start to map what content users need during their journey. More on those activities in Chapter 8.*

User stories—With this activity, your participants will create reality-based scenarios that their users might actually experience. I have people work in pairs or threes, each group taking one of the users identified in the previous exercise. Using a worksheet I provide (included in **Content Strategy Tool 7.2**), they write a story or scenario based on a literary pattern called A Hero's Journey (shown in the image on the next page), described by Joseph Campbell in his book

The Hero with a Thousand Faces. (I got this idea from a friend and former colleague, Matt Edwards.) As they write their scenario, they also record thoughts on what the user is thinking, feeling, seeing, and doing along the way. Then, they share their stories; they are often quite funny and extremely informative because they shed light on your stakeholders' assumptions about users' attitudes, behaviors, and experiences.

The resulting user stories, combined with what I learned from existing documentation and analytics, give me a lot to go on. User stories generated by internal stakeholders are not foolproof, but they give me something to work with. And if I am able to conduct research with actual people, I can refine it based on those findings.

RESEARCH WITH ACTUAL USERS

I really hope you get to do some real user research to validate and expand upon the insights you've already gathered. The saying "Nothing for us without us," coined by South African disability activists Michael Masutha and William Rowland is extremely important here. We're not talking with people so we can bestow on them something we created separately from them. It's acknowledging that the people we are designing for understand what they need better than we do and that the best way to meet those needs is to learn directly from them.

Some great user research resources go into much more detail than I'm going into here. One is *Observing the User Experience: A Practitioner's Guide to User Research* (2nd edition), by Elizabeth Goodman, Mike Kuniavsky, and Andrea Moed. Another is the User Research Basics section at www.usability.gov. And one of my all-time faves: *Just Enough Research* (2nd edition) by Erika Hall.

Before you jump in headfirst, spend some time thinking about the kind of people you want to talk with. For example, for our dentist client, you might want to recruit parents who have looked for and chosen a new pediatric and family dentist in the past six months so that the experience is fresh in their minds.

CONTENT STRATEGY TOOL 7.2

USER UNDERSTANDING WORKSHOP ACTIVITIES

Download the sample workshop plan to get more specific instructions for conducting the workshop described in this chapter's templates (including a Mural board for remote workshopping).

TIPS

- Keep a list of tasks that internal stakeholders assume people come to your site or app to do. It will come in handy later.

- During the user story exercise, listen in on participants' conversations to get even more insights that might not make it into their worksheet.

WHERE TO GET IT

Download the workshop plan at www.peachpit.com/register.

WHERE IT CAME FROM

Brain Traffic (www.braintraffic.com)

Now you can choose your research methods. I find two methods particularly helpful at this point in the project:

- **Interviews**—User interviews are similar to stakeholder interviews, and you can use much of the information about structuring and conducting the interviews from Chapter 6 to get ready. Ask questions that address attitudes and beliefs, concerns, experiences, behaviors, and motivations, as discussed earlier in this chapter. Whenever possible, conduct the interviews in person or on video so that you can observe facial expressions and body language for added context.

- **Observation**—Observation involves asking participants to visit a website or use an application while you watch. Ask them to talk you through what they're thinking and doing. Using the dentist example, you might visit another dentist's website and ask the user to walk you through what they would do on the site if they were researching dentists for their family or looking for a dentist in an emergency. Remember a little earlier when we discussed assumptions based on site analytics? Here's where you can validate them. In the previous example, you assumed that users clicked About Us because they wanted to learn more about the dentist. But maybe, instead, participants might say they clicked there because they assumed that's where the contact information would be and they needed to find it fast.

🔧 *TIP Remember that you don't need to talk with many people to get valuable insights. Three to five from each priority audience is all you really need.*

After you've completed your user research, go back to your User Understanding Matrix and fill in what you've learned. Be sure to include any new assumptions that arose from the research too.

NICE TO KNOW YOU, USERS

Do you realize how set up you are for making smart content strategy recommendations after all this user research work? I'm excited for you. Really, I am. I hope you are, too.

The next chapter talks about how you take your business and user insights into evaluating the current state of your content. The kind of assessment you can do now goes far beyond counting how many pages you have to knowing how well your content supports your business goals and satisfies users' needs.

CHAPTER 8

GET FAMILIAR WITH YOUR CONTENT

This is the time when you answer the question "What in the world is going on with our content today?" It may seem like this doesn't matter much because your strategy will tell you what to do with that content.

Although I don't think you need to know every single detail about every individual piece of content, to bring your content strategy to life when the time comes you do need to get a sense of what content exists today, why it was created, who created it, who is responsible for it, how it is structured, and where it's stored.

THE CONTENT ECOSYSTEM

In the first edition of this book, this section was called the "The Content Landscape." I have broadened the description based on the work of my friend and former colleague Scott Kubie. One of the key differences between the content landscape and the content ecosystem is that the ecosystem includes the places and channels (for example, websites, applications, social media, newsletters) where our audiences experience our content *and* the databases where content is stored and how it is accessed so that it can be delivered or displayed on or through those channels.

For example, let's say your company sends out a monthly email that is a roundup of the most popular blog posts published in the previous month. It's important to know that the monthly email is a content thing you do *and* it's important to know how it becomes the content thing you do. Some questions your ecosystem documentation should answer include the following:

- How is popularity determined?

- What information related to each blog post is included in the email (for example, title, author, summary)?

- Is the blog post structured in such a way for a person or machine to easily pull out the information to be included in the newsletter?

- Does someone manually put together the list of blog posts or is it automated?

- If it's automated, is it possible to modify the email if you'd like to remove or add a blog post?

Documenting and understanding the entire ecosystem of content is important for several reasons. Here are two big ones:

- You or your clients may not even know about all the places where the content lives. I once worked on a project in which my client told me they had three websites. They actually had 17, and they all contained different versions of their product information.

- The content ecosystem helps tell the story of the role that content plays within the organization and how mature the organization is in managing its content. Knowing whether content is considered a strategic business asset or an afterthought *or* whether there is a strong technology infrastructure or a flailing platform held together by metaphorical duct tape can help you ensure that your content strategy and recommendations are appropriate and realistic.

Let's document it!

STEP 1: MAKE A LIST

Your first step is to list all the content properties and types relevant to your project. Depending on the scope of your project, your list could be short or very, very long. **Table 8.1** provides some example project scopes and content that might be part of the ecosystem for each.

HINT *A content type in this context is content you publish in a specific format or with a specific purpose. Examples include product details, a how-to guide, a Facebook event, and an article.*

Typically, my initial list comes from stakeholder interviews. They will bring up web properties my client hadn't mentioned. I commonly hear about websites or blogs created on a whim once upon a time and never kept up to date. So when someone mentions a place where project-related content might live, write it down and get as much information about its purpose, history, status, and ownership as you can.

Next, poke around the content you knew about when you started the project. You can do this simultaneously with stakeholder interviews. But wait until after the interviews, when you'll have a bit more information to help put the content into context.

I almost always find links to or web addresses for additional websites, references to mobile applications, or calls to action to visit social media accounts I didn't know existed. More often than not, my client contact didn't know they existed either. And keep in mind that these surprise content properties and types can pop up on offline items, such as packaging, print collateral, signage, and technical documentation.

Add them all to the list. Then, you can follow up with stakeholders or do more digging if needed to find out the pertinent details (purpose, history, status, ownership, relationships, and so on).

TIP *Take Scott Kubie's advice and avoid overthinking as you pull together your list. Your goal is to be as accurate as possible, not perfect.*

TABLE 8.1 **PROJECT SCOPE EXAMPLES**

SCOPE	EXAMPLE	CONTENT TO CONSIDER
Enterprise—A project in which you are developing a content strategy for all the content the organization creates, curates, and solicits for and from all external audiences for all relevant purposes, such as sales, marketing, and customer support	Financial services organization—Sells its products through a network of advisers and needs a content strategy that encompasses content for sales, marketing, and customer support	▪ Sales presentations ▪ Customer support knowledge center ▪ Brochures and other collateral ▪ White papers ▪ Webpage content across all external-facing properties ▪ Client publications ▪ Transactional emails ▪ RFP (request for proposal) responses ▪ Mobile applications ▪ Point-of-sale signage ▪ Packaging ▪ Social media
Function, Audience, or Purpose—A project in which you are developing a content strategy for content created, curated, or solicited by a specific function (marketing, HR, customer support, and so on), in support of a specific purpose, and/or for a specific audience (internal, external, prospect, current customer, and so on)	Regional grocery store brand—Needs a content strategy that encompasses its marketing content for customers and prospective customers in all channels that marketing controls	▪ Promotional content on the company website ▪ Promotional content on store websites ▪ Social media content ▪ Promotional in-store signage ▪ Store circular creative
Property—A project in which you're developing a content strategy for a specific website, application, publication, or other singular channel	Private college—Needs a content strategy that encompasses the content it creates, curates, and solicits on its primary .edu website	▪ Content on the primary .edu site ▪ Content on other website properties the site links to or that link to the primary .edu site ▪ Social media content that drives to the website or to which the website drives
Parcel—A project in which you're developing a content strategy for a section of a web property, application, publication, or other singular channel	Merchant—Needs a content strategy for corporate and user-generated customer help content on a primary website	▪ Company-produced content on the website ▪ User-generated content on the website ▪ Support-related social media content ▪ Support content that lives in other places

STEP 2: DOCUMENT THE DETAILS

As I'm making my list, I use a spreadsheet (such as **Table 8.2**) or Airtable database to document what I learn. This file will be a valuable artifact for you and your client or stakeholders as you move through the project.

Some of the information I record includes:

- Name, such as *main site*

- Location, such as *www.mainsite.com*

- History, such as *was created during merger to satisfy legal requirements*

- Owner, such as *owned by marketing department*

- Technology, such as *built on the Contentful CMS*

- Relationships, such as *product details are automatically pulled in from our PDM (product data management) system, and there is little flexibility in how they can be displayed*

- Status, such as *still serves as main marketing channel for prospects*

- Audience, such as *prospective clients*

- Purpose, such as *help potential clients get familiar with our products and services before they contact us*

- Traffic or usage, such as *gets 1,230 unique visits per month.*

You might also want to specify whether you'll analyze the newly discovered content in more detail as part of this project. I almost always include notes about my early thoughts and questions on whether the property or content should stay in its current place or form, evolve, become part of something else, or go away completely.

Content Strategy Tool 8.1 is a detailed guide and spreadsheet/Airtable database for documenting the content ecosystem. Here's what it might look like.

CONTENT STRATEGY TOOL 8.1

CONTENT ECOSYSTEM MAPPING GUIDE

Download the guide and spreadsheet/Airtable template to document your content properties and types and relevant details about them.

TIPS

- Some of the stuff in Scott's guide is more relevant to the next chapter on content processes. Feel free to start documenting it now.

- Include everything you think might be relevant (rather than leave something off).

- Modify the information you include to match your project needs.

- You might find content that no one knows anything about, which makes you a hero in my book. If you found it, their audiences might, too.

WHERE TO GET IT

Download the spreadsheet at www.peachpit.com/register.

WHERE IT CAME FROM

Scott Kubie (www.kubie.com) & Meghan Casey (www.dobettercontent.com)

TABLE 8.2 **CONTENT ECOSYSTEM**

ID	NAME	LOCATION	HISTORY	OWNER	TECHNOLOGY	RELATIONSHIPS	
1	Main site	www.mainsite.com	Was created during merger to satisfy legal requirements	*Owned by the* marketing *department*	Built on Contentful	Product details are automatically pulled in from our PDM (product data management) system, and there is little flexibility in how they can be displayed	
2	Mobile website	m.mainsite.com	Was created because salespeople wanted to be able to look up some information about products on their phones and wanted some content on the main site to be accessible on mobile devices Marketing wanted some content on the main site to be accessible on mobile devices	*Owned by the* marketing *department*	Hard-coded	Developers use the PDM as the source and hard-code the needed information	

VISUALIZE THE ECOSYSTEM

Once you've documented the information that helps put all the content into context, create a "map" of the content ecosystem. The visualization is a way to sum up key information about the content, such as where it lives, how it's linked together, who it's for, who owns it, its place along the customer journey, how much traffic it gets, and what properties/channels are in scope or under consideration for your project.

Documenting all those details in one visual can get a bit complicated. So, pick the items that make the most sense to visualize for your purposes and include notes about the rest. You can do that easily using the IDs you included in your content landscape list.

✎ **HINT** *You may need multiple versions for different stakeholders. For example, the head of marketing might care about different details than the head of technology does.*

STATUS	AUDIENCE	PURPOSE	TRAFFIC	INCL. IN ANALYSIS	NOTES
Still serves as main marketing channel for prospects; a project is underway to make it responsive for mobile access	Prospective clients	Help prospective clients get familiar with our products and services before they contact us	Gets 1,230 unique visits per month	Yes	Recommend exploring whether it's possible to present product details from the PDM in more user-friendly ways.
Sales team has a separate sales support app now, but the site is still accessible to anyone online and it's not kept up to date Not kept up to date as information changes on main site	Sales team	Help sales reps talk about our products and services with potential clients	Gets 400 unique visitors per month	Yes	Since sales doesn't use the mobile site anymore, data suggests potential customers do. New site should be responsive rather than having a separate mobile property with product details that have to be entered and updated manually.

Here's an example of an ecosystem diagram that's focused on the outward-facing aspects of the organization's content properties and types:

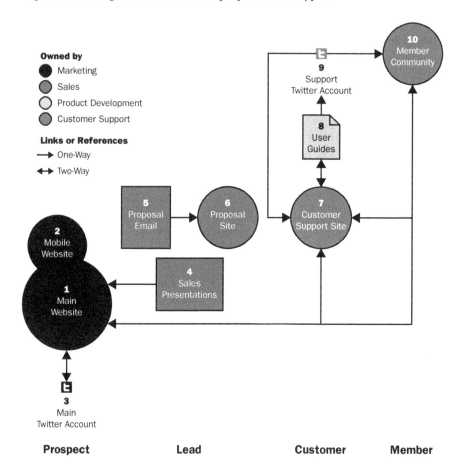

Prospect   Lead   Customer   Member

TIP
In your notes, try to avoid language that makes judgments about the content properties or types, even if you have st-hem.

Here are examples of notes, observations, or considerations you want to communicate to your stakeholders:

1 **Main website**—The primary marketing channel, which houses a lead-generation form that forwards inquiries to sales. Product information is pulled in from the PDM.

2 **Mobile website**—Contains a subset of content from the main website. This was primarily used by sales, but data suggests prospects use it too. It does not include the lead-generation form.

3 **Main Twitter account**—Used primarily to share opinions on recent events, studies, and so on that impact the industry, to drive awareness of offerings with prospects.

4 **Sales presentations**—Sales does not have a standard presentation or a reliable single source of truth for customer-centric language about products.

5 **Proposal email**—Each salesperson has created their own email template. These email templates are not stored centrally.

6 **Proposal site**—Sales reps can upload their proposals to a password-protected site that mimics a customized site for potential customers to review their proposals.

7 **Customer support site**—Public site customers can use this site for basic support questions and find user guides and other details about products. This site must be updated manually every time a change is made to user guides and other support content.

8 **User guides**—Guides are included as a hard copy with the products and are accessible online through the customer support site.

9 **Support Twitter account**—Customers can tweet at the support Twitter account if they need product help. One person monitors the Twitter account and follows up as appropriate. There is no library of common questions and answers. However, some support team members have created their own.

10 **Member community**—Site for customers who join the loyalty program. It has a message board where customers can discuss best practices (which are then manually curated into a knowledge base).

CONTENT SNAPSHOTS

OK, you now know—or mostly know—what makes up your content landscape. Let's get to analyzing, which I like to think of as taking snapshots of more specific aspects of your content.

Remember back in Chapter 1, "Identify Problems and Opportunities," when I talked about writing down your research questions before you look at what's going on with your content? You'll need to do that again. Here are some of the questions you'll likely want to answer:

- How much content is there?

- What content is in what places?

- What is the content about?

- Who is the content for?
- Does the content answer the questions users are likely to have throughout the customer life cycle and/or sales funnel?
- How does the content make users feel?
- What is the intended purpose?
- How is content connected to other content?
- Is the content clear, usable, and readable?
- Does the content contain a compelling call to action or next step?
- Is the content easy to find by users?
- Can search engines find the content?
- Is the content organized in a way that makes sense to the user?
- How is the content structured?
- Is the content relevant to users' needs?
- Is the content up to date and accurate?
- Who is responsible for the content?

That's a lot of questions. You might have to prioritize the questions you answer and/or scale the depth of your analysis based on your timeline, resource availability, and budget.

TABLE 8.3 **SAMPLE WEBSITE INVENTORY**

ID	NAME	URL	REFERENCES/LINKS TO	USAGE	
0.0	Home	www.confabevents.com	▪ Confab Central page ▪ Confab Intensive page ▪ Confab Higher Ed page	7 billion visits per month	
1.1	Confab Central	www.confabevents.com/events/central	▪ Speakers page ▪ Program page ▪ Venue page ▪ Registration page	4 billion visits per month	
1.1.1	Confab Central: Speakers	www.confabevents.com/events/central/speakers	▪ Registration page ▪ Convince your boss page ▪ Talk pages ▪ Speaker Twitter pages	3.5 billion visits per month	

I can't tell you precisely what to prioritize or how to decide, because that's influenced by your business and project goals. I can provide methods and tools for learning about the current state of your content once you know what answers you need.

INVENTORIES

Content inventories—which are like lists of all the content you have or are considering for your project—are best for answering quantitative and objective questions, like these:

- How much content is there?
- What content is in what places?
- How is content connected to other content?
- How is the content structured and stored?
- How much traffic does the content get?
- Can search engines find the content?

So how do you get answers to those questions? It usually involves a combination of automated and manual tasks. The output can be a spreadsheet (or Airtable) with columns for the data you're collecting. Start with the information you can automate, and then add columns for the stuff you'll record manually. It might look something like the spreadsheet shown in **Table 8.3**.

STRUCTURE	SEARCH ENGINE OPTIMIZATION (SEO): TITLE	SEO: DESCRIPTION	SEO: H1 TAGS
Headline, intro text, image, and text block for each event	Home: Confab Events	Content Strategy: Mission Critical. Confab is the world's best content strategy conference. Improve your work. Find your people. Expand your universe.	Content Strategy: Mission Critical
Event title + date and location line. Event detail tabs, Headline, Intro text, Image and sub-page titles (4)	Central: Confab Events	Confab Central is the world's premier content strategy conference. It takes place each year in Minneapolis, Minnesota.	Content strategy's biggest event
Event title + date and location line. Event details tabs, Headline, Intro text, Button links, Speaker photo, Speaker name + Title + Twitter handle + Linked talk titles	Speakers - Confab Events	Check out the smart folks who will be presenting talks at Confab Central.	Speakers

You can structure your spreadsheet (or Airtable) in a number of ways, depending on how you want to analyze the data. If you want a big picture representing all properties and pieces, put everything in one sheet and include columns that distinguish between a website or a piece of collateral, for instance. If you're going to analyze each type of content or property separately, it might be easier to put each property (such as a website or application) or content type (such as brochures) in a separate sheet. But filters can be used in either scenario to look at a subset of the larger list.

WEBSITES

TIP

If your site contains 500 or fewer pages, you can probably look at every page to understand structure, SEO information, related content, and so on. If your site is larger than that, run a crawler program to do most of that work for you.

If you're looking at a website, you should be able to get a list of all the URLs from your content management system (CMS), your analytics tool, or a site crawler (I use Screaming Frog). The data you can get depends on what tools you use. For example:

■ Your CMS might be able to spit out a list of pages based on the hierarchy of your sitemap.

■ You can use many free and paid options for site crawlers that provide different information. For example, some tools grab all the SEO information (page title, meta description, h1 tags, and so on) and can identify broken links, orphan pages, accessibility issues, and more.

■ Your analytics tool might be able to pull a URL list with traffic numbers or other data.

Since no one tool likely does everything you need, you might have to manually record some information. Even if it does, I find it valuable to do some manual work to aid in my own understanding of the content. Examples include following links from a page on your site to other pages, websites, applications, and PDFs, and documenting the structure of your pages (main content, image, supporting content, and so on) whether or not that structure is built into your CMS templates.

PRINT

You might be able to automate the process of creating inventories for offline content too. Find out if your organization maintains a collateral library or uses a print-on-demand service that manages a catalog of print pieces before you try to find and record them on your own.

If you have to record them on your own, start by asking stakeholders what print collateral they produce or own. Then, categorize them in meaningful ways, such as audience, product, sales cycle stage, industry, and location.

APPS

I haven't found a good tool to inventory all the content within an application. Hopefully, you have a map or diagram showing all the screens and scenarios. But if you want to get a good sense of what content it included, you'll likely have to walk through all the screens and scenarios and record what you find. Ask for a test account and dive in.

CONTENT AUDITS

Content audits are best for answering more qualitative or subjective questions like:

- What is the content about?

- Who is the content for?

- What is the intended purpose?

- Is the content clear, usable, and readable?

- Does the content contain a compelling call to action or next step?

- Is the content up to date and accurate?

- Who is responsible for the content?

OK, so those last two could be considered objective questions, but I included them here anyway. Determining the answers likely involves a person who is familiar with the context of both the content and the organization.

Back in Chapter 1, I talked about content audits as a way to figure out what's wrong with your content. You're doing the same thing here, but perhaps on a larger scale, in more detail, or with a different set of criteria. (If you did a large-scale, detailed audit at the beginning of your project, you just might be finished with this part.)

The first step is still to define the attributes you'll assess, what questions those attributes relate to, and what you'll look for to make your assessment. **Table 8.4** shows the example from Chapter 1 with some different attributes.

You're probably wondering if you need to audit every single page of your site. The answer is either "maybe" or "probably not." (I know, crystal clear.) So how do you decide? Consider the following:

- Can you get help? Perhaps content owners audit their own pages or sections.

- How much time do you have? Think about how much you can realistically do in the timeframe you have, especially if auditing won't be your primary job during that time.

TIP

Don't forget to get a list of error messages used on your websites and applications. Whenever possible, try to replicate the situations when they occur to understand the context.

HINT

Download Content Strategy Tool 1.1 Audit Spreadsheet to create your audit spreadsheet and record your findings.

TABLE 8.4 **EXAMPLE AUDIT CRITERIA**

ATTRIBUTE	CELL VALUES	RESEARCH QUESTION	WHAT YOU'LL LOOK FOR/RECORD
Topic	*<Product/Service>* *<Industry Trend>* *<Help Topic>*	What is the content about?	Record primary topic; note secondary topics.
Purpose	Inform Convince/Persuade Engage Unknown	What is the intended purpose of the content?	Record primary purpose, not secondary purposes.
Ownership	Marketing HR PR Product Team	Who is responsible for ensuring the content is accurate and up to date?	Note specific person or role if known.

Will a sample answer your questions? On a larger site, patterns will quite likely emerge after auditing a portion of your content.

No matter what you decide, some auditing will be better than no auditing. If you look at the whole site, you'll have some more prescriptive and specific details to share in your recommendations. If you do a sample, you'll know what needs to be addressed at a high level and you can communicate those themes.

> **TIP**   *On most websites I've encountered, the top 100 or so visited pages make up a huge chunk of a website's traffic. If nothing else, use those top 100 pages as a sample. Just filter out the home page (still look at it, but don't include it in the 100 pages) and watch for any weird things happening. For example, on a current project 35 of the top 100 pages on a higher education website for potential students were how-to articles about Microsoft Office functionality. I filtered those out.*

CONTENT MAPS

Content maps are a way to bridge the business and user perspectives. They help to answer questions like these:

- Does the content answer the questions users are likely to have throughout the customer life cycle and/or sales funnel?

- What is the intended purpose?

- What content is missing?

People use the term *content maps* for many things. I'm referring to a diagram that depicts what your users want to do or know, what you want your users to do or understand, and what content you have to serve those purposes. I usually do a content map workshop activity at the same time I'm learning about my stakeholders' perceptions and assumptions about users. (I talked about that in Chapter 7, "Learn About Your Audience and Users.")

HINT   *The Miro and Mural boards included with this toolkit contain a template for facilitating the content map exercise described here.*

Here's how it typically works:

1   On a physical or virtual whiteboard, I write a set of labels representing the purchase path or user journey. It might be something super simple like *Before* (engaging with you), *While* (engaging with you), and *After* (engaging with you). Or it might be more along the lines of a sales funnel like Awareness, Research, Consideration, and Purchase.

2   I ask workshop participants to brainstorm all the questions they think users would have and all the tasks users would want to complete for each stage of the user journey.

3   I ask participants to work together to cluster the questions and tasks underneath the purchase path or user journey and consolidate duplicates.

4   I have participants write on sticky notes the high-level answers to the consolidated questions and the calls to action (CTAs) to the consolidated tasks. They place them next to the corresponding questions and tasks.

5   I have them brainstorm what content they have that fulfills the questions and tasks in each phase of the customer journey or purchase path. Through this process, participants identify where the gaps are in their current content.

AWARENESS		RESEARCH		CONSIDERATION		PURCHASE	
QUESTIONS	MESSAGES	QUESTIONS	MESSAGES	QUESTIONS	MESSAGES	QUESTIONS	MESSAGES
TASKS	CTAS	TASKS	CTAS	TASKS	CTAS	TASKS	CTAS
EXISTING CONTENT		EXISTING CONTENT		EXISTING CONTENT		EXISTING CONTENT	
CONTENT GAPS		CONTENT GAPS		CONTENT GAPS		CONTENT GAPS	

USER TESTS

User tests can help you answer questions like these:

- Does the content answer the questions users are likely to have throughout the customer life cycle and/or sales funnel?
- How does the content make users feel?
- Is the content clear, usable, and readable?
- Does the content contain a compelling call to action or next step?
- Is the content easy to find by users?

I group user test types into four main categories: findability, relevance, readability and comprehension, and favorability. What categories you include in your tests depends on what you want to learn.

Let's go back to our dentist example from Chapter 7 (except now they have a live website) to walk through the test types. Then, you can download **Content Strategy Tool 8.2 Sample User Tests** to make your own test plan.

FINDABILITY

Findability refers to how easily users can find what they came for on your website. Why they came might be to find information or to complete a task.

The types of questions you might ask include "How would you go about finding the dentist's hours?" and "Where would you go to find out whether the dentist does cosmetic dentistry?"

RELEVANCE

Relevance helps you understand if the content contains the information a user needs and would expect in a given situation. So, you might frame up a scenario like, "Let's say you were looking to book an appointment with a new dentist. What information would you expect to find on the appointments page of the dentist's website?" Once you get responses from a few people, you can go through the page on your own to see if the content matches the users' expectations.

Another method that I use to understand relevance is telling test participants the name of a page on your website and asking them to write down or tell you three questions they think content on a page with that title should answer. Then have them read the actual content and see if they were able to find the answer to those questions.

CONTENT STRATEGY TOOL 8.2

SAMPLE USER TESTS

Download the sample user tests for descriptions of tests (and instructions) you can use to get user insights about your content.

TIPS

- Avoid trying to do too much in one testing session. Aim for about 45 minutes tops.

- Recruit people in the right phase of their customer journey for the content you're testing. For example, if you're assessing sales and marketing content, choose people who have recently made a decision about your offering rather than long-term customers.

- Make it clear to users that you are testing your content, not them.

- Compensate test participants to show you value their time. Gift cards are a good choice.

WHERE TO GET IT

Download the sample user tests at www.peachpit.com/register.

WHERE IT CAME FROM

Meghan Casey (www.dobettercontent.com and Brain Traffic (www.braintraffic.com)

READABILITY AND COMPREHENSION

Readability and comprehension suggest how easy your content is to digest and understand. (I dislike the word *digest* for content, but I haven't come up with anything better.)

In a test like this, you ask test participants to read a page or snippet of your content and then answer questions about what they read. So you might show them the dentist's services content and then ask them questions like "Does the dentist offer cosmetic dentistry?" and "What's the youngest patient they will see?"

TIP *There are some neat tools you can run your content through to see how it measures up for readability and comprehension. My personal favorite for a quick check is www. hemingwayapp.com.*

FAVORABILITY

Favorability looks at how your content makes people feel and how that influences their behaviors. The super-simple user test from Chapter 1 is an example of a test that falls into the favorability category. To jog your memory, that's the one in which you ask people to highlight content with different colors depending on how it makes them feel.

Another example of a favorability test is to ask users to respond to two variations of the same content. You could show them a snippet about the dentist's and a competitor's patient-care philosophy or show them the current version and a revised version. Then, ask questions about how the content made them feel, what dentist they would be more likely to choose, and so on.

CONTENT CONSCIENTIOUSNESS

Now you're swimming in information about your current content, and you probably have a lot of ideas for how to make it better. Hold those thoughts. Before you do that, you'll want to align on a strategic foundation for your content and set your content compass. We'll cover that, starting in Chapter 10, "Align on a Strategic Foundation."

But first in Chapter 9, "Evaluate Your Processes," we'll talk about how to evaluate your content processes. Figuring out what's working and not working will be key to executing your strategy.

CHAPTER 9

EVALUATE YOUR PROCESSES

If I were to guess, I'd estimate that at least 80 percent of the time when prospective clients ask for help with content, it's the people and process stuff that's keeping them from doing content well.

In this chapter, I'll outline four key characteristics of optimized processes—often referred to as *content operations*—and how you might identify the areas of opportunity or improvement for your organization:

- Right people, right skills, right work

- Role clarity and decision-making authority

- Standards, guidance, and enablement

- Built-in collaboration and iteration

Content Strategy Tool 9.1: Process Assessment Guide will help you document and synthesize what you've learned.

RIGHT PEOPLE, RIGHT SKILLS, RIGHT WORK

One of the most important content strategy concepts to understand is *aligned autonomy*. The concept comes from Spotify, and I first learned the term—although I've been talking about the idea of it for years—in an article published on Medium.com by Neil Perkin called "Why we need aligned autonomy in marketing" (https://medium.com/@neilperkin/why-we-need-aligned-autonomy-in-marketing-95ec1f84fd4c).

Essentially, aligned autonomy means that everyone working on content (in our case) understands what your organization is trying to achieve with their content and is trusted to bring their skills and insights to bear in service of those goals. It comes down to leadership and culture.

Of course, aligned autonomy can be realized only when your organization has the needed expertise to prioritize, plan, and implement on-strategy content.

HOW TO ASSESS LEADERSHIP AND CULTURE

I won't lie—this can be tricky, especially when reporting to leaders who may not want to hear what you learned. The best assessment methods are observational research and interviews with folks from all levels and departments who touch content in some way.

The questions you want to answer are ones like

- Do team members feel like they know how their work supports organizational goals?
- Are leaders confident in the teams' abilities to deliver?
- When faced with competing requests, do team members know how to decide which is more important?
- Do team members feel they can provide feedback to leaders?
- Do team members feel they have the direction they need to make decisions about tactics and activities independently?
- Is the culture a safe place to experiment, fail, and learn?

While those are the questions you want answers to, they are not always the questions you want to ask. More often than not, the answers to those questions surface from less-direct questions, like

- How do you plan what to work on when?
- What are some of the pain points or challenges in your work?

- What obstacles do you run into in your day-to-day activities?

- What's one thing about how you do your work today that you would change if you could?

- What about the content at your organization keeps you up at night?

Observational research, also known as *contextual inquiry*, is another way to understand the culture around content. Ask to sit in on relevant strategy and planning meetings to see how information flows to the people responsible for content strategy and content. Consider things like who is invited to the meetings; what purposes the meetings serve; and how questions, concerns, and recommendations are addressed.

HOW TO ASSESS CAPABILITIES

Most organizations I've worked with have some gaps in the capabilities needed to do content well. That's not necessarily a bad thing, because it often makes sense for some capabilities to be outsourced. But you can't determine what to outsource until you know where your gaps are.

Over the years, I've developed a list of core capabilities organizations must be able to do to be successful with content. I got the initial list from my friends at Content Strategy, Inc., and I've evolved it from there. Here's what an organization must be able to do:

- **Analysis**—Ability to gather strategic business and user insights through stakeholder interviews, documentation review, content audits, competitor review, and so on

- **Strategy**—Ability to develop a vision for content, such as setting the editorial strategy, providing actionable recommendations, selling the strategy and securing alignment, identifying the artifacts needed to support people in executing the strategy, measuring the success of the content strategy, and managing the behavior change required to be successful

- **Content Design**—Ability to translate strategy into content requirements through deliverables like content models, taxonomy schemas, sitemaps, wireframes, and so on.

- **Storytelling**—Ability to translate brand, business goals, and audience needs into relevant, uniquely positioned narratives that bolster conversation, provoke emotion, and spur action

- **Writing**—Ability to execute the content strategy and content design with website content that meets core web writing best practices for readability, usability, accessibility, and usefulness

- **Audio/visual content production**—Ability to produce quality content such as podcasts, videos, animation, learning modules, and presentations to support the content strategy

- **Search engine optimization**—Ability to investigate search terms and search intent to make recommendations about what content to produce and what terminology to use in your content; ability to provide guidance and requirements to content creators, developers, and so on for optimizing content for search engine optimization (SEO).

- **Process design**—Ability to analyze content-related processes, including workflows and roles, to recommend improvements and lead teams through the implementation of new processes and evolution of existing processes

- **Content enablement**—Ability to identify and develop standards, guidelines, and templates, as well as evaluate and source technologies, that enable teams to prioritize, plan, define, create, distribute, measure, and manage on-strategy content

- **Author experience design**—Ability to research and define the content entry experience for people who create, input, review, and publish content in the content management system, including integrating standards, guidelines, and requirements

Similar to analyzing culture and leadership, I learn a lot about capabilities from conducting stakeholder interviews. I'll often ask specific questions about the capabilities. For example, the answer to the question "How do you determine what words to use to describe <concept>?" tells me a lot about how mature my client's SEO capability is. A lot of the insights, however, come from less specific questions where details about capabilities organically arise.

Observation of strategy and planning meetings, working sessions, content review check-ins, and so on also provide a lot of information about how an organization stacks up against the outlined capabilities. And finally, I like to facilitate a self-assessment when I'm able to do working sessions about content operations.

The image on the next page is a partial example from a Miro board, which is a whiteboarding tool, where I had workshop participants work in two groups to discuss and agree on an assessment of their key content capabilities. The details of running this activity are included in **Content Strategy Tool 9.1: Process Assessment Guide** (later in this chapter).

TIP

You'll note that the capabilities in the capabilities assessment example don't match up exactly to what I outlined above. It's totally okay to tweak based on the client and project!

Content Capabilities

1. Break into two groups.
2. Discuss each capability and jot down some notes from the discussion.
3. Align on an assessment of the capability and put the appropriate face in the circle.

☺ We are good at this!
☺ We could improve on this.
☹ We struggle with this capability.

Capability	Group 1	Group 2
Analysis Ability to gather, interrogate, and translate strategic business and user insights through stakeholder interviews, documentation review, content audits, competitor review, etc.	◯	◯
Strategy Ability to develop a vision for content such as setting the editorial strategy, providing actionable recommendations, selling the strategy and securing alignment, identifying the artifacts needed to support people in executing on the strategy, measuring the success of the content strategy, and managing the behavior change required to be successful.	◯	◯
UX and content design Ability to investigate user needs and translate strategy into user experience and content requirements through user research and deliverables like user journeys, personas, user flows, content models, taxonomy schemas, sitemaps, wireframes, communications plans, editorial calendars, channel selection, etc.	◯	◯

CONTENT STRATEGY TOOL 9.1

PROCESS ASSESSMENT GUIDE

Download the guide to get step-by-step guidance (see what I did there?) and templates for assessing content processes against the four factors outlined in this chapter.

TIPS

- Make it yours. If something I've outlined doesn't make sense for your organization, change it.

- Keep an eye out for processes, templates, and so on that are too over-engineered to be helpful. Those situations are the ones that derail people from following processes.

- Listen. Listen. Listen. The documentation of workflows and capabilities is important, but the conversations will be chock-full of insights.

WHERE TO GET IT

Download the workshop exercises at www.peachpit.com/register.

WHERE IT CAME FROM

Brain Traffic (www.braintraffic.com), Meghan Casey (www.dobettercontent.com)

ROLE CLARITY AND DECISION-MAKING AUTHORITY

Commonly, content problems are symptoms of a lack of clarity about what work to do, who should do it, and who has the final say-so about content-related decisions.

If any of the following situations sound familiar, you have an idea of what I'm talking about:

- Your website has become a dumping ground for all content ever created for no other reason than no one knew what to do with it.

- The people who make decisions about what work you should do don't have an understanding of what the people who use your website want or need.

- Leaders often bypass established processes to request work on a pet project that's not in the work plan.

- The home page is a hodgepodge of unrelated content blurbs from all areas of the business.

- You're about to launch a new product, and no one knows where the content for the website is coming from.

- A blog post was just published that is so far off brand that it's laughable, yet no one wants to rock the boat by saying it should be taken down.

- You just found out that the human resources department launched its own careers microsite with an outside agency because they didn't want to wait until technology resources were available to build something on the main site.

- You got an email from a coworker inviting you to a planning kickoff for the new company blog, but your boss just asked you to lead what sounds like the same project.

- Your team of two is on the hook for twice the amount of work you have time for—and it's all considered top priority.

HOW TO ASSESS ROLE CLARITY

Role clarity issues occur when multiple people have (or think they have) the same responsibilities. For example, a web content specialist's job description might include creating and editing help content on the website, while someone in the customer support department sees that as their job. The resulting negative effects include uncomfortable politics between the two departments, wasted time and money, and an inconsistent experience for customers who use the content.

Conversely, sometimes a task needs to be done that no one believes (or knows) is part of their job. A recent example with one of my clients is that the marketing planner for a division wasn't sure whether it was their job to ensure the copywriter knew about other in-flight or upcoming projects that relate to the one they were working on together or whether the copywriter was responsible for finding out about those projects.

Another more tactical example I've run into involves ensuring that content that needs to be created and stored in two places is in sync. Let's say that your product database and your content management system (CMS) don't talk to each other and a change is made to the product details in the product database. If the person who made that change doesn't know that they need to alert the web team so that the details can be updated on the website, your content isn't consistent. In some cases it might not be that big of a deal, but some changes—say, price adjustments or legal information updates—could cost the company money or damage its reputation.

You can find these role clarity issues in several ways—and you guessed it, stakeholder interviews is one of them! Again, a lot of role clarity challenges will come up organically in your interviews.

Here are some targeted questions you might ask about an individual's own experiences with content work:

- Are there times when you have assumed someone else was taking care of something, and it became clear later that the task fell through the cracks?

- Are there times when you feel a certain task or decision should be your responsibility but someone else thinks it is theirs?

- What are your most important tasks or responsibilities?

- What would your boss say are your most important tasks or responsibilities?

Other ways to dig into role clarity include the following:

- **Job description audit**—To do this, I get copies of all the job descriptions of people working on content and make digital sticky notes (using collaboration tools like Miro or Mural) for the responsibilities in each job description—one color sticky per job description. Once I have all the stickies made, I group like responsibilities together to see how much overlap there is. I also look for responsibilities that don't seem to be represented anywhere or tasks that I would recommend a certain job title be responsible for.

- **Job studies**—This ethnographic approach is one I borrowed from friend and colleague Christine Benson. I provide team members with a worksheet, where they record what they do over a one- to two-week period.

When I get their worksheets back, I analyze where they are spending most of their time, how what they do overlaps with what other people do, and how their task list matches or doesn't match their job description.

HOW TO ASSESS DECISION-MAKING AUTHORITY

Who is or isn't empowered to make and enforce content decisions is a key factor in defining and implementing your content strategy. More often than not, the problem with authority is when no one has any.

Two types of authority exist regarding content: strategic and implementation. Both are important.

Without *strategic authority*, figuring out what content to produce and distribute is nearly impossible. Strategic authority belongs to the person who ultimately is responsible for the site objectives, resources and budgeting, and content planning.

HINT
A job description audit online whiteboard template and a job study worksheet are included with Content Strategy Tool 9.1: Process Assessment Guide *(later in this chapter).*

When no one is in charge, you're likely to spend time and money on content that doesn't help achieve business goals.

Without *implementation authority*, the strategic vision and related content guidelines don't get enforced. If no one is empowered to say "no" to content requests that don't address business goals or support user needs, you end up with muddled messages, unclear calls to action, and confused customers and prospects.

Unsurprisingly, stakeholder interviews are a key way to identify issues with decision-making authority. You might ask questions like these:

- Can you think of a time you were asked to work on something you didn't think was on strategy?
- What is the process for vetting content ideas and requests?
- How does your team determine what content projects to work on?
- Who has the final say if a leader requests a content project that doesn't align with your team's priorities?

Contextual inquiry is also helpful to identify challenges with authority. Sit in on meetings, review content submissions, and sift through chat messages and email chains to see where tension arises.

STANDARDS, GUIDANCE, AND ENABLEMENT

Standards, guidelines, and enablement are like the engine of your content operations. Without them, team members are often forced to make things up as they go along, which leads to fragmented, inconsistent processes.

This might not seem like that big of a deal in smaller organizations or in organizations that don't create much content. But I'd say it's still a big deal. It's an even bigger deal for larger, more complex organizations that create a lot of content for various purposes.

Consider an example where a subject matter expert (SME) works with several folks to define and review content. Each of these folks employs different processes, uses different tools, and has set different rules for the content they work on. Can you imagine how difficult it is for that SME to keep track of what's needed from them? Sounds awful. And what about the wasted time on learning new processes and tools, sifting through emails to find out what they need to do, and providing the same information over and over. Also awful.

FIRST, SOME DEFINITIONS

Before we dig into how to assess standards, guidance, and enablement, let's define those terms:

- *Standards* are the ultimatums for content across your organization.

- *Guidance* encompasses the suggestions, rules, requirements, instructions, and training for meeting your standards.

- *Enablement* refers to the processes, tools, technologies, templates, checklists, and so on that support your content efforts from ideation to archival.

Table 9.1 is an example of how these elements work together.

TABLE 9.1 **HOW STANDARDS, GUIDANCE, AND ENABLEMENT COME TOGETHER**

STANDARD	GUIDANCE	ENABLEMENT
We have a plan for measuring the effectiveness for every piece of content we create.	▪ Content metrics matrix ▪ Guidelines for choosing metrics and measurement methods	▪ User testing plan and script template ▪ User testing report template ▪ Analytics dashboard

HOW TO ASSESS STANDARDS, GUIDANCE, AND ENABLEMENT

I imagine you know what I'm going to say now... stakeholder interviews! Here are some questions you might ask:

- Are there any documented or undocumented rules for content at your organization?

- What applications or software do you use to complete your content work?

- What are some challenges you run into throughout the content processes?

- What's working well with your content processes?

In addition to the information you can glean from stakeholder interviews, I recommend collecting and analyzing any documentation of standards and guidance that does exist, as well as any templates. You can learn a lot from contextual inquiry as well. Ask to observe people as they use applications and software, templates, and documented standards and guidance.

Finally, a really great way to get some insights is to lead a workflow workshop. In these workshops, I bring together team members who work on content and ask them to co-document the steps of their workflow process and include places to record details about standards, guidance, and enablement as they go. A template and instructions are included in Content Strategy Tool 9.1: Process Assessment Guide.

The image on the next page is an example of what a "filled out" process step that includes information about standards, guidance, and enablement might look like.

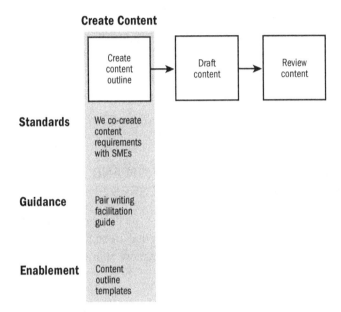

BUILT-IN COLLABORATION AND ITERATION

In my experience, collaboration along the journey of ideating, planning, and maintaining content is much more effective than working on content in silos. And purposeful iteration typically makes for more user-centric content.

COLLABORATION AND ITERATION EXAMPLES

Here are some of the ways teams can collaborate on content:

- Hold content prioritization meetings where stakeholders agree on what content is most important to work on in a defined time period.

- Facilitate a content-first design studio with UX designers and visual designers.

HINT
A whole guide
on pair writing is
included in the
downloadable
tools. We'll talk
more about it in
Chapter 15, "Specify
Content Structure
and Requirements."

TIP
I find that pair
writing reduces the
rounds of revisions
with SMEs.

- Use a technique called *pair writing* (I first learned of this technique from fellow content strategist Richard Ingram) to define content requirements.

- Set up regular meetings with the development team to collaborate on how to "model" your content. (More on that in Chapter 15.)

- Teach stakeholders how to assess their content so that they can help identify content that should be updated or removed.

On to iteration. To be clear, I am not talking about endless rounds of revisions with SMEs. I'm talking about iteration based on feedback from the people who will be using your content and reviews for user-centricity, specifically. Here are some examples of how this iteration can happen:

- Develop review criteria for writers and strategic reviewers that help ensure content caters to user needs and follows best practices for readability.

- Test content with actual people who will be using it to identify ways of making it more relevant and usable.

HOW TO ASSESS THE WAY COLLABORATION AND ITERATION ARE BUILT INTO YOUR PROCESSES

Stakeholder interviews. I sound like a broken record. But you'll learn some things about collaboration with more general questions like "What are some challenges with your content processes?" But you could ask some more pointed questions as well. For example:

- How do you work with SMEs?

- Does content get created before or after UX and visual design?

- Do you test content with users before publishing it?

Another great way to suss out how collaboration and iteration fit into content processes is to build upon the workflow workshop I mentioned in the previous section. Add details about who does what at each step to identify where collaboration is—and more importantly isn't—happening. Document where in the process content is refined based on user or strategic feedback.

The image on the next page is an example of a "filled out" process step that includes observations about collaboration and iteration.

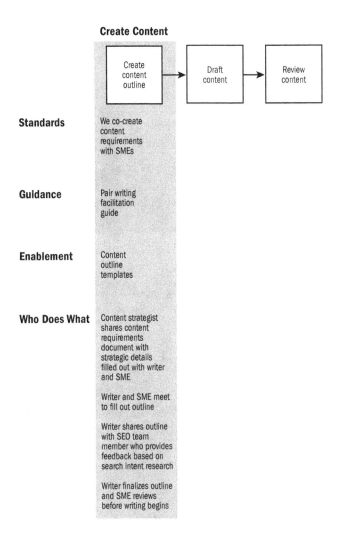

Create Content

| Create content outline | → | Draft content | → | Review content |

Standards — We co-create content requirements with SMEs

Guidance — Pair writing facilitation guide

Enablement — Content outline templates

Who Does What — Content strategist shares content requirements document with strategic details filled out with writer and SME

Writer and SME meet to fill out outline

Writer shares outline with SEO team member who provides feedback based on search intent research

Writer finalizes outline and SME reviews before writing begins

PROCESS EVALUATION STATUS COMPLETE

You just wrapped up the last bit of your discovery activities. And your head is likely swimming. All these insights will come in handy as you make recommendations for optimizing your content operations.

Chapter 10, "Align on a Strategic Foundation," walks you through how to pull together everything you've learned and facilitate alignment with your stakeholders on the strategic approach for content. Exciting!

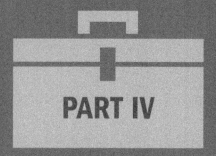

PART IV

ARTICULATE YOUR STRATEGY

Your stakeholders are ready to see a finished product. And honestly, you are too. Ideas are bubbling faster than you can remember them all. That's great. It really is. Write them all down. Every idea. Every possibility. Now, put them aside.

Before you go too far into designing a solution, you need to set the strategy. It might be really apparent by now. Document it. Communicate it. Get everyone onboard with it. Then you can revalidate your ideas and possibilities to ensure they're on strategy. Then get to work on what everyone wants to see finished.

CHAPTER 10 Align on a Strategic Foundation

CHAPTER 11 Set Your Content Compass

CHAPTER 10

ALIGN ON A STRATEGIC FOUNDATION

I hope you're feeling good about all the work you've done so far. More important, I hope you feel confident that it will help you develop a solid content strategy and make meaningful recommendations.

What comes next? Now is the time to check in with your stakeholders, especially the ones who have decision-making power or a lot of influence. (Don't forget the derailers.)

RUNNING A STRATEGIC ALIGNMENT WORKSHOP

I used to prepare a strategic alignment summary and present it to stakeholders at this phase of a project. And I still do sometimes. But whenever possible, I bring stakeholders back together for a workshop to align on the following:

- The business goals the project should help the organization achieve and how you might measure success

- Who makes up the priority audiences and what tasks they need to complete

- How content should help audiences complete their tasks and aid the organization in achieving its goals

I've found this approach extremely useful in achieving consensus across the organization about the strategy for content. Here's an overview of the exercises I find to be the most productive. **Content Strategy Tool 10.1** is a guide, with Miro and Mural online collaboration templates, to help you run an alignment workshop yourself.

EXERCISE 1: LEVELS OF WHY

A *Levels of Why* exercise helps you dig deeper into the issues that are driving the project you're working on. You may be familiar with the iceberg model as a way to understand systems thinking. This model was first introduced by Edward T. Hall as the Cultural Iceberg Model in the 1970s to analyze the visible and invisible levels that make up an organization's culture.

The following image is an interpretation of Hall's Cultural Iceberg Model from the webpage "Iceberg Model: Learn About the Theory and Practice of System Thinking" (https://ecochallenge.org/iceberg-model).

To summarize the model, there are four levels to consider to fully understand any situation (there are lots of online articles if you'd like to learn more):

1 **The Event Level**—The event level is like the weather report... what happened or is happening. This level is what we are typically reacting to when we start a content project. And it's the level that is visible above the water in the iceberg metaphor.

2 **The Pattern Level**—This level is about looking beyond the event to see if what happened or is happening is part of a larger trend. With this knowledge, we can anticipate when it or something like it could happen again in order to prepare for it or prevent it.

3 **The Structure Level**—The structure level helps us understand why the thing happened or is happening and how it relates to other things going on in the organization. It helps us start to think about how we can design something different.

4 **The Mental Model Level**—Mental models refer to the attitudes, beliefs, values, and expectations prevalent in an organization or on a team—typically espoused by leadership. Understanding how mental models play into the event at hand sets us up to transform the mental models or integrate them into our solution.

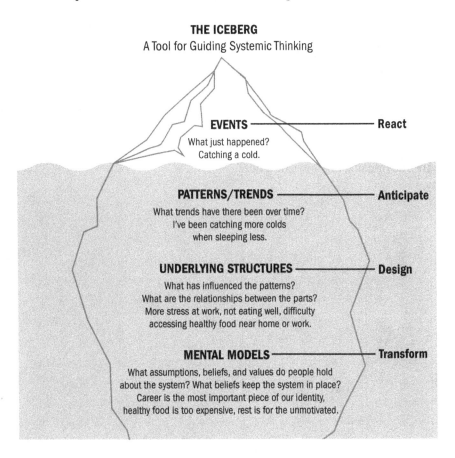

THE ICEBERG
A Tool for Guiding Systemic Thinking

EVENTS ———————— React
What just happened?
Catching a cold.

PATTERNS/TRENDS ———————— Anticipate
What trends have there been over time?
I've been catching more colds
when sleeping less.

UNDERLYING STRUCTURES ———————— Design
What has influenced the patterns?
What are the relationships between the parts?
More stress at work, not eating well, difficulty
accessing healthy food near home or work.

MENTAL MODELS ———————— Transform
What assumptions, beliefs, and values do people hold
about the system? What beliefs keep the system in place?
Career is the most important piece of our identity,
healthy food is too expensive, rest is for the unmotivated.

The Levels of Why exercise is a low-barrier way to uncover or validate what's happening beneath the surface and define the true motivations for and goals of the work.

To begin, each person in your workshop gets a column of seven sticky notes to answer the "Why are we doing <*this thing*>?" or "How will doing <*this thing*> make a difference?" question. After they answer the question on their sticky note, workshop participants are prompted to specify why their answer is important. Sometimes I'll assign them a lens to consider in their responses, like the following:

- How will reenvisioning our website make a difference for our organization overall?

- How will reenvisioning our website make a difference for the people who use it?

- How will reenvisioning our website make a difference for the content team?

- How will reenvisioning our website make a difference for the recruiting team?

Here are some examples of a Levels of Why exercise:

Once everyone has filled out the bottom of their column, I ask workshop participants to share what they wrote. Like most workshop exercises, the ensuing discussion is just as important as what is written on the sticky notes. This exercise gives folks an opportunity to deepen their understanding of their own thinking and the thinking of their colleagues.

	Kai	Riu	Zulmïra	Alula
Why is Content University re-envisioning its website?	For today's prospective students and their families, it is all about experience—we must give them the best possible experience on the web as part of their college search process.			
Why is this important?	Because these students and their families can choose to go anywhere.			
Why is this important?	Because we want them to attend CU.			
Why is this important?	Because once they attend CU, they will love it and become an ambassador for the University.			
Why is this important?	Because the more ambassadors and alumni we have who have had positive experiences with CU, the better chance we have to continue recruiting like people.			
Why is this important?	Because we need to make money to sustain our business.			
Why is this important?	Without students, we wouldn't exist.			

EXERCISE 2: LOOK OF SUCCESS

The Look of Success exercise builds on the Levels of Why activity. Once everyone has read their column, help them come up with one or more key performance indicators (KPIs) related to their "whys." Put the KPI in the middle of a cluster of physical or digital sticky notes and brainstorm together how you might measure success against that KPI.

In the Levels of Why activity, the bottom *why* for a higher-education institution was, "Without students, we wouldn't exist." In our Look of Success exercise, that "why" was translated to the KPI "Increase applications from qualified candidates."

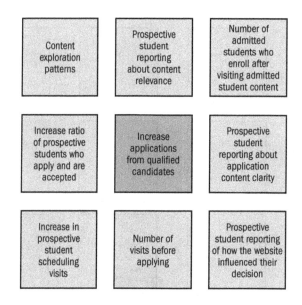

EXERCISE 3: AUDIENCE CHARACTERISTICS

The *Audience Characteristics* exercise is one I learned from my friend and fellow content strategist Cameron Siewert on a recent project we worked on together. I like it because it's a little less scary for my clients to prioritize characteristics of potential audience groups than prioritize (or deprioritize) a category of people. And even though it does help us prioritize and deprioritize categories of people, we end up with a more nuanced understanding of who we are prioritizing.

With this exercise, you facilitate a discussion around different spectrums of audience characteristics that you glean from the interviews and other discovery work you've done. I like to do this exercise twice, once for who they think their content is designed for today and once for who they think their content should be designed for based on the Levels of Why and Look of Success exercises.

For each spectrum, you can either

- Have workshop participants first work individually to place a dot on each spectrum and then bring them together to talk about why people placed their dots where. With this approach, you won't necessarily reach consensus, but you'll have fruitful conversations that will inform your proposed audience prioritization.

- Jump right into a discussion to come to consensus on where the dot should be placed on each spectrum. You'll still have the fruitful conversation to get there, and you'll have achieved alignment on the spot.

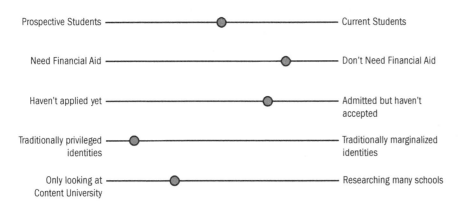

Audience Characteristics - Today

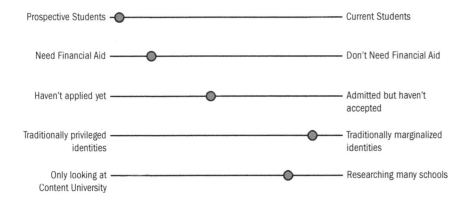

Audience Characteristics - Future

EXERCISE 4: THE MADLIB

This fill-in-the-blanks activity is a great way for workshop participants to synthesize their whys and perspectives on audience prioritization. It also helps them—and you—think about what your audiences need and why.

When in person, I hand out worksheets with spots to fill in the blanks. When I'm facilitating a workshop remotely, I use sticky notes. Depending on how much time is left in our session, I ask people to share their MadLib. It's generally quite fun and informative. After the session, I go through the responses to gather insights about areas where the organization is aligned or misaligned, organizational priorities related to our content project, and language to use in my strategic alignment summary and recommendations.

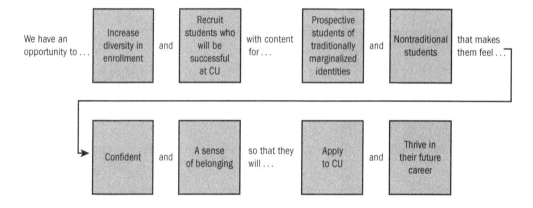

CONTENT STRATEGY TOOL 10.1

STRATEGIC ALIGNMENT WORKSHOP GUIDE

Download the guide and get links to the online collaboration boards (Miro and Mural) to plan and facilitate a strategic alignment workshop.

TIPS

- My activities are suggestions of methods that have worked for me. You might not like them. That's OK. Do something different. The key is to get to some sort of alignment of goals, audiences, and content objectives.

- You could plan this workshop for the beginning of your project, before you conduct your stakeholder interviews. I've found that I feel better about the outcomes when I complete the workshop after I've acquired a good amount of domain knowledge.

- For smaller projects or ones with an aggressive timeline, I sometimes plan this workshop as my primary stakeholder discovery activity. Afterward, I can let my clients know about gaps in knowledge that I'd like to fill with additional discovery activities.

WHERE TO GET IT

Download the guide and remote workshop boards at www.peachpit.com/register.

WHERE IT CAME FROM

Meghan Casey (www.dobettercontent.com)

PREPARING A STRATEGIC ALIGNMENT SUMMARY

Whether or not you do a strategic alignment workshop at this stage, you'll want to put together a Strategic Alignment Summary (or any other name you want to call it). Its purpose is to

- Help get project stakeholders aligned on why you're doing the project and what it will help the organization achieve.

- Serve as a guidebook for team members to ensure that the resulting strategy and recommendations are addressing the right business goals, user needs, challenges, and opportunities.

Before moving on to the document, here's a big ol' caveat: You may not need to separate this strategic summary from the next step of setting your content compass (which we get into in Chapter 11, "Set You Content Compass").

How do you know? Read through the considerations in the matrix in **Table 10.1** and circle or keep track of your answers. Then add up your points to help determine whether your organization is ready.

TABLE 10.1 **IS MY ORGANIZATION READY?**

YES	NO	CONSIDERATION
1	0	Do you feel your stakeholders are already aligned on what challenges or problems your project should help solve?
0	1	Do you need your stakeholders to fill in some gaps in your knowledge or understanding before you can move on to specific recommendations?
0	1	Do you think filling those gaps could drastically change your current thoughts on the high-level strategy?
1	0	Will preparing and waiting for feedback on a separate document compromise your timeline?
0	1	Do you think you've uncovered anything in discovery that will be a big surprise to your stakeholders?

If your score is between 0 and 2, you should probably get stakeholder buy-in on the Strategic Alignment Summary before moving on to the strategy phase. If your score is between 3 and 5, you're probably safe to combine the strategic summary with your strategy document.

OK, let's move on to putting your discovery findings together.

ORGANIZE FOR CLARITY AND ACTION

This document's job is to clearly define what challenges or opportunities your content project addresses. It can help connect the dots between what you want to solve or take advantage of and the steps needed to do it.

One way to tell the story is to organize the document using the opportunities or challenges. I typically start with an introductory section that includes the following:

- An overview of the document purpose

- Some project context, such as what triggered it, the timeline, and what discovery activities you completed

- The current understanding of the business goals and project objectives

- A high-level summary of the challenges or opportunities

- A list of the next steps and due dates

The introductory section might look something like the sample document shown here for a membership organization that wants to attract and retain members and drive revenue through the sale of premium content.

ABOUT THIS DOCUMENT

Our approach to content strategy consists of defining a core strategy with recommendations on four key components:

- **Editorial:** What kind of content do you need, and what messages does it need to communicate to your audience?

- **Structure:** How is content best prioritized, organized, stored, and displayed?

- **Workflow:** What are the optimal processes, tools, and human resources required to support the content strategy?

- **Governance:** How are key decisions about content and content strategy made?

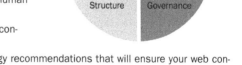

This document sets the stage for effective content strategy recommendations that will ensure your web content is useful, usable, purposeful, and profitable. Its purpose is to align your stakeholders on the following:

- Business goals and content objectives

- Challenges or opportunities your core content strategy and related recommendations must address

The information in this document was derived from the discovery phase. To arrive at our findings, we conducted stakeholder interviews and workshops, did research with users, and analyzed your current content ecosystem.

NEXT STEPS

- Provide feedback and clarification by February 7.

- Once finalized, we will begin work on the core content strategy and related recommendations.

BUSINESS GOALS AND CONTENT OBJECTIVES

Based on information during discovery, we've summarized your business goals and related content objectives as follows.

Business Goals	Content Objectives
Attract new members.	– Demonstrate the value the association provides for professionals just entering the profession or industry. – Describe the benefits of becoming a member of the association.
Retain new members beyond the first year.	– Showcase content created by members, for members. – Demonstrate how long-term members of the organization have advanced the profession.
Increase purchases of publications and training among prospective members and existing members.	– Drive visitors from free and member-only content to value-added paid content on the same topic. – Learn visitors' demographics, interests, and preferences to automatically serve up content they are likely to find relevant.

SUMMARY OF OPPORTUNITIES

We've identified several opportunities that will help you achieve your business goals and content objectives:

- Define the content product to ensure what we publish and curate helps us attract and retain members by helping industry professionals excel in their jobs and build their reputations in the industry.
- Organize content to move visitors along a path from non-member to member in ways that incrementally demonstrate our value.
- Develop content guidelines and tools to help content creators, contributors, and reviewers produce on-strategy content.

Then, I'll dive into each challenge or opportunity with a short introduction. The introduction typically explains why I believe it's important, which usually is because it addresses a business goal or user need. The introduction also suggests what evidence I considered to arrive at the conclusion—was it indeed an opportunity or a challenge? And, it hints at how the content strategy and related recommendations should or will help the organization address the challenge or take advantage of the opportunity.

Here's an excerpt of how I might introduce an opportunity for a membership association in an actual Strategic Alignment Summary:

OPPORTUNITY

Define our content product to ensure what we publish and curate helps us attract and retain members by helping industry professionals excel in their jobs and build their reputations in the industry.

One of the biggest revenue drivers for our company is membership dues, thus making member acquisition and retention a key business goal. The primary way we provide value to members is through content that helps them excel in their jobs and build their reputations in the industry.

Based on our research with users, we're not providing or soliciting the kind of content that members and prospective members believe is helping them excel or giving them opportunities to demonstrate their expertise. Our content strategy must define what content we need to produce and curate to take advantage of opportunities to convert non-members to members and members to long-term members.

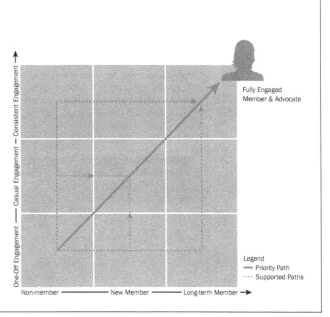

In this case, the opportunity is important because it helps them meet a business goal of increasing membership revenue. The evidence is that users don't feel the website content helps them do their jobs better or build their reputations in the industry. The content strategy must help define the right kind of content to publish and curate to attract and retain members.

Then, I'll provide whatever evidence led me to include the challenge or opportunity, which helps stakeholders understand why it's relevant and important. The evidence helps you as you develop strategy and recommendations. You can return to this document often to make sure you've addressed the key challenges or opportunities.

Building on the example opportunity, here's what an excerpt about evidence might include:

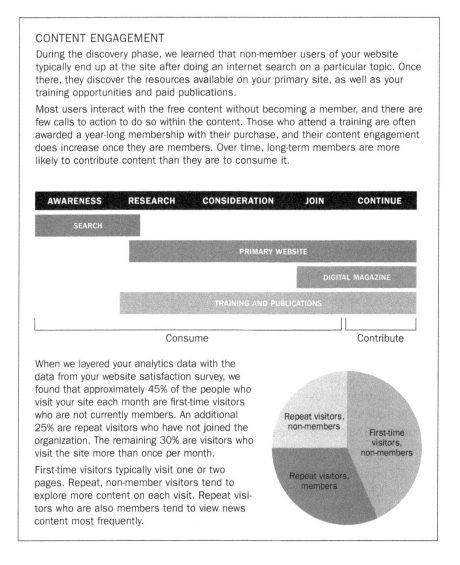

CONTENT ENGAGEMENT

During the discovery phase, we learned that non-member users of your website typically end up at the site after doing an internet search on a particular topic. Once there, they discover the resources available on your primary site, as well as your training opportunities and paid publications.

Most users interact with the free content without becoming a member, and there are few calls to action to do so within the content. Those who attend a training are often awarded a year-long membership with their purchase, and their content engagement does increase once they are members. Over time, long-term members are more likely to contribute content than they are to consume it.

When we layered your analytics data with the data from your website satisfaction survey, we found that approximately 45% of the people who visit your site each month are first-time visitors who are not currently members. An additional 25% are repeat visitors who have not joined the organization. The remaining 30% are visitors who visit the site more than once per month.

First-time visitors typically visit one or two pages. Repeat, non-member visitors tend to explore more content on each visit. Repeat visitors who are also members tend to view news content most frequently.

And finally, I provide an example of how the challenge or opportunity might be addressed in the content strategy. Sometimes this is a simple statement such as, "The content strategy and specifications will define the appropriate calls to action for non-members to explore more content or join the organization and for members to contribute content and re-up their memberships."

Other times, you might provide a little more of a taste for what the recommendations might entail. I often get a bit more explicit when clients have difficulty envisioning what content strategy recommendations include and look like.

IMPLICATIONS FOR CONTENT STRATEGY

The content strategy and specifications will define the appropriate calls to action for non-members to explore more content or join the organization and for members to contribute content and re-up their membership. In the following example, the calls to action are geared for a logged-in member whose membership will expire in the next 60 days.

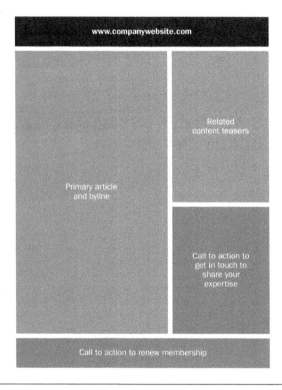

ANALYZE AND SYNTHESIZE

So how do you identify the opportunities or challenges you'll include in your summary? Before you started the project, you likely had some hunches about what they were. As discussed in Chapter 1, you may have used those hunches with a small data set to get project funding.

Keep those handy, but don't get overly attached to them. I usually use one of two methods to organize my findings into challenges or opportunities. For both, open your insights engine (Content Strategy Tool 6.4) or whatever other tool you used to record your notes during the discovery phase.

The first method works best when I'm confident my hunches are accurate and I don't have much time to spend on the summary. I create a document listing each hunch as a heading (or you can use **Content Strategy Tool 10.2** to collect and organize your thoughts). Then, I dig through my insights engine and look for notes and data that relate to each challenge or opportunity.

▚▚▚▚▚ HINT Use the built-in filtering capabilities to narrow your insights by interviewee, document, topic, and so on.

CONTENT STRATEGY TOOL 10.2
STRATEGIC ALIGNMENT SUMMARY STARTER DOCUMENT

Download the starter document so that you don't have to start from scratch. It contains an outline based on this chapter's discussions along with some questions and considerations to help you put your document together.

TIPS

- Avoid being wordy. Short, simple, and straightforward is better. You can always add detail if stakeholders ask for it.

- Don't feel you have to include everything you learned. Some information may not be relevant anymore, and you don't want to bog down stakeholders with unnecessary information.

- When possible, include quotes from stakeholders and users and examples from documentation or content to strengthen your narrative.

WHERE TO GET IT

Download the starter document at www.peachpit.com/register.

WHERE IT CAME FROM

Meghan Casey (www.dobettercontent.com) and Brain Traffic (www.braintraffic.com)

Without wordsmithing (which I find hard not to do), I pull in those notes and data and add a few notes about why the information is important. Try to move quickly; you can worry about sounding awesome later.

TIP
If you're using Miro or Mural, you can easily create individual sticky notes from a copy and paste from your insights engine.

The second method works great if you have more time and want to challenge your assumptions a bit. Grab lots and lots of physical or digital sticky notes. Go through your notes and write each individual important piece of data or bit of information on a note. Then, start to group them to identify your challenges or opportunities. Sometimes I end up with a whole new set of challenges or opportunities—different from the ones I had in my head.

All right. You have your challenges and opportunities and the source content for your document. As you prepare the summary, the intent is not to just regurgitate what you learned. Instead, analyze and synthesize the information to provide your point of view about why the information matters.

For example, regurgitation might be something like:

> We have 17 web properties, 3 of which we publish to regularly. The rest haven't been reviewed in a year or more.

Instead, add some context about the information's importance:

> We have 17 web properties, 3 of which we publish to regularly. The rest haven't been reviewed in a year or more. User research suggests that our audiences don't know where to go for what information. Our target audience is most likely to go to www.siteexample.com, but that's a site we haven't been maintaining. The information is out of date, and the messaging doesn't represent our brand very well.

At this stage, it's difficult not to make formal recommendations even if you're pretty sure what you want to recommend. Specific strategy recommendations are risky because your stakeholders need to get onboard with your findings first. That's why this interim step is so important in cases where you need to ensure that stakeholders are aligned before moving forward.

I think you're ready to go. Download **Content Strategy Tool 10.2**, and get started!

GETTING TO THE STRATEGY

OK, you have the document, and it's fabulous. Now, you want to strategically share it to get alignment and proceed.

I like to start with an informal presentation to my key stakeholder. The benefit is that they can call out any major red flags or areas where the language needs a little softening. And they're likely the one who's on the hook for a successful project.

TIP

Never deliver a Strategic Alignment Summary by itself without a conversation. Get people on the phone or in a room and walk through it. I usually won't even send it in advance unless my client feels super strongly about getting it first.

After I make any necessary revisions, I prepare an executive summary presentation for the more strategic stakeholders. Although I prefer to deliver that presentation myself, sometimes I prepare a presentation for my client to deliver.

Make sure you put this presentation in a business-focused context: goals and results versus process. Pull out the key items they will be most interested in, and highlight how they affect the bottom line. Expect a lot of discussion. A lot. It's normal—and actually productive—even if it feels annoying at the time.

Your role is to listen and answer questions about your conclusions. You may hear comments that change your mind, in which case you can update the document (and your thinking). You may hear conversations that suggest the organization isn't quite ready to change the way it does things or put a new stake in the ground. That's OK.

It's not a failure to have to make some changes based on new information or a realization that you have more work to do to get aligned. I've facilitated meetings where I told clients that I don't think they should proceed just yet.

And then there are the meetings where productive discussions lead to a shared vision for the project. Then, it's time to talk with the people who will be doing the work.

Whenever possible, I also ask to present to the implementers and influencers. They need to understand the vision agreed on by their leaders and to get a chance to react and provide feedback. You may tailor your presentation slightly to address this audience. The conversations you'll hear will probably be mostly tactical. Let them happen; more than likely you'll get good insights that will inform your strategy.

DISCOVERY: THAT'S A WRAP

OK. So you have alignment on the project vision. It's time to get to work on the strategy. Keep your Strategic Alignment Summary handy to remind you, your stakeholders, and your team why you're doing this project and how it should help your organization and your users.

Next up, you'll set the content compass that helps you provide the right content, to the right people, at the right time, and for the right reasons. You know all that stuff now. So this will be a breeze!

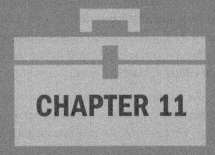

CHAPTER 11

SET YOUR CONTENT COMPASS

OK. Stop and breathe for a second or two. You have accomplished a lot so far. You've done all the right things to make sure you know what your organization or client is trying to achieve. And you've diligently made sure everyone who matters is on board with those goals.

Now you'll define your content compass, which gets specific about the following:

- The purpose of your content, including relevant business goals, prioritized audiences, and content objectives

- The concepts your content should communicate to fulfill that purpose

- How you'll measure whether your content is working and how you'll communicate your findings

Before we start pulling together your content compass, I'll talk about how your project's scope affects your content compass.

CONTENT COMPASS SCOPE

Your content compass can be super broad or quite narrow, depending on the scope of your project and what's been documented before. Keep in mind that your project's place in the organization's content universe *affects* what you're able to control or influence. It also is *affected by* the formal and informal strategies guiding content efforts throughout the organization.

Content strategy for an entire organization and across all channels is super complex and steeped in business management and operations. Some call that *enterprise content strategy*. For the purposes of illustrating a useful content compass, this book focuses on the three main project types I've encountered most outside of enterprise content strategy: function, property, and subset.

FUNCTION

Function refers to a functional unit within an organization, such as sales, marketing, communications, customer service, or human resources. Of course, every organization is set up a bit differently, so yours could have different names for similar functions.

Very often, my client is a senior leader within one of these functions who wants help with content strategy across all the content types and delivery channels. Marketing and customer experience are probably the most common.

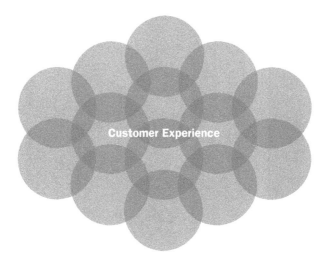

PROPERTY

Property refers to a single digital destination, such as a website or an application, or even a social media channel, such as Facebook. Most of my digital property projects are for new website launches or existing website refreshes or redesigns. They could be a client's primary web presence, a customer portal, an employee intranet, or a microsite (for something like a campaign, product launch, or event), to name just a few.

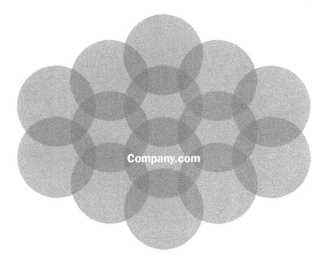

SUBSET

Subset refers to any defined portion of content on a digital property or content of a function of the organization (like Human Resources or Marketing), regardless of where it's published. You can define that subset by where it lives in the site, such as the Help or the About Us section. Or you may define it by whom the content is for (current customers, prospective customers, and so on) or what the content is about (products, company information, area of expertise, and so on).

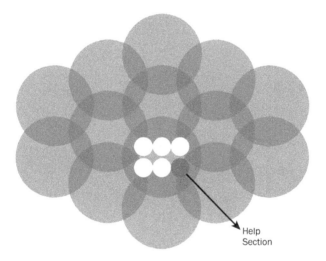

Help
Section

CONTENT COMPASS COMPONENTS

Next, I'll walk through some helpful artifacts for documenting, communicating, and using your content compass.

ARTICULATE YOUR CONTENT PURPOSE

The content purpose is the central component of your content compass. It answers the fundamental questions for providing the right content, to the right people, at the right time, for the right reasons. **Table 11.1** summarizes the three questions a core strategy statement must answer. These should seem familiar if you're reading this book in order.

TABLE 11.1 **CORE PURPOSE QUESTIONS**

Business goals	What outcomes does providing this content help us achieve?
Audience	Who, specifically, is that content for?
Content objectives	What content should we produce, procure, curate, and share, and why do our audiences need it from us?

HOW DO YOU DOCUMENT YOUR CORE PURPOSE?

There's no one right way to articulate your core purpose. The ones I've documented over the years have taken on different formats depending on what I think the client will be receptive to and the complexity of the concepts the core purpose might need to communicate. Let's look at three examples: a simple statement, an annotated statement, and a framework.

SIMPLE STATEMENT

The example in this figure is a one-sentence statement that identifies four key components of the content purpose:

- Business goal
- Content substance
- Audience
- Content objectives

ANNOTATED STATEMENT

For this example, I've used the same sentence and added some annotations to demonstrate key concepts for the strategy.

Reviving Revenue
Our website exists to generate revenue from new customers and existing customers.

Success Stories Sell
Our content paints a picture of how real customers have met their fitness goals eating our meals.

To increase new and recurring orders, we will provide motivating content that demonstrates how our meals for busy, Paleo-minded athletes who eat on the run fit into their lifestyles and help them eat to perform.

The Sweet Spot
People who have already bought into a Paleo diet and who are always on the go represent our biggest revenue potential.

Fit to Thrive
Our audience cares the most about one key thing... how do I get healthy means that help me achieve my fitness goals when I don't have time to shop or prepare?

FRAMEWORK

The last example, shown in the following figure, is a slightly more detailed version that I use when it's harder to describe the audience and content objectives in a shorter statement. You'll notice that I added a couple details that aren't specified in the previous two examples.

HINT
You might find it helpful to create a statement or annotated statement and a framework with some additional details. The simpler statement could be a good summary for leadership, while the framework can offer some specifics that people doing content work find valuable.

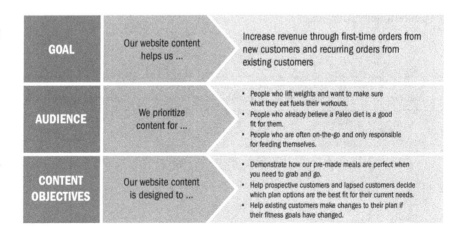

GOAL — Our website content helps us ...
Increase revenue through first-time orders from new customers and recurring orders from existing customers

AUDIENCE — We prioritize content for ...
- People who lift weights and want to make sure what they eat fuels their workouts.
- People who already believe a Paleo diet is a good fit for them.
- People who are often on-the-go and only responsible for feeding themselves.

CONTENT OBJECTIVES — Our website content is designed to ...
- Demonstrate how our pre-made meals are perfect when you need to grab and go.
- Help prospective customers and lapsed customers decide which plan options are the best fit for their current needs.
- Help existing customers make changes to their plan if their fitness goals have changed.

HOW DO YOU CRAFT YOUR CONTENT PURPOSE?

The best part about putting together your content purpose is that you already have all the information you need from the discovery phase. Even better, your stakeholders have agreed on the important aspects: who the content is for, why they need it, and what the organization is trying to achieve.

Now you just need to put all that together and add some specificity about the kind of content to produce, through either a collaborative or an individual approach. I typically start by opening a blank slide presentation (for example, Google Slides, Apple Keynote, or Microsoft PowerPoint), the digital collaboration board I used for the strategic alignment workshop, and my insights engine.

Using the collaboration board and insights engine, I'll just start writing words and phrases that relate to the business goal(s), audience(s), and content objectives. The board... and my thinking... will often seem scattered and never polished. Trust the process.

Then, I'll sit there for a few minutes staring at the screen, trying to get started. True story. That's often how it works. I bet you can relate. So, I'll take a break and work on something else, play with the grandbabies, practice my ukulele, take a nap—you get the idea.

At some point during this period of what I call "productive procrastination," concepts start to become clearer in my mind. That's when I go back to my blank document, go to a new slide, and take a first pass at writing a purpose statement.

This is when I form a pretty good idea about whether it needs to be a statement, an annotated statement, or a framework. If I can't clearly summarize the purpose in 35 words or so by the end of my revising and finessing, I will grab my framework template and fill that in. Of course, there will be more finessing and revising with the framework as well.

Once I feel good about where it's at, I'll go through a mental "definition of done" exercise, where I make sure that it includes a measurable business goal, clear audience definition, and content objectives that tie to audience needs.

I'm not quite done yet, though. Before I show the proposed core purpose to my client, I like to test it out.

One way I test is to present the core purpose with a colleague or even a friend (redacting as necessary for confidentiality). Then, I'll present the purpose in whatever format I've used and ask them to recap the purpose in their own words or ask more direct questions like these:

- How would you describe who we create content for?
- Why do you think those people need that content?
- What does providing the right content to the right people help my client achieve?

If people who don't have much context for the project can get the gist and explain the content purpose back to me, it's usually in pretty good shape.

The next thing I do is make sure it's prescriptive enough to help my client make decisions. To do that, I will look for some examples of content they have published or produced in the past and make a determination about whether that content aligns with the core purpose.

Let's say, for example, that the fake client in our example had published an extensive primer about the history of the Paleo diet. Using the core purpose, I would deduce that such content is not aligned because our audience is already sold on eating a Paleo diet.

After a few more of those kinds of examples, I'm ready to present it to my client so they can start using it. I'll often use the examples I walked through in my presentation deck to show how it helps with decision-making. After all, that's the whole reason for it to exist.

HOW DO YOU USE YOUR CONTENT PURPOSE?

As I mentioned, the whole idea behind articulating a content purpose is to help organizations make smart decisions about content. With this in mind, it can be used a few ways:

To decide what to keep of the content you already have

TIP
Once your purpose is defined, you can add columns to your content assessment spreadsheet or Airtable for alignment with your strategy.

You can use your content purpose to go back through existing content to determine whether it should be kept, repurposed, or archived. For example, perhaps there is content in that extensive history of the Paleo diet primer I mentioned that does fit the strategy, even if the entire piece is not applicable.

To decide what content ideas to pursue

When you get requests for content, you can use your content purpose to decide whether they make sense. I find it most helpful to have a group of stakeholders go through ideas together and come to agreement based on the strategy. **Table 11.2** shows some additional examples to evaluate for the example content purpose. Before looking at what I decided, try deciding what might be in or out for yourself.

TABLE 11.2 **IDEAS FOR CONSIDERATION**

YES	NO	IDEA
		Page about Paleo foods to eat on workout days
		New site section with Paleo recipes
		Blog post about feeding your family Paleo style
		Videos featuring athletes talking about how our Paleo meals helped them achieve their fitness goals
		Page featuring information about the benefits of eating Paleo and tips for making the switch

Here's what I decided and why:

- *Yes* to a page about foods to eat on workout days because the purpose is to help athletes eat to perform in the gym; this page should have a call to action (CTA) to explore meal plan options.

- *No* to a new section with Paleo recipes because we want people to buy our meals.

- *No* to a blog post about feeding your family Paleo style because our target audience is responsible for feeding only themselves and needs something they can eat on the go.

- *Yes* to videos featuring athletes talking about how our Paleo meals helped them achieve their fitness goals because we want people to see what's possible when they choose our meals.

- *Yes* to a page featuring information about the benefits of eating Paleo and tips for making the switch because our target audience is already sold on the Paleo lifestyle.

To ensure content is on strategy as it's being planned and created

When I help my clients define planning processes, one of the things that's almost always included is a strategic content brief. Within it is a section to describe specifically how the content you're proposing or planning fits with the content purpose.

Similarly, when I create editorial checklists for writers and reviewers, I will include line items for audience appropriateness and content objectives.

HINT
Hang with me until the last chapter where I'll talk about building briefs, checklists, and other enablement artifacts into your content playbook and show you some examples.

CREATE YOUR MESSAGING FRAMEWORK

A messaging framework clarifies what you want your audiences to know and believe about your organization and suggests how to prove that what you want them to believe is true.

As a component of your content compass, the messaging framework helps ensure that every piece of content you create supports the framework. If it doesn't, it doesn't belong or needs to be revised.

WHAT DOES A MESSAGING FRAMEWORK LOOK LIKE?

As with a core strategy statement, you can document your messaging framework in multiple ways. I tend to create something visual to show a hierarchy or progression. **Content Strategy Tool 11.1** contains three messaging framework examples and editable templates to save you some work.

CONTENT STRATEGY TOOL 11.1
MESSAGING FRAMEWORK TEMPLATE

Download the template for examples and editable versions of the three ways I have documented messaging frameworks for my clients.

TIPS

- If the labels don't work for your situation, change them. They need to make sense for your stakeholders and anyone else working on content.

- You can change the colors in the template to make it match your or your client's brand.

- Remember, this isn't external-facing messaging, but rather part of your compass to help people working on content communicate the value of the organization or its offerings to your target audiences.

WHERE TO GET IT

Download the template at www.peachpit.com/register.

WHERE IT CAME FROM

Meghan Casey (www.dobettercontent.com) and Brain Traffic (www.braintraffic.com)

The messaging framework is a nice foil to the content purpose. While the articulation of your purpose is more focused on the business, the messaging framework builds on the purpose by defining what you think your audiences want to know from their perspective (and hopefully get a chance to validate).

> **HINT** *My messaging frameworks rarely contain word-smithed messages to plop into copy. Instead, they represent concepts that your writers and creatives can bring to life.*

This example builds on the purpose we defined earlier and details the first impression you want athletes in the target audience to have when they visit the website, why the company's meals are valuable to your target audience, and what the organization will communicate to prove that value.

First Impression	Value Statement	Proof
What first impression do we want our audiences to have when they interact with our content?	What do we want our audience to know or believe about the value we provide?	What will demonstrate that what we want them to know or believe is true?
"They understand me."	*"I love that I can customize convenient meal options to give my body what it needs to reach my next goal."*	*"Meal plan options are available to nourish your body for whatever your fitness situation or goal—build muscle, lose fat, lift heavier, run farther, hit that personal record, "deload" week—we have a Paleo meal for that."* *"Athletes like you count on our meals to eat balanced meals that fuel their body—day in and day out."* *"Our meal plan options are as flexible as your fitness goals—change them up as often you want to match whatever workouts you'll be crushing."*

HOW DO YOU DEVELOP A MESSAGING FRAMEWORK?

The substance of your messaging framework can come from several sources, including stakeholder interviews, user research, and working sessions. Let's dig into a few ways to gather the info.

STAKEHOLDER INTERVIEWS

When I'm doing stakeholder interviews, I often ask interviewees to give me their version of the "elevator pitch" when asked about the organization they work for. Then, when I'm working on the messaging framework, I'll put all the concepts I heard from those answers (or other parts of the conversations where organizational messaging came up) on digital sticky notes and organize them into value statements and proof points. This is a great starting point.

USER RESEARCH

Social listening on related topics, your organization, or your competitors; interviews with existing and potential customers; and surveys or polls with people in your target audience can yield a treasure trove of information to help you understand what your audience cares about.

WORKING SESSIONS

When my projects allow the time—mine and internal stakeholders'—I like to bring everyone together to work through messaging. Sometimes I'm able to do this as part of my stakeholder alignment workshop, and sometimes it's a separate session.

The primary activity in this session is to talk through which messaging concepts resonate with both the organization and the target audience. To do that, I do the following:

🔧 **TIP**
If you can't get the right people back together, you can do this exercise on your own.

- Prepopulate a digital collaboration board with all the messaging concepts I've heard from the organization on sticky notes of one color on one side of the board and all the messaging concepts I've gathered from user research on sticky notes of a different color on the other side.

- Ask working session participants to look through the prepopulated sticky notes and add any they think are missing.

- Have participants work together to identify where there is overlap in messaging and move those sticky notes to the middle of the digital whiteboard.

HOW DO YOU USE YOUR MESSAGING FRAMEWORK?

Your messaging framework can guide you in evaluating content you currently have to identify necessary revisions and planning for and creating new content:

To evaluate content you currently have

When you go back through existing content to determine whether it is aligned with your content purpose, you can also assess whether it contains the right messages to demonstrate value and meet your audience's needs. For example, you may find that some content you deem still relevant needs to be edited to convey the appropriate messages.

TIP   Once your purpose is defined, you can add columns to your content assessment spreadsheet or Airtable for your messaging assessment. Aside from saying "yes" or "no" on whether key messages are represented, I like to note which proof points are specifically accounted for in the content.

To ensure content is on-strategy as it's being planned and created

Remember that content brief I mentioned earlier? It's a good idea to include a section on messaging with the content purpose details.

At the very least, you can identify which of your proof points or key messaging concepts the content you're planning relates to. You can also go deeper to specify precise key messages for the content you're proposing or planning.

And you've probably guessed that I recommend including a messaging line item in your editorial checklists. Editorial checklists can help content creators check their own work and remind content reviewers what concepts to look for when they are providing feedback.

DEFINE HOW YOU'LL MEASURE SUCCESS

A measurement framework is the final component of your content compass. It helps everyone working on content understand how success will be measured.

HOW DO YOU DECIDE WHAT TO MEASURE?

It's easy to get stuck on vanity metrics for "engagement" like views, likes, shares, and follows, oh my. As fellow content strategist Mike Powers says, "Engagement is not your goal. Your goal is your goal." That's why it's important to dig deeper to identify measurements that signal whether you are achieving your goal.

LET'S DEFINE SOME TERMS

Key performance indicators (KPIs), objectives, and metrics are words lots of people use, but not always in the same way. So let's start with defining how I'm using them in content measurement. If you think about them differently, that's OK—as long as the people you're working with know how you use them.

KPIs are how a company determines, through measurement, whether it's meeting its business goals.

Objectives refer to the ways you think your content can help your company meet its business goals and influence its KPIs.

Metrics refer to the quantitative and qualitative data and information you can analyze to understand whether you're moving the needle on your KPIs and content objectives.

CHOOSE THE RIGHT METRICS

Measuring content success involves determining whether your content efforts had an effect on specific business outcomes as well as supporting content objectives. To measure these, you'll need to combine quantitative (based on numbers) and qualitative (based on opinions) methods and metrics.

Quantitative and qualitative data will help you get a well-rounded picture of how your content is performing. Numbers provide some hard-hitting information; opinions and behaviors provide context to make sense of them. I categorize methods of measurement in three main ways: analytics, heuristics, and user feedback.

Before we dig into each, I want to point out that choosing the right metrics hinges on asking the right questions. **Table 11.3** provides some examples of the types of questions you can answer with each method category.

TABLE 11.3 **EXAMPLE QUESTIONS BY METRIC CATEGORY**

ANALYTICS	HEURISTICS	USER FEEDBACK
Are we providing the content people need and want from us?	Is our content easy to read and understand?	Does our content answer the questions people have?
Is the content that people need easy to find?	Is our content accessible and inclusive?	Does our content make visitors feel confident in our product?
Are our calls to action compelling?	Does our content guide users to appropriate next steps?	Is our content easy to find by navigating our website?

ANALYTICS

For my clients, Google Analytics is still the most widely used analytics tool. So, it's the one I'm most familiar with. With it, and others like it, you can dig into metrics like these:

■ Number of visits before a prospective customer did a thing you want them to do (for example, buy a meal plan)

■ What paths visitors took to get to the meal ordering page

■ What percentage of users ordered something after reading a page or blog post

■ Whether onsite search results returned relevant content

■ What terms visitors searched for to get to our site or on our site

■ How much stuff we sold

■ How long visitors spend on a page

HEURISTIC

A heuristic (or best practices) assessment looks at how your content measures up to commonly regarded standards for digital content. You can also mix in some strategic factors related to how well content supports your core purpose and conveys your messaging framework, like we discussed earlier in the chapter.

I really like the way Abby Covert (known as @abby_the_ia on Twitter) talks about heuristics. She combines some of the expert views from other practitioners, like Jakob Nielson and Lou Rosenfeld, into a mega heuristics framework that is the most comprehensive I've ever seen. The UX Writers Collective also put together a great compilation of heuristics in their document "UX Writing Checklist: Content Heuristics for Designers."

TIP

The same data point applied to various pieces of content can mean different things. For example, bounce rates (the percentage of people who come to your page and then leave) are typically considered to be negative. Yet, a high bounce rate might mean they got the information they needed (such as a phone number) and left. Keep in mind that context is everything.

Table 11.4 outlines Abby Covert's set of heuristics:

TABLE 11.4 **SUMMARY OF ABBY COVERT'S HEURISTIC FRAMEWORK**

HEURISTIC	EXAMPLE QUESTIONS CONSIDERED
Findable	Is the content easy to locate via search or navigation?
	Are there multiple ways to get to the information?
Accessible and Inclusive*	Is it available on all devices?
	Does it comply with accessibility standards for people with disabilities?
	Does the content consider the experiences and contexts of people of traditionally marginalized identities?*
Clear	At what reading level is the content written?
	Is the content straightforward and free from industry jargon?
	Does it provide the necessary information for a user to complete a task or process?
Communicative	Does the content clearly communicate the messages you want your users to understand?
	Does it provide a solid orientation of where a user is in a process or task?
Useful	Does the content provide information that the target user wants and needs?
	Does it anticipate what users might want or need next?
Credible	Is the information up to date?
	Is the content about a topic on which the organization is realistically known as an expert?
Controllable	Can you or your users modify what information they have seen or have access to?
	Do error messages provide the context necessary to fix a mistake or solve a problem?
Valuable	Does the content improve the customer experience?
	Does the content help the user assess the value of what you provide?
Learnable	Is the experience consistent and predictable?
	Can users grasp the concepts quickly?
Delightful	Does the content offer something extra or special that users can't get from competitors?
	Does it exceed users' expectations?

*I added "inclusive" as part of the "accessible" heuristic.

USER FEEDBACK

User feedback is critical for adding context to your analytics and heuristics findings. You can get feedback from your users in a couple of ways. User surveys or unmoderated tests focus on getting quantitative data. Moderated tests and interviews gives you more qualitative information about how your content is performing.

> **TIP** Make sure your survey asks some demographics questions so that you can slice and dice the data to look for patterns related to user characteristics, such as gender, age, customer or member status, or location.

Let's start with surveys. Examples of survey questions you might ask include the following:

- What kind of information were you looking for today?
- Were you able to find the information you were looking for?
- Did you get the answers you needed from our website?

You can do a lot of user feedback tests—moderated or unmoderated. The method that I find gives you the most value is one in which you show the participant the website or application and ask them to walk you through how they would go about completing a series of tasks you've determined are important for your strategy.

As they walk you through where they'd look for the information, you can ask additional questions like the following:

- What would you expect to find on a page with this title?
- What benefits do you think this product offers?
- Is the content on this page the information you'd need to make a decision about <*a thing*>?
- What do you think the next step would be if you wanted to <*do a thing*>?

> **HINT** Fellow content strategist Erica Jorgensen just released a book called Content Research for User Experience, published by Rosenfeld Media. It's brilliant. You should read it.

HOW DO YOU DOCUMENT WHAT YOU'LL MEASURE?

Before you do the measuring, you'll need to document your metrics and the methods you'll use to collect the data. I call this a *measurement framework*. You'll also want to document the measurement cadence, or how often you'll collect data for each metric. **Table 11.5** is an example of what a measurement framework might look like. I've included a couple of examples for each method of measurement (analytics, heuristic assessment, user feedback).

TABLE 11.5 **SAMPLE MEASUREMENT FRAMEWORK**

BUSINESS KPI	CONTENT OBJECTIVES		
Increase revenue through first-time orders from new customers and recurring orders from existing customers	▪ Demonstrate how our premade meals are perfect when you need to grab and go. ▪ Help prospective customers and lapsed customers decide which plan options are the best fit for their current needs. ▪ Help existing customers make changes to their plan if their fitness goals have changed.		
METRIC	**QUANTITATIVE OR QUALITATIVE**	**METHOD(S)**	**FREQUENCY**
Number of orders from new customers	Quantitative	Analytics	Monthly
Number of orders from existing customers	Quantitative	Analytics	Monthly
Amount of engagement with customer profile content	Quantitative	Analytics	Monthly
Attitudes toward customer profile content	Qualitative	User Feedback	Annually
Compelling meal plan choice decision support	Qualitative	User Feedback	Quarterly
Clarity of content about changing plan options	Qualitative	Heuristic Assessment	Annually
User comprehension of content about changing plan options	Qualitative	User Feedback	Quarterly

HOW DO YOU USE YOUR MEASUREMENT FRAMEWORK?

Pause for caveat… You've probably noticed that measuring content effectiveness is not quite an exact science. The numbers can tell you only so much by themselves. The qualitative data and insights will always be a bit subjective (because they come from humans). That's OK. Content measurement is about getting a sense for whether you're headed in the right direction and what you can improve.

Measuring content effectiveness involves documenting how your content is performing and reporting to stakeholders what you've learned.

DOCUMENT HOW CONTENT IS PERFORMING

All the work you did in the discovery phase prepared you to document your findings. Repurpose these tools to do it:

- **Audit Spreadsheet or Airtable database**—Set up your heuristic assessment using the spreadsheet as a starting point. Just as you did for your mini-audit in Chapter 1 and your larger-scale assessment in Chapter 8, define what you'll be looking for with each criterion—or in this case, heuristic.

- **Insights Engine**—You can use your workbook or Airtable to record insights you gather from user interviews and a review of your analytics. For analytics and user surveys, you'll have access to some nifty dashboards through the tools you use, but I recommend adding your thoughts on what the numbers might mean or suggest to the insights engine.

REPORT TO STAKEHOLDERS

Now, it's time to let your stakeholders know how your content is performing. Provide a high-level scorecard for each KPI with its related objectives and metrics. You can back it with a more detailed report if needed.

You may be able to automatically pull in some of your data, but it's likely you'll have to do some of it manually. I've yet to find a perfect solution for creating a scorecard, so I tend to manually create it and enter the data.

Table 11.6 is an example scorecard building on the example we've been using in this chapter. It contains the same KPI, content objectives, and metrics as the measurement framework, along with the following:

- An assessment of how content is performing against each metric
- Key insights or findings from the data
- Recommendations for improving the content based on content performance

You may do a full scorecard and report only once or twice per year, depending on how often you're conducting heuristic assessments and soliciting feedback from users. Although you may not feel you're doing enough measurement, that frequency is probably OK. The quantitative data is more accurate if you consider it over a longer timeframe versus a monthly snapshot. You'll get a better picture of how your content is doing and not risk acting on an anomaly if you don't have a knee-jerk reaction to a month or two of data. And you're less likely to attempt to micro-optimize something without considering the entire content experience.

TABLE 11.6 **SCORECARD SAMPLE**

BUSINESS KPI	CONTENT OBJECTIVES		
Increase revenue through first-time orders from new customers and recurring orders from existing customers	▪ Demonstrate how our premade meals are perfect when you need to grab and go. ▪ Help prospective customers and lapsed customers decide which plan options are the best fit for their current needs. ▪ Help existing customers make changes to their plan if their fitness goals have changed.		

METRIC	ASSESSMENT	FINDINGS/INSIGHTS	RECOMMENDATIONS
Number of orders from new customers	😐	We saw an increase of 25% in new orders this month. It's possible that this was due in part to new year motivation. We did see some drop-offs during the order flow, which might suggest some issues with content.	Monitor order increase to see if it drops off after January. Do some user testing of the ordering flow to identify any issues.
Number of orders from existing customers	🙂	Orders remained steady. We only saw about 5% of current customers upgrade to a recurring order plan.	Revisit recurring order messaging and calls to action. Do some user research/testing to assess what might persuade customers to set up recurring orders.
Amount of engagement with customer profile content	🙂	75% of new customers who placed orders viewed a customer profile story/video during their visit.	Consider creating additional profiles.
Attitudes toward customer profile content	😐	We haven't done any specific user testing/research on customer profiles, but video comments suggest that people generally like them.	Ask specific questions about the profiles in our next round of user testing.
Compelling meal plan choice decision-support	🙂	About half of new and recurring customers used the interactive meal recommender before placing their order. 90 percent of people who used the meal recommender quiz went on to place an order.	Nothing at this time.
Clarity of content about changing plan options	☹️	50% of people who started the plan change flow ended up calling customer service for assistance.	Conduct a best practices review of the flow and relevant content. Test the current flow with users. Propose changes to the flow for implementation in the next development cycle.

Content Strategy Tool 11.2 contains templates for your measurement framework and scorecard so you don't have to start from scratch.

CONTENT STRATEGY TOOL 11.2

CONTENT MEASUREMENT FRAMEWORK AND SCORECARD TEMPLATE

Download the sample for ideas on how to put together your own content measurement report.

TIPS

- There are a lot of ways to organize your measurement framework and communicate your findings. Take from these templates what makes sense and leave the rest.

- Make a commitment to use what you learn from measurement to make changes to your content. If you have trouble getting approval to make improvements, go back to Chapter 2 for a refresher on making the case.

- Even when you find that your content isn't performing well, find something positive to build upon. Conversely, when it's performing well, look for something small you could improve to make the content even better.

WHERE TO GET IT

Download the sample at www.peachpit.com/register.

WHERE IT CAME FROM

Meghan Casey (www.dobettercontent.com) and Brain Traffic (www.braintraffic.com)

All right, you're ready to measure once your new content is in place. Doesn't being prepared feel good?

TRUE NORTH

It's time to share your strategy far and wide. Schedule some time with the key teams who work on content—from leaders to subject matter experts to UX designers to writers to developers—to go over your content compass and how it should inform their work.

The next four chapters are all about designing an on-strategy content experience. And you'll have your compass to guide you.

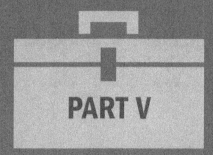

DESIGN YOUR CONTENT

Organizations and practitioners tend to jump into designing content before defining a strategy that clarifies what content users need and how it should support business goals. That's not going to happen here because you defined your content purpose first! In Part V, I discuss how your content purpose guides how you determine what content to create or curate and how to organize and present it so that users can easily find and use it.

In each chapter, we'll walk through an element of content design (prioritization, organization, definition, or specification), some methods for how you might accomplish and document it, and ideas for validating your work when applicable.

CHAPTER 12

PRIORITIZE BASED ON YOUR STRATEGY

Prioritization is how you determine what content you need to meet your audiences' expectations and how you can achieve your organizational goals. An information architect once told me, "I can organize the heck out of whatever content my clients give me. And most of the time, they ask me to organize stuff I bet no one cares about." That's the sad but true reality for lots of websites.

I call it the Marjory the Trash Heap phenomenon. Remember *Fraggle Rock*? Marjory was like an oracle to the Fraggles. She was made up of all the garbage from all time, and from that garbage came history and wisdom. A lot of organizations dump all the content they have ever created on their website and dare people to find what they need. Customers or other types of users could probably find some great stuff in there, and it certainly provides a comprehensive corporate archive. But is it the information their audiences need and that will move the needle on measurable business goals? Quite often, the answer is a resounding no.

Prioritization helps you cull that content down to the truly useful and relevant bits and pieces. So how do you figure out what content is most important? Let's get into it.

METHODS FOR PRIORITIZING CONTENT

Most, if not all, the methods described in this chapter could also be used to define your content purpose, which is a prioritization exercise in and of itself! I'll talk about them assuming you'll be using them post-purpose definition, but absolutely use them to better understand your audience's needs and current content in the discovery phase.

TWO-QUESTION USER SURVEY

You can use this method when you already have a website. It's especially helpful as a stand-in for user research if you haven't had the interest or budget to talk to your customers directly.

You can run this survey using a behavior analytics tool like Hotjar (www.hotjar.com) or Crazy Egg (www.crazyegg.com). I typically use the "pop-over" format, which displays the survey over the lower-right side of the website.

Technically, the survey consists of three, not two, questions because the first one asks whether the visitor wants to participate.

If they say yes, I use open-ended questions to understand who they are and why they are visiting the website.

Please describe in a sentence or two who you are. For example, "I work in procurement."

Please type here...

Please describe in a sentence or two why you visited our website today. For example, "I need to find out what services you offer, so I can decide whether to send your our request for proposals."

Please type here...

⚡ hotjar   Next

⚡ hotjar   Next

> **TIP**   It can be tempting to include a list of user groups and tasks or information needs, but I advise against it. Letting people use their own words can facilitate your understanding of who uses your website and how they think about and describe their needs.

The information gathered from actual site visitors can help you understand what information people need for what reasons. As you analyze responses, you'll be able to put content needs in priority order by frequency of need.

That prioritization will be one input into organizing your content (which we'll dig into in Chapter 13, "Organize for Intuitive Wayfinding"). Survey findings will also help you determine what words to use to describe the people who use your website, the information they need, and the actions you want them to take.

TOP TASKS IDENTIFICATION

A method called Top Tasks analysis was developed by Gerry McGovern, founder and CEO of Customer Carewords and an idol of many content strategists and information architects. I'll provide a high-level summary of how I've implemented Gerry's approach here, but I strongly recommend that you pick up a digital or paper copy of his book *Top Tasks: A How-to Guide* at www.gerrymcgovern.com.

TIP

Don't get too hung up on the word tasks. Tasks can be transactional, like "account balance," or more informational, like "flu symptoms." While Gerry suggests not including a verb in your top task description because your list gets difficult to scan, I sometimes start with verbs and then edit down to nouns. So, "Find out what symptoms are typical for the flu" becomes "flu symptoms."

Here's how it works:

1 Gather a long list of possible reasons your audience might visit your website (or app)—what they're looking to find or do.

These are your "tasks." Inputs to this list might include the following:

- Your organizational strategy, business plan, or product strategy
- Customer feedback, like the two-question survey we just talked about
- Call center or customer support logs
- Stakeholder interviews, which you already did
- Competitor websites
- Social media listening reports
- Analytics, like popular pages and downloads
- On-site and search engine terms (including search intent, which we'll cover after top tasks)

2 Narrow your list to 100 or fewer tasks.

You should consider several factors when whittling down your initial list. Here are some examples (see Gerry's book for more):

- Remove tasks that include formats. For example, "videos" is not a task on a project management software website. The task is related to what information the user needs, like "product features," that may be in a video.
- Look for duplicates. In Gerry's article, "What Really Matters: Focusing On Top Tasks" on the A List Apart website (https://alistapart.com/article/what-really-matters-focusing-on-top-tasks), he gives this example: "Bug toolkit" and "Debugging" can be combined into one task.
- Avoid lofty concepts or goals. For example, a leader's *goal* may be to build an efficient and high-performing team; the *task* is researching project management tools.
- Include subsets of tasks in parentheses if necessary. Examples of this from Gerry's work include: "Troubleshooting (bug fixes, diagnostics, guides)" and "Product availability (lead times, back orders, in my location)."

3 Ask internal stakeholders and customers to rank the narrowed list of tasks.

This is where it gets good. You'll do this with an online survey, which you can email to your internal stakeholders . You can email it to your users (if you have permission to do so), promote it via social media, or run it on your website, like the two-question user survey.

The survey consists of one question, which asks participants to select the five tasks that are most important to them. Optionally, you can have people rank those five tasks in order of importance to them. The following image shows how the survey instructions and first few tasks might look in Google Forms.

Yes, I know this seems like bad survey design. But it's very intentional. As Gerry explains in his A List Apart article,

> *We want to find out what really matters to people—what they do versus what they say they do. The very length and overload of the survey forces the gut instinct to kick in. You don't 'read' the list; rather, the tasks that really matter to you jump out.*

Gerry sees the same patterns every time he uses his methodology, and I've seen the same kind of results when I've used it. These patterns or findings include the following:

- The top 3–5 tasks get 25% of the vote. These are your top tasks.

- Around 10 tasks get 25–50% of the vote and 50–75% of the vote. These are your medium and small tasks.

- The remaining tasks (which are also most of the tasks) get 75–100% of the vote. These are your tiny tasks.

- Internal stakeholder and user survey results don't match, with internal stakeholder over- or under-prioritizing tasks compared with actual users/customers.

This image shows what that breakdown looks like.

Task Distribution

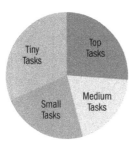

What you end up with after analyzing your findings is a table ranking all your tasks, from top to tiny. This ranking informs what content to prioritize when you organize your content and define content requirements for each page or screen.

I like to look at these results in context of the proposed content purpose to further prioritize and contextualize the findings. Every now and then, I might even find that the proposed purpose might need to shift a bit.

SEARCH INTENT ANALYSIS

This section on search intent research is basically my crib notes of Chapter 2 of Rebekah Baggs and Chris Corak's book, *SEO for Everyone*. This is another book I strongly recommend you get a copy of if you want to dig deeper. You can order it at www.abookapart.com.

So, what is search intent research? At its core, it is about understanding the intention or need behind the terms someone types in the Google, Bing, or other engine search bar. A main way search intent research is done is by analyzing search engine results pages (SERPs) for terms related to your organization, your products and services, your industry, and relevant topics/subject matter.

The Google algorithm is getting better and better at sussing out a user's intent and serving up the most relevant content. That's great news for content folks because we can take advantage of what Google has learned to understand our audiences' needs and design our content to meet them.

Let's walk through an example of how you might analyze a SERP to help you prioritize your content. We'll use my pandemic pastime, learning how to play the ukulele. (I've been having a blast.)

For this example, I started with the search term *play the ukulele*, as shown.

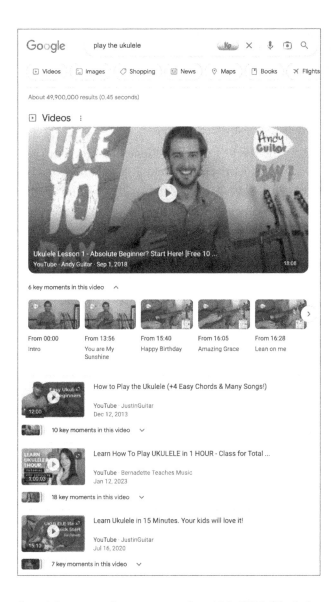

Surprising to me, there were no ads on this SERP. (If ads do appear, you can ignore them.) The first thing I notice about the videos that show up is that they are all geared toward ukulele beginners. That tells me that Google has likely determined that people searching for *play the ukulele* are looking for beginner resources. And I can look at the "10 key moments in this video" sections for even more insights on what people are looking for. Examples from the search include beginner songs, instructions for tuning your ukulele, information about holding and strumming your ukulele, easy chords, and picking a ukulele. So we've struck gold from just these two video search results.

Let's keep scrolling. The next set of results (shown in the next image) still focus mostly on beginners, but there are some topics for more experienced players as well. The "People also ask" section of the SERP is a literal treasure trove of insights into what people intend when they search for something.

And, beyond the page title of the results listings that follow, we'll want to pay particular attention to any links under the description. For example, the links under the description for How to *Play Ukulele Chord—Cordoba Guitars* suggest some nuanced topics we may want to consider, like reading a chord diagram and getting the best sound from our chords.

Further down the page are details about other search terms people use related to playing the ukulele. These can be a great jumping-off point to continue our research.

We're only halfway down the first page of results, and we already have some amazing information to help us prioritize content (should we have a website about playing the ukulele). When doing this kind of research, document the kinds of terms and topics you find. A spreadsheet, a Google Doc, or a digital collaboration board are all great places to make your notes and record screenshots for context.

TOPIC SORTING

Topic sorting is a great way to get your stakeholders involved in prioritizing content—with the added benefit of achieving alignment. I will typically do this by writing one topic each on physical or digital sticky notes. With a recent client that provided free legal resources, we did this with all the topics they currently had on their website.

We started the exercise by reviewing the content purpose they had aligned on. Then, I showed them the big ol' wall of stickies. There were 243 of them!

Then, I asked them to dive in and move each sticky from the wall of stickies into one of three columns, keeping their content purpose in mind: Must Have, Could Have, Don't Need. After all the stickies were moved, I asked stakeholders to review the list and put a question mark by the sticky notes they wanted to discuss because they disagreed with where their colleagues placed them or because they wanted their colleagues' opinion about where they placed a topic.

After that discussion, we ended up with the following:

- 81 topics in the *Must Have* column (about a third of their original 243 topics)
- 57 topics in the *Could Have* column (about a quarter of their original 243 topics)
- 105 topics in the *Don't Need* column (about 43% of their original 243 topics)

The next image shows how the sorting exercise shook out (using one-third of the stickies because 243 is a lot of stickie, and . . . you get the idea). They cut between about a half and two-thirds of their topics, depending on how many *Could Haves* they decided to keep.

That's the power of a clear content purpose!

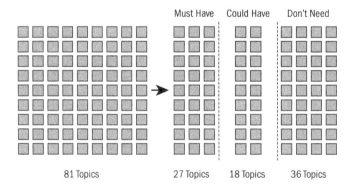

DOCUMENTING CONTENT PRIORITIES

Once you've identified your content priorities, it's important to document them in ways that are meaningful to your stakeholders and your team. While you could just make a list of priorities, it's helpful to contextualize them a bit.

Content Strategy Tool 12.1 is a series of editable templates you can use to document content priorities. One of my favorite ways to do this is to use a table with four equal quadrants:

- What content you should **focus** on because it's important to your business and your users

- What content you need to **guide** users to because it's important to them but not all that beneficial to your business

- What content you want to **drive** people to because it wasn't what they were looking for, but it's beneficial for you

- What content you'll probably include (I call it "meh" content) because you feel like you must, but it's really not beneficial or important to anyone

CONTENT STRATEGY TOOL 12.1

CONTENT PRIORITIZATION TEMPLATES

Download the templates to think through and communicate content priorities to your team.

TIPS

- You can use one template, multiple templates, or a combination of templates to document your content priorities and communicate them to your teams.

- Don't worry yet about how to organize the prioritized content. First, you must know what content you need.

WHERE TO GET IT

Download the templates at www.peachpit.com/register.

WHERE IT CAME FROM

Meghan Casey (www.dobettercontent.com) and Brain Traffic (www.braintraffic.com)

This image shows an example of a prioritization quadrant. The content most important to the business and the users is information about products, how to purchase products, and support content for their products. The company also wants to drive people toward content about product enhancements, making referrals, and social media channels. Users need information about returning products and getting refunds, which isn't great for the business but is still necessary. And the company history and awards they've received aren't that important to anyone and shouldn't be a priority.

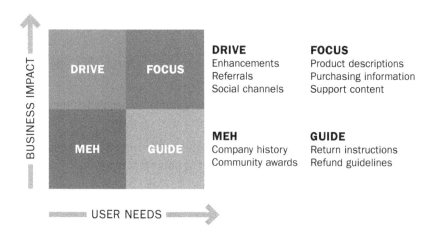

DRIVE
Enhancements
Referrals
Social channels

FOCUS
Product descriptions
Purchasing information
Support content

MEH
Company history
Community awards

GUIDE
Return instructions
Refund guidelines

You can take your topic lists a step further by combining them with user scenarios, calls to action, related content, and so on. **Table 12.1** shows what that might look like.

TABLE 12.1 **USER SCENARIOS AND TOPICS**

USER SCENARIO	SEGMENT	FOCUS	DRIVE	GUIDE
I'm researching products from various companies to find out which will be the best fit for my situation.	Prospect	▪ Product description and specifications ▪ Product reviews ▪ Pricing ▪ Comparisons to competitors' products	▪ Social media channels ▪ Product awards	
I've decided to buy a product from you and need to find out how to make a purchase.	Prospect	▪ Ordering instructions ▪ Shipping information and costs	▪ Add-ons and enhancements ▪ Referral program ▪ Social channels	▪ Returns and refunds information ▪ Warranty details
I'm thinking about upgrading my product and want to know how the newer model is different from what I have now.	Loyal Customer	▪ Product description and specifications ▪ Product reviews ▪ Pricing ▪ Side-by-side comparison		
I just got my product in the mail. It doesn't fit in my home, so I need to return it.	New Customer		▪ Troubleshooting and workarounds ▪ Information on exchanges	▪ Returns and refunds information

LIGHT THE WAY

Nicely done. You've just made whoever is going to organize your content very happy. Your stakeholders are hopefully feeling a bit clearer on your content purpose and how it helps the organization. And the people who are responsible for creating and maintaining content are likely breathing a sigh of relief.

Next up, we'll get into how to organize your content so that your audiences can find what matters to them. After that, we'll start to pull all that content together into a cohesive experience with just the right content.

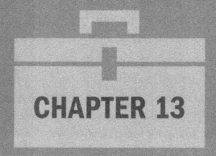

CHAPTER 13

ORGANIZE FOR INTUITIVE WAYFINDING

After you've determined what content your audiences need, you can organize it so that it's easy to find. Organization of content refers to the framework for grouping, labeling, and relating content to make it discoverable by people (meaning the people the content is for and the people who produce the content) and machines (such as search engines and your content management system [CMS]). The process of doing this work is commonly referred to as *information architecture*.

Common artifacts used to document how your content should be organized and related are sitemaps and taxonomies. In this chapter, we'll talk through ways to develop, document, and test these artifacts.

SITEMAPS

Sitemap diagrams are like organizational charts for your content. A sitemap visually demonstrates how the site is organized so that you can communicate the proposed structure to stakeholders and the people who will be building the website.

Sitemaps are especially helpful for websites with traditional navigation, such as tabs for each section of the website that link to a section landing page and sub-pages within that section. But they can also be used to communicate screens in an app. I'll be using sitemap examples in this chapter for more traditional websites, like this one for Voices for Racial Justice (www.voicesforracialjustice.org).

The sitemap for this example looks like this:

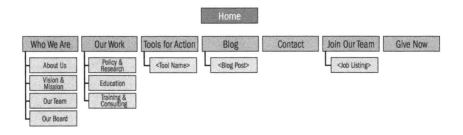

The Voices for Racial Justice (shout-out to my people!) website has a simple and flat hierarchy as you can see. So, a simple sitemap works quite well to document how the site is organized, what pages will need to be built, and how they are linked together hierarchically (more about the specifics of those pages and what they consist of in Chapter 14, "Define the Content Experience," and Chapter 15, "Specify Content Structure and Requirements").

For more complex organization requirements (such as those in the next image), you may need a more detailed sitemap to convey additional information like links between pages and key content to communicate in a section or on a page. I love the way my friend and colleague Callie Myers does this.

In this example of one site section from a project that Callie and I worked on together, note the following:

- The section landing page You Can Help is in a darker color to distinguish it from the other pages in the section.

- Under the section landing page and under most of the main pages in the section, there are details about what information goes on that page.

- When relevant, recommended links from pages in this section to other pages on the site are noted with angle brackets.

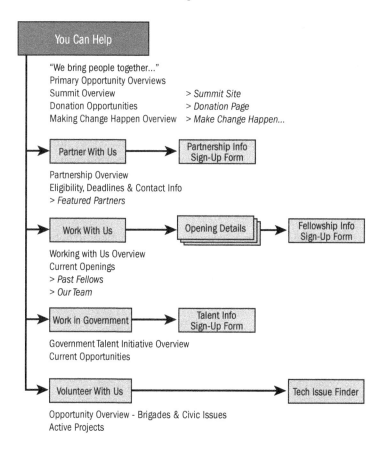

BUILDING YOUR SITEMAP

Before I jump into my somewhat organic approach to developing a sitemap, I want to recommend that you get a copy of the book *Everyday Information Architecture* by Lisa Maria Marquis (https://abookapart.com/products/everyday-information-architecture). Lisa Maria's approach is much more methodical than mine.

When we work together, our approaches can complement each other, which is one of the reasons I love working with Lisa Maria. Regardless of what kind of approach you take, these three principles for information architecture are universal:

- You want to make it easy for people using your website or application to learn how it's organized so that they know what to expect as they move throughout the site. This is particularly important if the user wants to compare content. For example, all products should have the same set of pages (such as features, success stories, how-to's) underneath them.

- You want people to be able to easily orient themselves to where they are on your website, no matter how they got there. For example, if they land on a page for a specific product and they want to explore other products in the same category, the information architecture should make it easy for them to back out a level to find all those products. The design of the navigation system plays a big role in orientation as well.

- You want to guide people to other relevant content and actions to help them complete their tasks. That's one reason I like to document in the sitemap where pages on the site link to other pages on the site. Another aspect of organizing information so that people can find it is enabled by taxonomy, which we'll get to in a bit.

HINT *Like most rules, guidelines, or principles, there are times it makes sense to break them. If I'm creating a sitemap for a digital product that contains content for audiences that are unlikely to overlap and need very different content, the organizational consistency within those content experiences is more important than consistency between them.*

That all sounds logical, right? But that doesn't mean organizing the content is easy or simple. So many factors are at play that can inform how you organize the content. And the truth is there is no one right way. So, creating your sitemap is a little bit art and a little bit science... and a lot iterative.

Let's walk through a couple examples of how I might think through ways to organize content.

In this first example, I knew that users of the website came looking for my client's services through one of three lenses:

- Location—Does the company have an office in my area?
- Industry—Does the company have experience in my industry?
- Service—Does the company offer the service I need?

The website's purpose was to help visitors decide whether the company fits their needs based on those three lenses. If the visitor liked the fit, we wanted to put them in touch with the most appropriate person who could help them.

So as part of developing the sitemap, I diagramed the content pathways based on those three lenses. The end of every pathway was to get people who were able to self-qualify as a potential customer to a means of contacting a sales consultant.

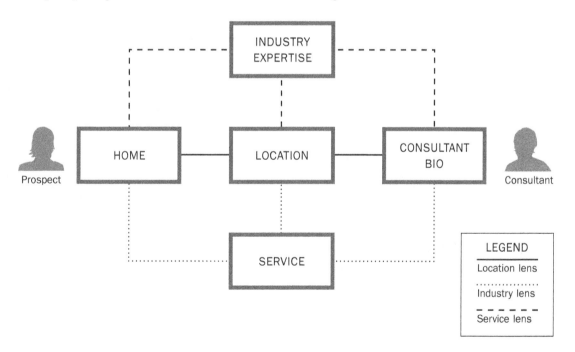

In this second example, I played around with mapping content to a site structure that followed their sales cycle. My organizing premise was that no matter where the users were in the sales cycle, they could easily find information they needed and take the next step in the path. I presented this high-level sitemap (mapped to the sales cycle) for feedback before moving ahead with developing a more detailed sitemap.

TIP   One way to help you think through possible ways of organizing your content is to do a card sort with people in your prioritized audiences. With a closed card sort, you have your categories already defined and ask people to sort descriptions of your content into them. With an open card sort, you provide the descriptions of your content and ask people to sort them into categories and name the categories.

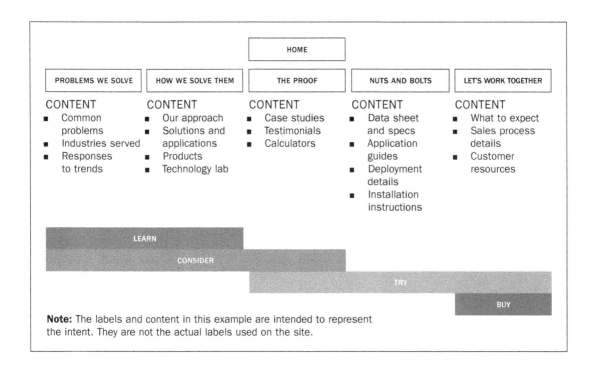

Note: The labels and content in this example are intended to represent the intent. They are not the actual labels used on the site.

Finally, in this third example (which is for the same client referenced in the detailed sitemap example that Callie Myers and I worked on from earlier in this chapter), Callie and I first developed a task-based framework for thinking about the site content. For this project, there were three buckets of tasks we wanted the sitemap to support:

- Helping people in our prioritized user groups decide whether they want to partner with our client

- Connect people in our prioritized groups with the appropriate partnership type

- Support partners with tools and resources to do the work they were partnering to do

Before we created our detailed sitemap, we obtained alignment from our client on this organizing framework:

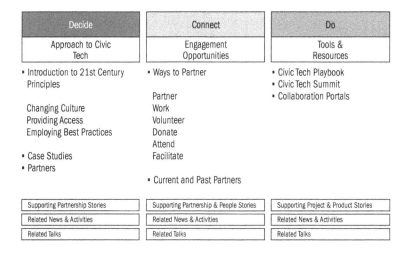

ITERATING YOUR SITEMAP

The first version of your sitemap is not likely to be the version you launch with for a couple reasons. The first reason is that you will hopefully iterate it with your team and then test it with actual people. And then you'll iterate again after that. The second reason is that as you start creating the content, stuff comes up that you perhaps hadn't accounted for. Sometimes it's stuff you missed (it happens), and other times it's because something changes (a product category is sunsetted, a product or service is added, and so on).

Let's talk about the iteration that happens on purpose, starting with iterating with the team working on the project and ending with testing with actual people in your prioritized audience groups.

INTERNAL ITERATION

The approach I like best is Dan Brown's from Eight Shapes Information Architecture Lenses. You can learn more about the approach and buy yourself a set of the cards on the Eight Shapes website (www.eightshapes.com/information-architecture).

The gist of this method is that you evaluate your proposed sitemap from a variety of perspectives. The categories of lenses, or perspectives, included in Dan's cards are as follows:

- How to flex
- How to present
- How to manage
- How to include
- How to explain
- How to guide
- How to classify
- How to engage

Each of these categories encompasses different lenses. For example, the *how to include* grouping contains a lens called *Who benefits?* Dan provides a description of each lens along with questions to help you analyze the sitemap from that perspective.

Sometimes I use Dan's method as he prescribes in his instructions, and sometimes I flex it a bit to meet the needs of my project, including what I know to be the biggest challenges or sticking points in getting alignment on the sitemap.

Here's an example of how I set up a team-working session to analyze a proposed sitemap for a higher education institution:

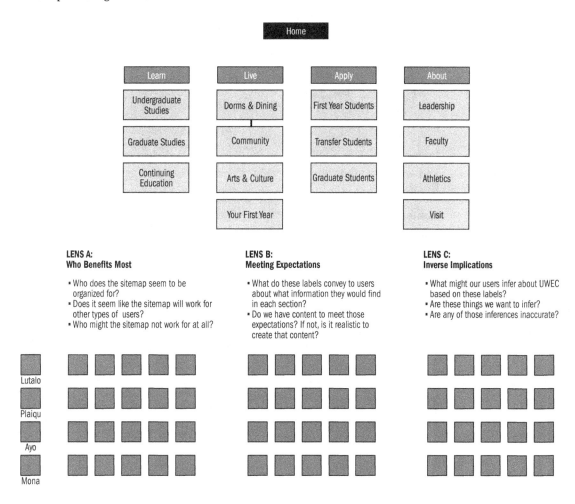

Notice that we used three of Dan's lenses (I switched up some of the questions a bit), and each person had a place to record their observations related to each lens. We worked through one lens at a time and discussed each before moving on to the next.

Then, each person had an opportunity to suggest how they might iterate on the sitemap based on our discussion and note what calls to action (CTAs) were more relevant for each section. This was homework, so I gave each person a blank table in Google slides. It looked a bit like **Table 13.1.**

TABLE 13.1 **SITEMAP ITERATIONS TEMPLATE**

<SECTION LABEL>	<SECTION LABEL>	<SECTION LABEL>	<SECTION LABEL>	<SECTION LABEL>
<Page or Content List>	<Page or Content List>	<Page or Content List>	<Page or Content List>	<Page or Content List>
<CTA 1> <CTA 2>	<CTA 1> <CTA 2>	<CTA 1> <CTA 2>	<CTA 1> <CTA 2>	<CTA 1> <CTA 2>

In this situation, I synthesized all the discussion and ideas into a revised sitemap and annotated the changes I made. Then, we discussed again and determined it was ready to test!

Content Strategy Tool 13.1: Sitemap Evaluation Working Session Exercises provides templates for analysis and iteration workshop activities.

CONTENT STRATEGY TOOL 13.1

SITEMAP EVALUATION WORKING SESSION EXERCISES

Grab the exercises from the Miro or Mural board to run your own sitemap critique session.

TIPS

- I highly recommend getting the Information Architecture Lenses from Eight Shapes (www.eightshapes.com/information-architecture) for ideas on perspectives to use to evaluate your sitemap.

- When working with people who don't make sitemaps for a living, setting up your sitemap iteration exercise with sticky notes or more familiar formats like a table helps those people become more comfortable with the exercise.

WHERE TO GET IT

Download the templates at www.peachpit.com/register.

WHERE IT CAME FROM

Meghan Casey (www.dobettercontent.com) with ideas from Dan Brown at Eight Shapes (www.eightshapes.com)

USER TESTING

I like a good Treejack test to learn whether the way the content is organized and the labels used to describe content make sense for your audiences. A Treejack test works a bit like this:

1 Identify a set of scenarios your site should support based on your strategic content purpose. For the higher education example I gave, tasks might include:

- What fields can you major and minor in at <college>?

- What kinds of academic resources are available to students?

- How much is tuition for <college>?

2 Build your sitemap in a Treejack testing application like Optimal Workshop (www.optimalworkshop.com). Depending on the complexity of your sitemap, you may want to test one level at a time rather than including the entire hierarchy in the first test. That way, you can iterate between tests.

3 Determine how you will field your test. Options include:

- Recruit through your testing tool. Optimal Workshop allows you to pay for test participants, but it can be difficult to narrow in on the right audience demographics.

- Send your test to people in your audience groups you have permission to contact.

- Publish your test on social media, in online forums, and so on.

4 Collect and analyze responses. The responses to your test can help you determine whether certain labels make sense to your users, how to connect content together to account for other paths people might take, and whether you're on track with how you've organized the website.

Here's what a Treejack test scenario looks like to the test participant in OptimalSort:

And here's the kind of data you get about how the task performed in your test. In addition to showing you how successful the task was, it tells you how directly people went to their final location. The directness score indicates how confident someone was that the location they selected was the right one.

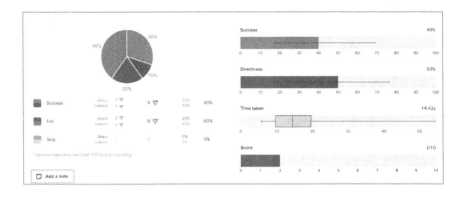

You can also get data and visualizations that show where people clicked first and what paths they ultimately took to the right or wrong locations.

After analyzing the data, you can come back with some recommendations about what to change and talk with the team about whether you want to test again or call the sitemap finished for now.

TAXONOMY

Okay, moving on to taxonomies. Taxonomy means ways of classifying content. I'm going to focus on how you might use taxonomy to "serve up" content based on what you know about people using your digital product and help people discover relevant content.

I can give examples of both scenarios—delivering content based on knowledge of the site visitor and based on the visitor's own discovery actions—using a digital product that has become an integral part of my life during the COVID times: DoorDash. When I open DoorDash to find a restaurant, I immediately see a row of cuisine types with some additional filters.

Those cuisine types and filters are based on taxonomies. And those taxonomies help me discover restaurants to order from.

A little farther down the page, I'm shown restaurants near me where I can get fast delivery.

And a little farther down, I'm shown restaurants that DoorDash thinks I might be interested in because I recently ordered Japanese food.

The restaurants that can deliver the fastest near me and the recommendations based on what I've ordered in the past use taxonomies to show me content based on what they know about where I am and what I like. So, the examples I've given represent both taxonomies that I as a user can click on to discover content and taxonomies that work "behind the scenes" and show me content *automagically*.

In summary, taxonomy is magic.

DOCUMENTING YOUR TAXONOMY

Let's look at the earlier example of the content pathways for people who may be looking for an industry, service, or location. That company may offer a service that's relevant for only some of the industries in which it has expertise. Or the service might be available in only some locations. If the description of that service should automatically populate only to the relevant industry and location pages, the company needs a taxonomy to associate the service with the appropriate industries and locations.

Taxonomies can sometimes be set up directly in the CMS. But often you'll need to put together a table or spreadsheet to define the taxonomies and the terms that they use. **Table 13.2** shows an example of how that might look, and **Content Strategy Tool 13.2: Taxonomy Documentation Template** is a template for documenting your taxonomy.

TABLE 13.2 **EXAMPLE TAXONOMY AND TERMS**

LOCATION	INDUSTRY	SERVICE
Chicago	Healthcare	Content Strategy
Barcelona	Finance	Web Design
Helsinki	Technology	Writing
Mexico City	Retail	User Experience
Hong Kong	Entertainment	Development

So let's say that Chicago is focused on the technology and entertainment industries and offers content strategy, web writing, and web design services. Using taxonomy, you can ensure that only information about those industries and services will appear on the Chicago location page.

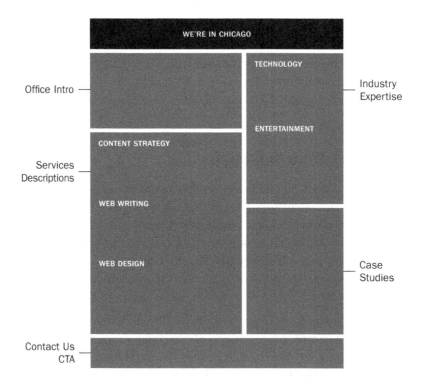

Pretty cool, right? Even cooler, some of the other stuff in that example could be pulled in via taxonomy. For example, you could tag every case study in the CMS with the appropriate location, industry, and service to automatically appear on relevant pages. Or maybe you could have a few versions of the Contact Us CTA.

You can associate the CTA with the locations, industries, and service pages on which it should appear.

 **HINT**   *The book* The Accidental Taxonomist *(www.hedden-information.com/accidental-taxonomist) by Heather Hedden is in its 3rd edition. If you want to dig deeper into taxonomy, I highly recommend you buy the book and check out Heather's blog at http://accidental-taxonomist.blogspot.com.*

CONTENT STRATEGY TOOL 13.2
TAXONOMY DOCUMENTATION TEMPLATE
Grab the Google sheet or AirTable template for a starter template to document your taxonomies.

TIPS

- Before going down a taxonomy rabbit hole, set a strategy for who you will use taxonomy. Don't do more than you have to. You can always do more later.

- If your organization is new to using taxonomy to serve up or personalize content, start small. Working with content in this way requires a major behavior shift, and you want to set your team up for success.

WHERE TO GET IT
Download the templates at www.peachpit.com/register.

WHERE IT CAME FROM
Meghan Casey (www.dobettercontent.com) and Brain Traffic (www.braintraffic.com)

ITERATING ON YOUR TAXONOMY

I'm going to turn toward a slightly different use case for taxonomy. Sometimes we are developing taxonomies that help internal teams store, access, and distribute content to the right people, at the right times, for the right reasons.

Storing information to be able to do that can require some robust taxonomies. Just off the top of my head, I brainstormed possible taxonomies for a large health-care organization I've worked with:

- Patient status—Is the content for prospective patients, current patients, lapsed patients, and so on?

- Plan member status—Is the content for prospective insurance plan members or current plan members, and if a current plan member, what plan do they have?

- Plan type—What plan type is the content related to?

- Conditions—What medical conditions is the content related to?

- Age group—What age groups do we want to provide this content to?

- Care type—Is the content related to preventive care, urgent care, emergency care, and so on?

- Campaign—Is the content related to a specific campaign?

- Restrictions—Are there restrictions on how the content can be used?

I could probably go on for at least a few more lines. Coming up with this initial list of taxonomy needs is likely a collaborative process in which you and your team document as many use cases as you can for finding and distributing content to the organization's audiences.

From there, you can build the terms or entries that fall under each taxonomy, such as the list of medical conditions you have content about.

Once you have an initial taxonomy in place, you'll want to test it in real-world situations. You could do this in a few ways. Two immediately come to mind:

- Grab a randomized set of content that has been produced in the last year or two and apply the taxonomies you've defined to it. Then you can analyze:

  - Were there taxonomy categories missing that would be helpful to provide?

  - Were there categories that were infrequently used, suggesting they might not be needed?

- Build a library of that same content with the taxonomies applied. Then, observe people as they navigate through the library to find content for their specific purposes and talk through what they're doing and noticing. Use those observations to iterate on your taxonomy.

ORGANIZED AND READY

You are well on your way to creating a content experience that delivers on your content purpose. The work you've done to organize your content is so important. And the people who use your website or other digital product will appreciate that work.

Next up, we'll cover how to pull your content together into useful and usable experiences that help your audiences do what they came to do. It's time to draw some pictures!

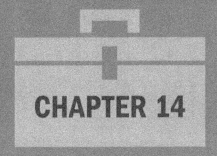

CHAPTER 14

DEFINE THE CONTENT EXPERIENCE

The sitemap is finished (although it may continue to evolve). Now it's time to contemplate how the people who need your website or other digital product will experience it. (We're going to focus on websites throughout this chapter.)

Defining the experience considers the likely pathways people will take through your website and defines how content should be presented to support people's needs along those pathways. Of course, we also need to consider that people can arrive at your site on any page and may not arrive at the right place for what they need.

In this chapter, you'll learn ways to formulate and document your content experience. And then we'll talk about how to test it with people who are candidates to visit your website.

FORMULATING THE CONTENT EXPERIENCE

You've likely already formulated some of the content experience as you organized the site and might have documented pieces of it. Remember this graphic from Chapter 13, "Organize for Intuitive Wayfinding"?

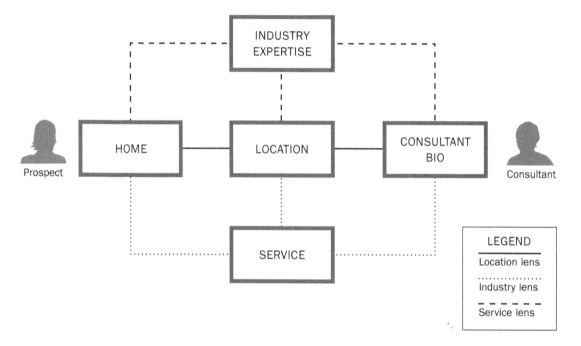

It's almost impossible to separate organizing the content from defining the content experience because the way the information is organized and the way people experience the content are necessarily intertwined.

Let's walk through how to use journey and flow mapping to help you determine what content is needed on key types of website pages so that they work within a defined user flow and can stand alone (because we can't control how people get to our sites or what they do when they get there). After that, we'll explore the Core Model, otherwise known as one of the best page-level content design frameworks ever.

Before we jump in, here are three principles that I've found apply to most projects I've ever worked on:

- People want to feel confident in their choices before they make a decision. For people to feel confident, the following typically must be true:

  - They believe they have and understand the information they need.

  - They feel like they have been able to consider their options.

  - They have an idea how their decision will impact them in real life.

  - They believe what they are about to decide reflects their values and priorities.

  Defining content experiences is all about building in the right information at the right times to support people in making confident decisions.

  Consider this example from some recommendations I put together for a former client, UCare, who provided Medicare Part C Plans. The pyramid in the image conveys five stages of information needs that people must have to make their decision and what kind of content my client could provide to satisfy those needs.

  - Absorb: At this stage, people are just getting a sense for the foundational information they need to understand a product, service, situation, and so on.

  - Align: At this stage, they are parsing information to determine what aspects match their values and priorities.

  - Apply: Here, they are imagining how what they've learned fits in with their daily lives or presumed needs.

  - Assess: At this stage, they are digging deeper into what makes sense for them and likely comparing options.

  - Act: Now, they have decided on a course of action!

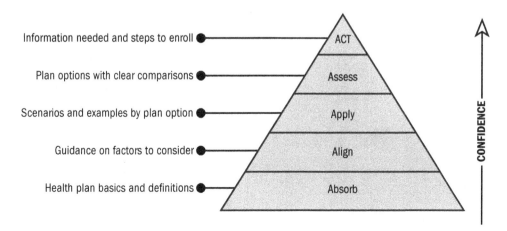

▪ People want to feel in control of their experience. That's why it's important to provide on-ramps and off-ramps with our content. I tend to think of facilitating this control a couple of ways:

▪ Ensure that the experiences allow for people to choose where to start or go based on where they are in their decision-making process.

This means organizing the content into a helpful flow, while allowing people to jump ahead or back up. As the Medicare example user flow shows, people can choose where to start in the process and can move between steps in the flow as needed.

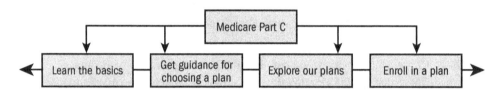

The design of the pages that support this flow make it easy for the user to choose their path. One design element that was implemented remained constant on the pages to help people navigate between them.

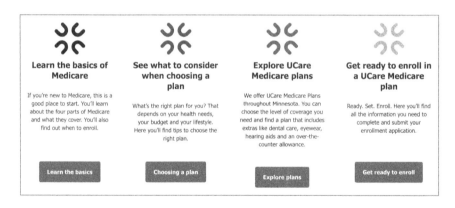

- Ensure you provide options for how people interact with you as they make their decision. Examples include offering the option to talk to a human if you can accommodate it or enabling other ways of discovering answers like search or chatbots.

In the Medicare example, a consistent part of the experience was the opportunity to talk to what the client called "Medicare de-complicators," as shown in the image. They didn't implement live chat or a chatbot because they didn't have the infrastructure to support it.

Chat with a de-complicator

Our licensed Medicare specialists can answer your questions or walk you through the enrollment process step by step.

Call
TTY users

- People tend to crave simplicity, and simplicity breeds credibility. David Dylan Thomas talks about this concept in his book *Design for Cognitive Bias* (https://abookapart.com/products/design-for-cognitive-bias), which is a brilliant book you should get right now. He says to "design for believability" to harness cognitive bias for good—people are more likely to believe (have a bias toward) that a digital "thing" is accurate, helpful, and so on if they perceive it to be simple.

Let's look at the 2016 version of the www.medicare.gov website. Not so simple, huh? Where would you even start?

Let's look at it now. Much simpler, right? The truth is Medicare has not become simpler, but the website is doing a better job at making the experience simple. Kudos to that team!

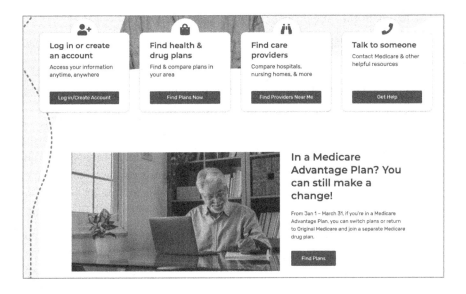

Ok, let's dig into mapping user journeys and flows.

USER JOURNEYS AND PATHWAYS

Let's talk about the difference between journeys and pathways first … or at least the distinction that I make between them:

- The *user journey* is a person's entire experience, which may lead them to a digital property or ecosystem.

- The *user pathway* is what happens once a person gets to the digital property or ecosystem.

As an example, let's say someone were to injure their wrist because they fell while ice skating (that someone was me). Some of the steps in my journey were:

1 Rock back and forth on the ice in pain.

2 Make my way to the warming house.

3 Tell the warming house staff what happened and fill out some forms.

4   Try to figure out on my own if my wrist is broken. (It was.)

5   Go to my insurance company's website from my phone and make an urgent care appointment.

6   Go to urgent care and be diagnosed with a broken wrist.

7   Check if my prescription for pain meds is ready so I can pick it up on the way home.

8   Call my employer to let them know that I won't be in tomorrow.

9   Go to my company's intranet site to figure out how to start a short-term disability claim.

10 Schedule my surgery and make a pre-operation appointment.

A few of those steps involved using a digital property to find information or do something. Those steps can be broken into user pathways or flows. For example, we can map out the pathway on a medical reference site for finding out how to tell if a bone is broken or the flow for making an appointment with urgent care.

Both journey mapping and pathway mapping can be helpful in defining your content experience. Journey mapping can help you empathize with your users' experience and understand how your content fits within it, and pathway mapping can help define optimal flows through site pages and page-level priorities.

So, how do we map journeys and pathways?

HINT   *While I'm focusing on websites in this chapter, I highly recommend you check out Noz Urbina's resources from an omnichannel perspective, meaning all the ways a company distributes content to their audiences. Check out his material at www.urbinaconsulting.com.*

I recommend you do it collaboratively with subject matter experts (SMEs) and your UX and visual design friends. The maps themselves and the process you use to create them can serve as a tool for understanding and perhaps even save some steps in your process. It can also be something you do on your own, depending on the team and who is responsible for what.

JOURNEY MAPPING

For user journey mapping, I typically set up an exercise that looks a little something like this image.

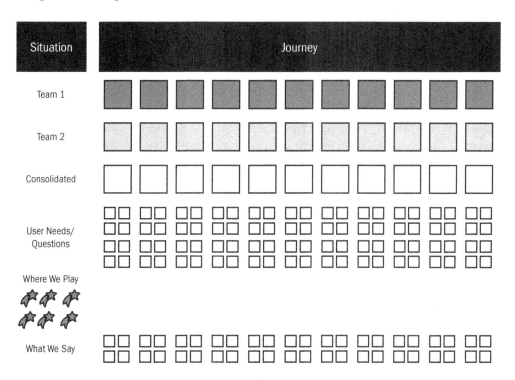

Here's how I facilitate the session using the structure in the image:

1 Write the scenario or trigger in the box at the top left. For example, from the journey I outlined previously, it could be something like: Person experiences an injury (or much more specific depending on your organization).

2 Break your team into two groups and have the groups work to outline the steps in the journey related to the trigger/situation you are working on.

3 Have each group share their journeys. Discuss where you overlap and diverge. Then, work together to consolidate into one journey.

4 Brainstorm the questions someone in that situation is likely to have or tasks they are likely going to need to complete at each step in the journey.

5 Place an icon of some kind on the steps in the journey that your organization's website might use.

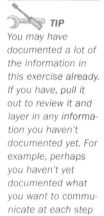

TIP

You may have documented a lot of the information in this exercise already. If you have, pull it out to review it and layer in any information you haven't documented yet. For example, perhaps you haven't yet documented what you want to communicate at each step where your website might be used.

You may wonder why you'd wait to do this after you brainstormed all those questions. Your brainstorming gives you a lot of context for what people are thinking about and doing before and after they use your website. And that information helps you craft user-centered content experiences.

6 For each step where your website might be used, brainstorm what you need to communicate to the user to answer their questions or help them complete their task.

PATHWAY MAPPING

For pathway mapping, I typically start with a visual of the sitemap as an image to orient people (or myself) to the pages planned for the website. Let's use one of the sitemap examples from Chapter 13 for Voices for Racial Justice.

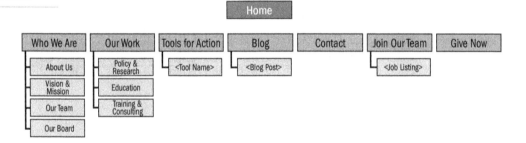

Then we need to decide what user needs we need to create pathways for. Luckily, you already know what tasks users are trying to complete based on previous work like journey mapping and top tasks analysis (from Chapter 12, "Prioritize Based on Your Strategy").

For this example, let's say that the task is deciding whether to apply for a job at Voices for Racial Justice. Like the user journey mapping, I'd facilitate a discussion to define the desired or presumed pathways a visitor to our site might take in that scenario.

1 Brainstorm any assumptions we want to make about the scenario. For example, one of the assumptions in our example is that the person is not familiar with Voices for Racial Justice.

2 Brainstorm questions the person is likely to need answers to as they decide whether to apply.

3 Using the sitemap for reference, plot out likely paths the user might take through the website to answer those questions.

4 Connect questions with the pages to include the right content that answers the questions.

The following figure shows what the result might look like.

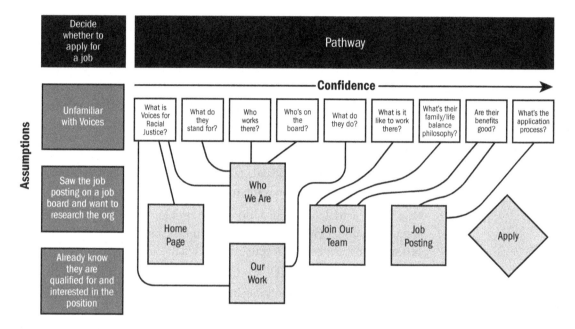

Mapping the pathways and relating questions to pages can help you plan out what should be on each page. And that's a perfect segue to the Core Model.

THE CORE MODEL

In 2006, Are Halland developed the Core Model to take the focus off website homepages as the crown of digital experiences and design. A second impetus was developing a way for people to collaborate across disciplines.

> **HINT**   Are made some updates and wrote a book on the Core Model titled Core Content (www.kjernepar.no/are-halland). If you read Norwegian, you can order it now. An English translation version is coming out in 2023. Because I haven't used his new versions yet, I'm sticking with the original version in this chapter.

CASE STUDY: CONTENT FOR CANCER

I first learned about the Core Model when I heard Ida Aalen of Netlife Research present a case study for the Norwegian Cancer Society (NCS) (www.kreftforeningen.no). It truly blew my mind.

Instead of trying to tell the story, I'm going to use Ida's own words from her *A List Apart* (www.alistapart.com) article, "The Core Model: Designing Inside Out for Better Results" (https://alistapart.com/article/the-core-model-designing-inside-out-for-better-results), which was published on January 6, 2015.

Ida describes what you need in order to use the Core Model. You'll note that Netlife Research also uses Gerry McGovern's Top Tasks Analysis methodology:

To use the Core Model, you need the following:

- Business objectives: Prioritized, measurable objectives and subobjectives. What does the organization want to achieve?

- User tasks: Actual, researched, prioritized user tasks. What is it that people want to get done? (We usually conduct top-task surveys to identify the user tasks, which is a great tool if you want to align the organization on what tasks your website needs to support.)

Ida goes on to explain how analyzing business goals and user tasks helped identify the site's core pages. This piece is very similar to what I talked about back in Chapter 12. I called them *focus* pages; Ida calls them *cores*. She explains how identifying your core pages can also help you create pathways to pages users might not be looking for initially but that you want to drive them toward:

An example from the NCS is its page dedicated to information about lung cancer. Our user research identified a huge need for qualified and authoritative information on the many forms of cancer—and seeing that one of the objectives for the NCS is to educate Norwegians about cancer, this is a clear match of the users' needs with the organization's larger objective.

"But what happens with pages like "Donate"? Our research showed that users did not typically search the site for information related to fundraising, but being able to receive donations online is essential if the NCS is going to raise more money for cancer research. This is where the Core Model truly shines: If you create good cores, you'll also be able to create good pathways to other, less-requested pages on your website, regardless of where they are placed in the information architecture. A core page should never be a blind alley.

Next, she describes the purpose of the Core Model and what you get out of it in the end:

> It helps the graphic designer know which are the most important elements to emphasize in the design. It helps include clients or stakeholders who are less web-savvy in your project strategy. It helps the copywriters and editors leave silo thinking behind and create better content.
>
> ⋯
>
> With a prioritized list of what kind of content and modules needs to be on the most important pages, it's a lot easier for the team to get to work, regardless of whether they are user interface (UI) designers, graphic designers, or content strategists.

TIP *As I've mentioned throughout the book, you don't always have the opportunity to collaborate with your clients or others in your organization during your project. It's best if you can. But you can use the Core Model on your own or with a small team, if necessary.*

TIP *One note of clarification on identifying the core pages: If you feel confident after your top-tasks analysis or mapping work that you know which pages should be the core pages (and you think stakeholders will agree), you can come to the workshop with a list. Or you can brainstorm and prioritize core pages with workshop participants.*

Then, the exciting part: She explains how to hold a Core Model workshop. Here are my crib notes. See **Content Strategy Tool 14.1: Collaborative Design Studio Workshop Plan** for all the details and templates.

1 Identify your cores.

Identify your core pages by matching the business objectives and the user tasks. The top-tasks analysis, which we talked about in Chapter 12, and pathway mapping from earlier in this chapter, are great inputs into identifying your cores.

Let's use the example of a cancer type template, for example "lung cancer," where you match the following tasks and objectives:

Business objectives:

- Helping patients and their friends and family
- Increasing knowledge about cancer and prevention

User tasks:

- Learn about different forms of cancer
- Identify symptoms of cancer
- Get tips for preventing cancer
- Find information about treating cancer (therapies, adverse effects, risks, and prognosis)

Core page: <u>Form of cancer (example: "lung cancer")</u>

Business goals (achieve at least one)   **User tasks**

<u>Helping patients and their friends and family</u>   <u>Cancer forms (symptoms, prognosis, treatment)</u>

<u>Increasing knowledge about cancer & prevention</u>   <u>Symptoms of cancer</u>

_____   <u>Preventing cancer</u>

_____   <u>Treatment of cancer</u>

Inward paths   **Core content**   **Forward paths**

2 Plan for inward paths.

Instead of jumping into content creation and detailing that page, map out the inward paths. This is where you'll look carefully at any user research findings to help inform decisions. How might people find this page? How did they get here?

This approach is a simple way to prompt your client to think about the page from a user's perspective. In the example of the lung cancer page, plausible inward paths include the following:

- Doing a browser search for lung cancer

- Doing a browser search for symptoms

- Clicking a link on the homepage

- Finding a link in a printed brochure

3 Determine core content.

Begin talking about the core content. What content do you need on this page for it to achieve the goals of both the organization and the users? What kind of modules or elements do you need?

In this task, the participants are using all the information they have on their worksheets: the user tasks, the business objectives, and the inward paths. Considering this information, what are the most important things that should go on that page—and in what order? Having a solid user research foundation at hand will make this process much simpler. In the case of the NCS workshop, the user research had identified cancer prevention as a top user concern, which made it clear that we needed to say something about prevention—sometimes even for cancer types that cannot be prevented.

4 Set forward paths.

This is key to the Core Model's success. After visitors have their questions answered, where do you want to send them next? At this point, you can allow yourself to think more about business goals in a general sense.

For the lung cancer page, it could be forward paths like these:

- Cancer help line (so they don't diagnose themselves)

- How to prevent all forms of cancer, not just this specific type of cancer

- Patient rights, if they are reading about treatment

- Information about the political work and lobby work NCS does (for example, trying to reduce treatment waiting times)

Do this in the context of user tasks. If someone is visiting the website in a fearful state, hoping to find solid information about melanoma, do you really want to conclude their journey with a flashy "Donate!" message? No—that would just be rude and insensitive and is unlikely to encourage donations anyway. However, many users do look for general information on cancer research, and in this context, you can frame it more specifically: "If you think cancer research is important, you can help us by donating." (And in fact, this more considerate approach might end up increasing donations, as it did for the NCS.)

Core page: Form of cancer (example: "lung cancer")

Business goals (achieve at least one)	**User tasks**
Helping patients and their friends and family	Cancer forms (symptoms, prognosis, treatment)
Increasing knowledge about cancer & prevention	Symptoms of cancer
	Preventing cancer
	Treatment of cancer

Inward paths	**Core content**	**Forward paths**
Googling "lung cancer"	Symptoms first!	Cancer line
Googling a symptom	Make sure you go to the doctor; don't diagnose yourself from a website!	Prevention
Homepage?	Survival rates	Rights
"Lung cancer" brochure	Not all cancer forms can be prevented. Risk factors and causes too, not just prevention efforts.	NCS opinion on this subject

---

5 Think mobile to prioritize.

After all these steps, participants are usually excited. Their worksheets are full of ideas for content, modules, and all sorts of functionality.

The enthusiasm is great—that's something we want—but a worksheet full of discursive ideas is difficult to work with. Are all these things equally important?

That is why the final step in the workshop is to use mobile-first thinking to prioritize all the elements. Give the participants a slightly different version of the worksheet and ask them: If you had just a small screen available, in which order would you place the elements you've identified throughout the workshop? They'll also need to place those forward paths they've written down in the context of the main content.

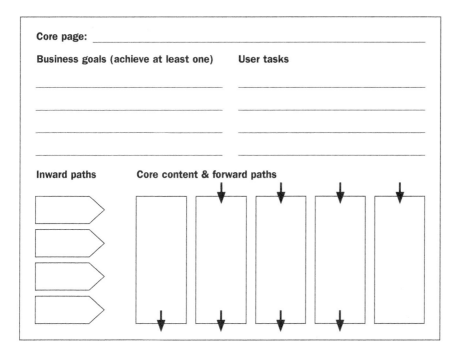

Keep in mind that you must still figure out what content is needed for your lesser priority pages, the ones you drive and guide people to (and even the "meh" pages because you'll probably have some).

You know I would never leave you without a tool or template by now, don't you? **Content Strategy Tool 14.1: Collaborative Design Studio Workshop Plan** contains links to Miro and Mural boards with exercises for user journey and pathway mapping and the Core Model.

CONTENT STRATEGY TOOL 14.1
COLLABORATIVE DESIGN STUDIO WORKSHOP PLAN

Get links to the online journey and pathway mapping working session exercises in Mural and Miro and all the updated material for the Core Model.

TIPS

- Don't try to do it all. Pick the activities and scenarios that will get you, your stakeholders, and your team the most clarity for the highest-priority user needs/tasks.

- Leave the homepage for last. Your core pages will influence what goes on the homepage.

- Have fun. This is yet another way to keep stakeholders engaged and get them aligned on the project.

WHERE TO GET IT

Download the templates at www.peachpit.com/register.

WHERE IT CAME FROM

Meghan Casey (www.dobettercontent.com) and Are Halland, creator of the Core Model (www.kjernepar.no/are-halland)

DOCUMENTING THE CONTENT EXPERIENCE

How you document the content experience depends on the following things (at least):

- Your role on the project and what you're responsible for delivering

- How you have and will collaborate with who needs the documentation to do their work

- The complexity of the content experience

Let's walk through a few examples to demonstrate. I'll go from simpler and scrappier forms of documentation to more complex ones.

In this first example, I was brought in after the sitemap had been developed, and it was a very simple website. We were also moving very fast toward a launch date.

The people who would be using my documentation were the developer and the visual designer:

- The developer was going to match content priorities with content components that came "in the box" for the website theme the client was using.

- The visual designer was going to use the documentation to create mock-ups of the pages to share with developers to inform how to style the components.

My documentation was probably the scrappiest I have ever delivered. I just outlined the page priorities in a Mural board we were collaborating in ahead of each sprint (an Agile methodology timeframe for getting work done). This image is an example of the three pages for their first sprint:

Page Outlines - Sprint 1

Home Page	Shop Collections	About
0 Could we have an optional Banner of some kind at launch. It would be about delivery/fulfillment area.	**1** Category teasers One-sentence description of each category. Imagine this same text would be used at the top of the corresponding collection page.	**1** Why we exist Combines mission with story
1 The Plant Lady story > Links to About > Shop		
2 Our Products > Shop by category		**2** Our founders
3 Testimonials	**2** The Plant Lady Says Promo of a relevant blog post, maybe something that details when you might want to choose a specific product type.	**3** Our plans for the future Talk about launch and future plans for brick and mortar, etc.
4 The Plant Lady Says > Blog preview		
5 Upcoming Events	**3** Delivery model teaser with link into details.	**4** The Plant Lady Says Optional list of recent blog posts
6 Email/Text Signup Widget	**4** Do we need any kind of disclaimer about not offering medical advice, etc.?	**5** Optional Upcoming Events

A likely scenario for this second example is what I might produce after a working session with the UX designer and client SMEs where we perhaps used the Core Model to think through the desired content experience. It's a low-fidelity drawing of the page priorities. In a case like this, I always make it clear that I am not suggesting where things should "go" on the page, but rather the priority so that the visual and UX designers have a reference for how to bring the page to life. It can also serve as an alignment artifact to ensure the client is on the same page.

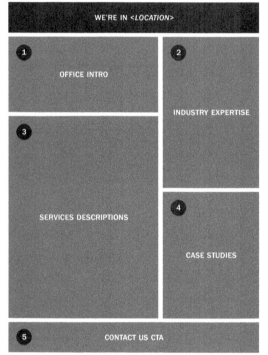

OBJECTIVE

Demonstrate the capabilities and expertise of the location, and provide contract information for the sales lead.

Content Priorities

1. Highlight the key differentiator of the location selected.
2. List the industries the location specializes in and why that expertise matters. (Industry descriptions will prepopulate based on the taxonomy.)
3. List the name of the service and a short description about our approach to providing it and the results a customer can expect.
4. Provide short teasers for case studies (up to three), focusing on the results of the work.
5. Include the key contact for the office with a short bio and contact information.

PREPARING FOR LAUNCH

- Create the taxonomy and map service descriptions, industry experience, and case studies to the appropriate locations if you'd like to auto-populate that content.
- Each office will need to choose a key contact to include on this page.

The final example is something that I might hand off to a client for review when there are predetermined content components that I need to consider as "containers" for the content. With this approach, I can mock up actual content. This partial example shows the content direction alongside a content mock-up. If I'm able to get into the CMS and create a page that my client can preview, as in the next image, I'll do that instead. It's always better when we can cut steps between documentation and distribution-ready content!

DO BETTER CONTENT CONSULTING HOME

1- VALUE PROPOSITION Short statement that summarizes the philosophy of the organization	 ABOUT SERVICES CONTACT TESTIMONIALS **Equity-and-inclusion-minded consulting for organizations that do good and want to do content better**
2- MY CLIENTS Overview of the kinds of projects we do and who we like to work with.	**Better Content Together** Do Better Content Consulting works with businesses, organizations, and campaigns that care about making the world a just place for everyone. And especially people whose stories, experiences, desires, and needs are too often an afterthought if they are thought of at all. If your work centers those who most in the margins and you want your content to prove it, let's talk. GET IN TOUCH
3- MEET YOUR CONSULTANT Client-need-focused heading and a short bio.	**Meet Meghan**  Looking for a content consultant to help you bring order to content chaos? Look no further. **Meghan Casey** has more than 20 years experience in communications, marketing, content strategy, and stakeholder whispering. Eight of those years were at Brain Traffic, the consultancy that put content strategy on the map.
4- SMARTS Teaser for The Content Strategy Toolkit.	Meghan's book The Content Strategy Toolkit: Methods, Guidelines, and Templates for Getting Content Right has become a go-to guide for new and seasoned content professionals alike. "Quality content increases value. Poor-quality content destroys value. It's as simple as that. Meghan's book has specific, practical, and immediately actionable ideas that will help you increase the quality of your content." —Gerry McGovern, CEO, Customer Carewords 

Content Strategy Tool 14.2: Content Experience Documentation Templates contains example templates like the ones shown for documenting the content experience when you don't have the ability to create directly in the CMS or, like me, you are not a designer. There's no one right way to document. It's all about who needs to know what to approve the direction or do the work that comes next.

I've literally sent my UX and visual collaborators pictures I drew with crayon and pen to demonstrate my recommendations for content. Like this one:

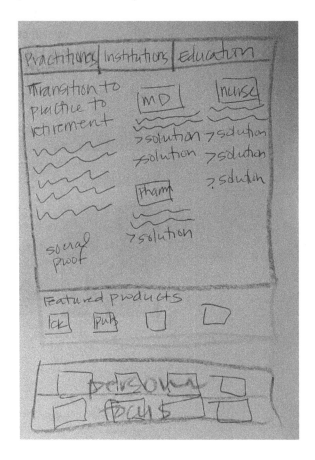

TIP *Tools like Figma (www.figma.com) can be a brilliant way to play with content substance and form, especially if you already have established patterns and components. Just be sure to document the content direction in a way that's accessible and usable for the people who will be creating content when you're not around.*

CONTENT STRATEGY TOOL 14.2

CONTENT EXPERIENCE DOCUMENTATION TEMPLATES

Get examples and templates to help you document your content experience.

TIPS

- Don't overthink it. Ask yourself what level of fidelity is needed to get the go-ahead to move forward from decision makers and provide your collaborators with what they need to do their work effectively.

- You might use different types of documentation with different people. Stakeholders might need something a bit more fleshed out, whereas your collaborators might be fine with a napkin sketch.

- Don't be afraid to show work in various stages. Iteration and collaboration make your work better. Perfectionism can hold you back from finding an elegant solution.

WHERE TO GET IT

Download the templates at www.peachpit.com/register.

WHERE IT CAME FROM

Meghan Casey (www.dobettercontent.com)

TESTING THE CONTENT EXPERIENCE

To test the content experience, I recommend moderated testing (that is, personally interacting with test participants) with three to five people per audience segment. If you did a Treejack test (or tests) to validate your sitemap, you can—should—use the same scenarios for your content experience testing. That's because those scenarios represented the top reasons people come to your website. And those scenarios likely guided what user journeys and flows you worked through in the process of defining the content experience.

Let's walk through the methodology as you might set up your test plan. Remember that we talked about user testing of content back in Chapter 8, "Get Familiar with Your Content." The method we'll look at next is included in **Content Strategy Tool 8.2: Sample User Tests.**

But, first, what exactly should you test and at what level of fidelity? That depends… every content strategist's favorite words. The number 1 recommendation I can give you is to test with close-to-final content.

HINT   *Remember, you aren't testing the entire website because you're focusing on top tasks. And even within top tasks, you might choose a representative product, service, or scenario to validate the experience.*

Beyond that, here are a few things to consider when you're deciding whether you should test something that's still pretty sketchy (think black-and-white wireframes turned into a clickable prototype) or something polished that resembles a real live website or *is* a real live website. Keep in mind that these are things to think about, but I do not have all the answers.

- Are you reusing design patterns without any modifications and are you able to plug new content into either a staging site or something like Figma without a ton of extra design work?
    - Yes. Test something that resembles the live website.
    - No. Go lower fidelity so that what you learn can inform new design patterns and components.
- How confident are you in what you know about your audiences and their journeys?
    - Super confident. Test something on the side of higher fidelity because the tweaks will likely be minimal.
    - Not so confident. Test something lower fidelity to make it easier to iterate.
- Will you have an opportunity to repeat the test at a higher level of fidelity?
    - Yes. Start with something lower fidelity and add fidelity after the first round of testing.
    - No. Test in as close to a live website state as possible that won't hinder you if you determine significant tweaks are needed.

METHODOLOGY DETAILS

Now let's dig into what to include in your user testing plan and how you'll facilitate the user interviews.

TEST PURPOSE AND APPROACH

The objectives of your test will likely be something like these:

- Understand how easy or difficult it is for test participants to find information or functionality associated with validated top tasks.

- Determine whether content associated with validated top tasks flows intuitively, meets users' needs and expectations, and is clear, complete, relevant, and useful.

Here's an example of how I describe the methodology:

- Ask participants to walk through how they would get to the page that would allow them to find/do what's asked in a series of scenarios.

- If they don't get to the page(s) we want them to, note that and direct them so that we can ask questions about the content itself.

- Ask relevant follow-up questions based on users' behaviors and narration.

PARTICIPANTS

As I've mentioned previously, you'll get the best results if you're talking with people who are in your prioritized audience(s). In my test plan, I'll note what specific audience groups we want to test with and how many of each we'd like to include.

I tend to get three to five people per prioritized audience if possible to participate in the tests to get enough insights to act upon with confidence. I've had good luck recruiting people from previous Treejack tests. You can also recruit from test panels that various user research and testing companies offer. Get as close to a realistic representation of your audience characteristics as you can.

TEST SCENARIOS

When I present the test scenarios to my client and team, I include the research questions each scenario will help us understand. **Table 14.1** is an example of what that might look like for a website about juices. You'll note there is one scenario for all participants and one for each priority audience group.

TABLE 14.1 **EXAMPLE TEST SCENARIO**

PARTICIPANTS	RESEARCH QUESTIONS	SCENARIO
All Participants	Does the label Juice Bundles make sense to participants? Do people understand what a bundle is and why they might choose it?	Where would you go to find out if you can get a variety pack of juices?
Cleanse Customer	Can people find the juice cleanses? Do they understand the differences between the cleanses?	Where would you go if you were looking for juices that help you detox your body?
Everyday Juicers	Can people find the juices geared for everyday drinking? Do they understand the health benefits of the various options?	Where would you go to find a juice option to add to your daily routine?

HAPPY PATHS

In most test plans, I also include the pathways to guide people through our content experience. Including this information is a way to make sure we've accounted for all the pages our prototype should feature and reminds the team what we designed and why.

Table 14.2 is an example from our juice example scenarios.

TABLE 14.2 **EXAMPLE TEST SCENARIO**

PARTICIPANTS	SCENARIO	HAPPY PATH(S)
Everyday Juicers	Where would you go to find a juice option to add to your daily routine?	Home > Shop Juices > Everyday Options

TEST SCRIPT

The last piece is putting together a test script that will help you or whoever is doing the research guide participants through the scenarios. The script is made up of three parts typically:

1 An introduction to orient participants to how the test will work. In your introduction, be sure to mention things like

- This is a test of our website, not of you.

- Not everything you'll see will be clickable.

- I may direct you to places to click throughout the test.

2 The test itself that walks through each scenario. It might look something like this:

Let's say that you wanted to find a way to buy multiple juices of different varieties without having to add them individually to your cart. Where do you think you could find that?

Listen to their answers and prompt for more explanation as follows:

- If they navigate to the Juice Bundles page, say:

   "Take as much time to look through this page. Like you've been doing, please talk through what you see and what you think it means. We may ask a few follow-up questions along the way."

- If they don't specifically talk about what they'd expect Juice Bundles to be, ask them.

- If they don't navigate to the Juice Bundles on their own, say:

   "Could you click the link that says Juice Bundles in the middle of the homepage? Thank you. Take as much time to look through this page. Like you've been doing, please talk through what you see and what you think it means. We may ask a few follow-up questions along the way."

3 Test wrap-up. Be sure to thank the participants. It's always a good idea to offer a token of appreciation, like a gift card.

USING YOUR FINDINGS TO ITERATE

Once you've finished your interviews, it's time to synthesize what you learned. I like to keep a list of key observations from each interview as I go. Then at the end, you can turn those observations into digital stickies and organize them into themes.

At that point, I like to pull my collaborators together and collectively discuss how we might iterate on the experience to address what we learned. From there, you can decide whether you want to iterate and test again or whether you feel confident that the changes you plan to make will address the issues that arose.

DEFINED, DESIGNED, AND REFINED

You are doing it. You've designed a truly user-centered experience and are ready to move into some of the nitty-gritty details.

Next up, we'll cover how to break your content experience into chunks that will make it easier to create, publish, and reuse. We'll also explore how to get specific about what content goes on each page to enable writers (and other types of producers) to create amazing useful and usable content.

CHAPTER 15

SPECIFY CONTENT STRUCTURE AND REQUIREMENTS

You just defined how you want to guide people through your website content based on what information they need and tasks they want to complete. Now, you're going to take it all apart.

My analogy for thinking about structuring your content is kind of silly, but it seems to work. A few years ago, there was a restaurant trend for menus to include deconstructed dishes, like deconstructed lasagna. To make deconstructed lasagna, you must know what goes into regular lasagna, right?

When you defined the content experience, you made "lasagna." Now you are going to deconstruct the lasagna into its smaller components, and those components will be available to use in other dishes. After that, you'll start specifying content requirements for the pages of your website and mapping current content (if you have current content) to your new sitemap and page structure.

SPECIFYING CONTENT STRUCTURE

Before I go any further, I need to give a shoutout to all the people in the content community who have taught me so much about the concepts I'll talk about in this section. I couldn't have written this material without them.

Let me start with Eileen Webb, who first introduced the concept of the author experience. A lot of what I'll say in this chapter is directly drawn from the work she has so graciously and generously shared. Next up, I want to mention Jeff Eaton, who proves to us all that developers who are advocates for content are the best developers to collaborate with. Next up is Mike Atherton and Carrie Hane, who wrote the amazing book *Designing Connected Content: Plan and Model Digital Products for Today and Tomorrow* (www.pearson.com/en-us/subject-catalog/p/designing-connected-content-plan-and-model-digital-products-for-today-and-tomorrow/P200000009416/9780134763385), which helped me further my understanding of structured content and content modeling. And finally, my thanks to Deane Barker, whose books *Real World Content Modeling: A Field Guide to CMS Features and Architecture* (https://deanebarker.net/books/real-world-content-modeling) and *The Web Project Guide: From Spark to Launch and Beyond* (https://webproject.guide), which he co-wrote with Corey Vilhauer, are also excellent resources.

This chapter draws from the expertise of these very smart people I'm honored to have learned from. The chapter does not go super deep into content modeling; rather, it summarizes the key concepts that you should understand to be a collaborative partner in structuring and modeling content. Let's start with a primer.

STRUCTURED CONTENT PRIMER

Structured content is how you break down repeatable content patterns (or templates) into smaller parts or components that can be authored within a template or as a separate content item and used across webpages, applications, and other platforms.

Structured content is the magic that brings together these three concepts:

- **Content experience:** In this context, the content experience is how people interact with and engage with your content everywhere it is. In the previous chapter, we focused on websites, but the content experience can cross delivery channels, formats, and so on.

- **Author experience:** The author experience is the content management system (CMS) that people who work with content use to create and relate content for the intended audience.

- **Content model:** The content model details the content types and components and how they relate to each other. It serves as a translation layer between the content experience and the author experience and a collaboration tool between content strategy and software development.

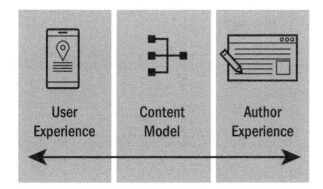

STRUCTURED CONTENT AND THE CONTENT EXPERIENCE

One of the best examples for demonstrating structured content is a recipe (the actual recipe part, not the novella you have to read these days to get to ingredients and how to make the thing). The recipe example, shown in the following images, in a workshop that Eileen did several years back is what made a lot of these concepts click for me.

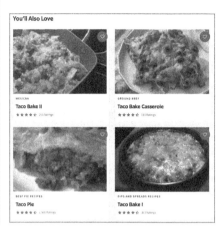

Ingredients

- 1 pound ground beef
- 1 (1 ounce) package taco seasoning mix
- 1 cup salsa
- ½ (15 ounce) can black beans, rinsed and drained (Optional)
- 1 (8.5 ounce) package corn bread mix (such as Jiffy®)
- ⅓ cup milk
- 1 egg
- 1 tablespoon honey
- 1 tablespoon corn oil
- ½ cup corn (Optional)
- 1 cup shredded Cheddar cheese
- 1 cup corn chips, partially crushed

Directions

Step 1
Cook and stir ground beef in a skillet over medium heat until brown and crumbled, 7 to 10 minutes; drain grease. Add taco seasoning; mix well. Stir in salsa and black beans; remove from heat.

Step 2
Grease a 9-inch pie pan or casserole dish.

Step 3
Mix corn bread mix, milk, egg, honey, and corn oil together in a bowl until batter is smooth; stir in corn. Pour batter into pie pan. Layer ground beef mixture over batter; sprinkle with Cheddar cheese. Top with corn chips.

Step 4
Place in a cold oven; set temperature to 350 degrees F (175 degrees C). Bake until sides are golden brown, 30 to 35 minutes.

WWW.ALLRECIPES.COM/RECIPE/254818/QUICK-TACO-BAKE-PIE

If you were to look at the content entry for that recipe in a CMS, you would likely find the following information (although I made up that they had a video of someone making the recipe):

- Recipe name
- Tagline
- Contributor
- Rating
- Prep details
- Main photo
- Photos
- Long video
- Short video
- Ingredients
- Directions
- Nutrition info
- Short teaser
- Long teaser

Of that information, the items bolded below would apply to the recipe page shown in the example images:

- **Recipe name**
- **Tagline**
- **Contributor**
- **Rating**
- **Prep details**
- **Main photo**
- **Photos**

- **Long video**
- Short video
- **Ingredients**
- **Directions**
- **Nutrition info**
- Short teaser
- Long teaser

That same recipe entry in the CMS stores the information that might populate a teaser for the recipe on a page that contains a collection of recipes. The teaser might contain the following bolded information:

- **Recipe name**
- Tagline
- **Contributor**
- **Rating**
- Prep details
- **Main photo**
- Photos

- Long video
- Short video
- Ingredients
- Directions
- Nutrition info
- **Short teaser**
- Long teaser

That entry also might store the information used in an Instagram post featuring the recipe. The items likely to be included in such a post are bolded here:

- **Recipe name**
- Tagline
- **Contributor**
- Rating
- Prep details
- **Main photo**
- **Photos**

- Long video
- **Short video**
- Ingredients
- Directions
- Nutrition info
- Short teaser
- **Long teaser**

As the example demonstrated, structured content provides a lot of value for the people who make and distribute the content and the people who use the content. Structured content:

- Enables flexible design and delivery of your content
- Future-proofs your content for platforms that don't even exist yet
- Provides a single source of truth
- Supports consistent, predictable, and contextual content design and delivery

STRUCTURED CONTENT AND THE AUTHOR EXPERIENCE

A structured author experience is an easier author experience for several reasons:

- Content authors don't typically know how to code, nor should they have to.
- Content authors are typically not visual designers, nor should they have to be.
- Content authors like support and guidance because they want to do a good job.
- Content authors who have support and guidance make better content.

When we don't structure content in the CMS, content authors see entry forms like this giant, blank WYSIWYG (what you see is what you get) editor:

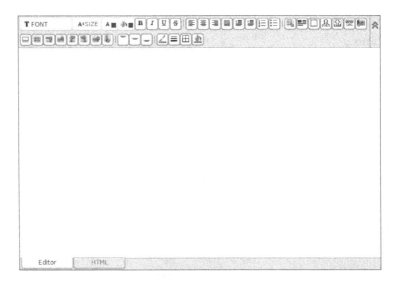

That looks hard, right? This next form (an example from the Craft CMS Recipe Plugin, https://nystudio107.com/docs/recipe) looks much easier for a couple of reasons. First, the form specifies exactly what information to enter where. Second, it provides some guidance for how to enter the content. (I like to provide even more guidance when I can, but this is straightforward.) Third, the author doesn't have to know what fonts, font styles, colors, and so on to use to build the recipe.

> ✎ **HINT** *Eileen Webb wrote an article for A List Apart called "Training the CMS" (https://alistapart.com/article/training-the-cms) back in 2014. You should read it.*

STRUCTURED CONTENT AND CONTENT MODELING

The content model is the basis for building an easy and intuitive author experience. It defines how content is structured and stored, which provides the backbone for flexible and adaptable content delivery. It also serves as an effective tool for collaboration, conversation, and understanding between teams.

So, what goes (or can go) in your content model? Let's walk through the kinds of information you'll want to include:

- **The content people will see or perceive** wherever they experience your content. This includes text, of course, and other formats like images, videos, and files.

- **Data about the content**, including things like who the content is for, what the content is about, where it should be available to publish, what kind of content it is, what phases of the customer journey it applies to, meta description, browser title, shortened URL for sharing, who owns it, when it was last updated, when it should be updated next, and so on.

- **Guidance** that *helps* people writing or entering the content ensure the content is on-strategy and usable. This can include things like suggested character limits or, a description of how the information entered is used, or for some types of pages and components, more descriptive guidance, like "Make sure to cover the key message for the page in the first paragraph."

Without getting too far into the weeds, here's a quick summary of how that information might get entered:

- For the content people see or perceive when using your site, you're likely to include field types like these:

  - Plain text (that's what most of the fields in our recipe example were)

  - Formatted text (hopefully used sparingly and sometimes an option when you want to allow for a little flexibility in how the content is displayed)

  - Date chooser (for events, webinars, deadlines, and so on)

  - Selector (for choosing related content to include or pull in)

- For the data about the content, the most common field types include the following:

  - Selector (to identify things like audience, topic, owner, customer journey phase, and so on)

  - Date chooser (for things like when it was last updated, when it should be reviewed, and when it should be unpublished or unavailable for publishing)

  - Plain text (for browser title, meta description, or any other notes you need to associate with the content)

- For guidance, this is not something the people who write or enter the content can control, but rather something they see when they use the content entry forms. Some guidance is built into the CMS, and some is customizable by people with very special permissions (like the back-end developer or back-end content strategist).

HINT
If you want to get into the weeds of structured content and content modeling, definitely check out the books I mentioned earlier.

Before I get into a process for modeling your content, I want to share just a few other concepts to keep in mind:

- **Authored versus reference:** Some audience-facing content is authored (or typed in) directly in the CMS content entry form, and other content is pulled in through references based on your taxonomy for things like audience, topic, and so on.

  The content that is referenced can be available to choose in some kind of selector. For example, you might select a testimonial that has been tagged to be available on the page you're working on.

  Or it can be automatically populated based on the taxonomy, such as in Chapter 13, "Organize for Intuitive Wayfinding, " when we showed the example taxonomy that included locations and services offered. The CMS can be set up so that it "knows" what services to show and on which location pages.

  In some CMSs, you can enter a bit of content you want to include in the content entry form for a page and it will be automatically added to the library for that content type. For example, let's say you have a new testimonial. You could either add the testimonial separately and then go to the page you're building so that you can pull it in, or you could add it directly from the page you're building and it will be available for other pages/posts based on how you tag it.

- **Locked down in versus customized:** There may be some content, like section subheads, that you want to be the same across all pages. An example might be something like a section of a recipe page for related recipes in which every single recipe page would include a subhead for that section called something like "You may also like." In that case, the person entering the content would not be able to change that subhead. In other cases, you may want to allow for more editorial discretion, which would mean that the form would include a text field for people to specify the text.

A CONTENT MODELING EXAMPLE

Most of the content in this chapter so far is based on a workshop I did at Omnichannel X (Noz Urbina's content conference) called "Content Modeling: The Translation Layer Between Teams." I cannot tell a lie—I am proud of what I put together. This section walks through some of the steps from that workshop. And **Content Strategy Tool 15.1: Content Modeling Tutorial for Content Professionals** gives you access to that workshop, the Mural board I created for the workshop activities, and an Airtable template for documenting your content model.

Let's dig in. We're going to walk through how to model the page intro from this example in Chapter 13:

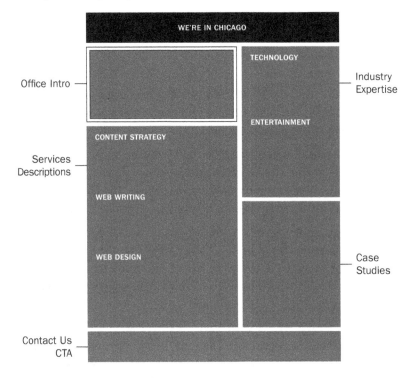

To do that, we need to think about what makes up the introduction and what kind of guidance we want to provide for authors. Here's what I think should be included:

- The copy for the introduction that will appear on the webpage

- A call to action (CTA) appropriate for the page

- An image that relates to the content of the page

Table 15.1 shows how I would document the content model to give my back-end developer a sense of how the authoring form should be built in the CMS.

TABLE 15.1 **CONTENT MODEL DOCUMENTATION**

FIELD LABEL	SOURCE	FIELD TYPE	REQUIRED	GUIDANCE	NOTES & QUESTIONS
Introduction copy	Authored	Plain text (See Notes & Questions)	Yes	The introduction should be one or two paragraphs introducing the content and clearly conveying the value proposition.	Is it possible to allow bullets but no other formatting options?
CTA button	Reference	Selector	No	A CTA in the introduction is optional. Choose a CTA only if it makes sense based on our content strategy.	All CTAs are available to this page type. The CTA link destination should be included in the CTA component, so all the author needs to do is select the CTA.
Image	Reference	Selector	No	Adding an image is optional. Images should add meaning to the content and not be purely decorative.	The alt text for the image will default to what's in the image record. Should we (can we) allow editing the alt text?

DOCUMENTING THE CONTENT MODEL

How you document the content model depends on a couple of things:

Who do you need to communicate the content model to and for what purpose?

You may end up documenting the content model more than one way depending on who needs to see and approve it. For example, the people who will be authoring in the CMS probably don't care about all the little details you would need to tell the back-end developer. So, you might instead mock up the content entry form (like the example recipe entry form from earlier in this chapter) and show them how they'll use it.

How do the people who will be building the CMS forms want the content model documented to facilitate their work?

When I'm working with developers, sometimes they give me a template they want me to use. Other times, we talk about what would be the most helpful and then I provide that. Still other times, we walk through the content experience I've documented, and my developer documents the content model however they want. (Those are often the best times.)

Content Strategy Tool 15.1: Content Modeling Tutorial for Content Professionals contains a template and some examples of how you might document your content model in an Airtable database. Have I mentioned how much I love Airtable?

CONTENT STRATEGY TOOL 15.1

CONTENT MODELING TUTORIAL FOR CONTENT PROFESSIONALS

Get access to my content modeling workshop, an Airtable template to document your content model, and examples of other ways you might communicate your content model to your team and stakeholders.

TIPS

- Gather a group to watch the content model workshop video so that you can work together on the exercises.

- Take the time to figure out what kind of documentation different stakeholders and team members need. This can save you time and help you socialize the concept of structured content if it's not something your client or organization are familiar with.

- Don't be intimidated. This is a topic that scared the bejeezus out of me until I had a couple great experiences with back-end content strategists and developers who made it easier for me to grasp and even made it fun!

WHERE TO GET IT

Download the templates at www.peachpit.com/register.

WHERE IT CAME FROM

Meghan Casey (www.dobettercontent.com) with a whole lot of learning from the folks I mentioned at the beginning of this chapter.

GETTING SPECIFIC ABOUT CONTENT

In this section, we'll talk about how to determine what specifically needs to go on a page of web content (or any other delivery mechanism for content) based on the content experience you've defined. Then, we'll discuss how to map your old content to your new site sitemap.

PAGE-LEVEL CONTENT SPECIFICATIONS

Now that you've identified what pages will be on your site, what content components make up those pages, and what pages and content are most important, you can start being specific about what goes on each page. I typically use something called a *page table* to document these specifications. **Content Strategy Tool 15.2: Content Specifications Templates and Pair Writing Resources** includes some variations of a page table template.

HINT   *Tools like Gather Content (www.gathercontent. com) can be set up to take the place of a more traditional page table prepared in a word-processing document or spreadsheet.*

The difference between what you documented for the content experience and a page table can be summarized like this:

A *content wireframe* or page sketch documents high-level details about unique or repeatable page types.

A *page table* details the specific information to include based on your content wireframe or page sketch.

Let's look at an example. This next image is the example of a content wireframe from Chapter 14, "Define the Content Experience." It lays out requirements for all location pages.

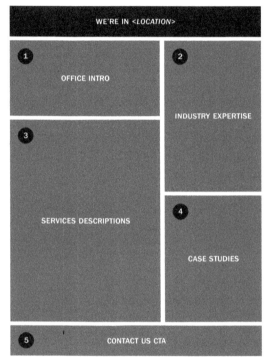

OBJECTIVE

Demonstrate the capabilities and expertise of the location, and provide contract information for the sales lead.

Content Priorities

1. Highlight the key differentiator of the location selected.

2. List the industries the location specializes in and why that expertise matters. (Industry descriptions will prepopulate based on the taxonomy.)

3. List the name of the service and a short description about our approach to providing it and the results a customer can expect.

4. Provide short teasers for case studies (up to three), focusing on the results of the work.

5. Include the key contact for the office with a short bio and contact information.

PREPARING FOR LAUNCH

■ Create the taxonomy and map service descriptions, industry experience, and case studies to the appropriate locations if you'd like to auto-populate that content.

■ Each office will need to choose a key contact to include on this page.

The following page table example contains specifications for messaging and detailed information for writing about a particular offering. The thumbnail sketch at the top right of this example represents the content wireframe that defined the content requirements for all offering pages.

4.1 CLASSROOM TRAINING

Page objective: Familiarize prospective clients with our classroom training offering, and help existing clients choose between training options.

Source content: Training handbook

Phase: 1 (Launch)

SME/Content owner: Jane Fisher, training manager

Page Title	Classroom Training: Getting you up to speed
Priority 1 content Main content	Present an overview of the classroom training program and its benefits: ■ Tailored to each client organization and audience. ■ On-site at the organization's location(s). ■ Training team includes experienced educators and programmers/technologists. ■ Talk about the mix of lecture, exercise, and activities.
	Assets: Image of the classroom
Priority 2 content Virtual classroom	Discuss how the virtual classroom brings the classroom experience to remote employees. Links to the Virtual Classroom page [Link to 4.2]
	Assets: Screen grab
Priority 3 content Ongoing support	Talk about how training continues throughout life of the product via our support services. Links to the Support section [Link to 5.1]
	Assets: None

■ **Content creation implementation:** The source content is not public facing. The content will need to be edited significantly.

■ **Maintenance frequency:** May need to be updated bi-annually after our corporate retreats.

■ **Outstanding questions/risks:** None

 TIP

To create your content specifications, I find a method called pair writing with the subject matter expert (SME) an extremely valuable way to communicate the content strategy and content design and collaborate on determining what content is needed to bring it to life. Content Strategy Tool 15.2 also includes some resources on pair writing.

Page tables can include lots of different information, depending on who is using them. The example shown here (from *Content Strategy for the Web, 2nd Edition*, by Kristina Halvorson and Melissa Rach) is bare bones. I often include search engine optimization (SEO) details as well, such as meta description, search intent details, the browser title, user tasks, and key messages. And I usually include the template name and the names of the components that each content priority will be created in. **Content Strategy Tool 15.2: Content Specifications Templates and Pair Writing Resources** provides resources for creating content specifications.

CONTENT STRATEGY TOOL 15.2

CONTENT SPECIFICATIONS TEMPLATES AND PAIR WRITING RESOURCES

Find templates and guidance for documenting content specifications and an overview of the pair writing process with links to lots of resources.

TIPS

- Include just what's necessary for who will be using the content specifications, or risk confusing your stakeholders, developers, and content creators.

- Avoid deliverables with overlap and redundancies, which would cause you to update two or more documents when something changes.

- Mix, match, and evolve to suit the needs of your project and collaborators.

WHERE TO GET IT

Download the templates at www.peachpit.com/register.

WHERE IT CAME FROM

Meghan Casey (www.dobettercontent.com) and a bunch of smart people who have written about pair writing

CONTENT MAPPING

Content mapping is how you determine what to do with the content you already have (assuming you are working on a website that already exists). The exercise of mapping your content has three primary purposes:

- Determine content to keep based on content purpose. Often this means noting who the content is for and what the content is about.

- Correlate current content to your new sitemap, which can mean:

  - Mapping of an existing page to the new sitemap

  - Identifying pages that won't be on the new sitemap but that contain information that can be used as source content

  - Determining what to do with any "meh" content (from Chapter 12) that you must keep

- Check for content you decide to keep that is out of date so that you can make sure it's updated.

How you do this mapping depends on how much content there is, who is equipped to make the determinations you need to make, and resources available for getting it done.

For larger sites, I like to prepare audit spreadsheets or Airtable tabs that can be divvied up among content reviewers and train folks on how to map the content. This approach helps make the process go more quickly and prepares content reviewers for future content maintenance audits (more on that in Chapter 16, "Define How You'll Govern Your Content").

You'll use the results of content mapping in a few ways. Here are some examples:

- Determine what URLs from your current site can stay the same.

- Gather source content for content creators.

- Identify gaps in source content for the new site.

- Archive content you don't need anymore.

- Develop a sense of how much work it will be to create or migrate existing content.

HINT
The giant Airtable database you'll get in the tools and templates contains a tab for how you might set up a content-mapping spreadsheet.

THE BEST-LAID PLANS

You probably thought I was going to say that even the best-laid plans have been known to fail, or something like that. You know that is true. There is no way to completely mitigate content messiness. But seriously. You have done so much work. Your stakeholders know it. Your development team is thankful for you. And the collaboration going on between content people and design people and UX people is downright awesome.

Nicely done. You have laid the groundwork for an amazing content experience. Really, you have. The next chapter discusses how you'll govern your content on-strategy over time. And then, the final chapter digs into creating a content playbook to help you and your teams kick some serious content behind forever and ever.

PART VI

IMPLEMENT AND EVOLVE

As I was sitting down to write this final section of the book, friend and content strategy godmother Kristina Halvorson sent me a brilliant blog post by Hilary Marsh, another content strategist who's been at this a long time. It was a brilliant way to sum up what content strategy is and why it matters.

The article is titled "Your deliverables are not your content strategy" (contentcompany.biz/blog/your-deliverables-are-not-your-content-strategy). In the post, Hilary discusses the various types of documents and artifacts we put together as people who do content work. Most of them are included in this book. She goes on to say that the deliverables are not the most important work we do, and explains that the most important work is the actions we take—actions like training people on effective content practices, setting and enforcing standards and guidelines, and facilitating collaborative processes for our teams.

That, folks, is what this section is all about. The final chapters are:

CHAPTER 16 Define How You'll Govern Your Content

CHAPTER 17 Build Out Your Content Playbook

CHAPTER 16

DEFINE HOW YOU'LL GOVERN YOUR CONTENT

Here's an important fact about content and content strategy: You can't just set it and forget it. And you certainly can't let anyone in the organization publish anything they want whenever they want. Yet that's exactly what happens with lots of websites or other digital properties.

Organizations don't do it on purpose (usually). They don't have time, or they haven't put anyone in charge of creating and enforcing a strategic approach to content. Why? Probably because they didn't think about it before they launched or redesigned their site. This chapter covers how to avoid this pitfall and make sure your content starts on-strategy and stays on-strategy until you archive it.

Content strategy and governance, at their core, is about aligning on and operationalizing four key points (Kristina Halvorson and I arrived at these recently for an engagement with a client, and they have become a bit of a framework for me):

- How business strategy, brand promise, and audience journeys inform the **content purpose.**

- Who makes what **decisions** about the content strategy and its implementation.

- A **decision-making process** for planning content efforts that align with the content purpose.

- What approach to **content ownership** the organization will follow and what that means for content owners.

- The **playbook of standards, guidelines, and enabling tools, templates, and process** that enables teams to create and manage on-strategy content.

In this chapter, we're going to focus on who makes what decisions, a framework for making those decisions, and approaches to content ownership. **Content Strategy Tool 16.1: Governance Definition and Documentation Guide** is a collection of working session exercises, instructions, and templates to help you define and document how you'll govern your content.

CONTENT STRATEGY TOOL 16.1

GOVERNANCE DEFINITION AND DOCUMENTATION GUIDE

Get a host of exercises, instructions, and templates to set up governance that helps your organization make smart decisions about content.

TIPS

- Before shaking things up too much, consider what you already have in place that's working. Governance should build upon what's going well so that it becomes more extensible.

- Reach out to content strategy folks at other organizations to learn from them what has worked and not worked related to content governance.

- Avoid becoming the content police. The best governance I've seen empowers and enables people to make smart decisions.

WHERE TO GET IT

Download the collection of templates at www.peachpit.com/register.

WHERE IT CAME FROM

Meghan Casey (www.dobettercontent.com) and Brain Traffic (www.braintraffic.com)

THE CONTENT LIFE CYCLE

To determine how to govern your content, you must understand the content life cycle. That's because content governance is all about helping your client or organization make on-strategy decisions throughout the content life cycle. In the first edition of this book, I included the content life cycle authored by content strategist Erin Scime. It included five phases: strategize, plan, create, maintain, and audit. It still holds up, although I have modified it slightly, changing a couple of the phase labels and including *learn* in the center.

Here's a diagram depicting the phases I now use, with a summary of each phase:

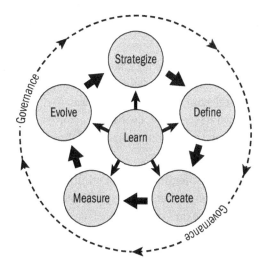

- **Strategize**—This is the work you've done to define the content purpose, the messages you want to communicate, and how you'll know whether you're successful. To get to that point, you've *learned* a lot about your business environment, your audiences, and your current content. Another part of strategizing is planning what content to focus on when, which makes that content something you revisit frequently.

■ **Define**—This is all the work you did in Part V: "Design Your Content." You have continued *learning* about your audiences and have used that data to shape and refine the content experience. The Define phase can also encompass your content ecosystem beyond a single website, application, and so on.

■ **Create**—Everyone working on your content learns during this phase, from adopting new standards, guidelines, and processes to understanding the subject matter. You will *learn* more about producing content when we discuss content playbooks in the final chapter.

■ **Measure**—This (often missing) piece of the content life cycle prepares us to work out our content strategy and our content. You've defined as part of your content compass how you'll know whether your content is successful. When you measure, you *learn* valuable information that helps you form insights for how to evolve your content.

■ **Evolve**—This phase is a mash-up of the audit and maintain phases from Erin Scime's original diagram. Most content should be reviewed regularly to make sure it's still accurate, timely, and relevant, and audits are a way to do that and then update content based on what you found. Evolve also refers to what you've *learned* from measuring the success of your content and the changes you made based on those findings.

This is a continual cycle. Evolve flows into strategize because nothing is static in this world—priorities change, what our audiences need and expect changes, what organizations sell or provide changes, and so on. And all those changes require that we evolve our strategy for content.

The concept that surrounds the work and decisions needed in these phases is *governance*. Let's dig into some details about who makes what decisions and a framework for decision-making.

WHO MAKES WHAT DECISIONS

When no one or no team of people is empowered to make and enforce content strategy and content implementation decisions, your strategy doesn't have the backbone it needs to be effective.

People or teams need to be empowered to make a couple of the main types of decisions: strategic decisions and implementation decisions. Each is important if you want to avoid situations like the following:

- A crowded homepage cluttered with all the content that everyone thought was the most important yet that provides no value to the audience

- Entire sections of content that no one ever visits

- Scads of expensive one-off microsites that business partners created to circumvent the strategy

- Eleven versions of the same information spread across those expensive microsites

- Teams of people trying to do the right things feeling deflated and defeated

Strategic decisions should be made by the person or team ultimately responsible for achieving the content strategy and demonstrating its success. This person or team needs to be able to say no even if the CMO comes to the table with a bright shiny idea that can't be tied back to the strategy.

Implementation decisions should be made by the people who have the more day-to-day content responsibilities, such as managing the homepage editorial calendar, triaging requests for unplanned content updates, coordinating the maintenance process, and providing editorial oversight. These people need to be empowered to tell people something they've created is not on-strategy or to decline a content request that wasn't included in the content plan for a specified time period.

The people who are empowered to make strategic and implementation decisions have associated responsibilities. We'll explore those responsibilities next, along with how you might use content councils and communities of practice to bolster your decision-making effectiveness.

RESPONSIBILITIES OF STRATEGIC DECISION-MAKERS

I recommend that the strategic decision responsibility sit with one team with one role being ultimately accountable, even if some of the work is done collaboratively (more on that in a bit). Some common titles for people with strategic responsibilities are Director of Digital Experience, Director of Content Strategy, and Director of Content Products.

Here are examples of responsibilities these people might have:

- Leads efforts to set and evolve the content purpose as business goals and priorities change

- Prepares the budget for annual content efforts

- Determines the staff resources necessary to achieve the content strategy

- Manages the process of creating and aligning on the content roadmap and communicates decisions to business partners

- Ensures that content tools, standards, and guidelines are in place to support content creators, reviewers, and publishers

- Defines content success metrics, ensures that content effectiveness is measured, and proposes content-improvement projects based on measurement efforts

- Serves as the content advocate and liaison in discussions about web operations, interactive marketing, technology enhancements, and so on

THE ROLE OF A CONTENT COUNCIL

I've found that forming a content council—made up of leaders from marketing, product development, business intelligence, customer insights, creative, user experience, technology, and so on—as a governing body can be quite helpful for these reasons:

- People with strategic roles throughout the organization come together to set and evolve the content strategy from a place of comprehensiveness, rather than silos.

- People on the content council become necessary champions and advocates in their areas of influence.

I recommend that defining the role of the content council be co-created, rather than something the strategic decision-maker bestows upon them. For example, for my clients, I've conducted a workshop exercise to brainstorm a job description for the content council. Here's what that looks like:

Job Description

Just as you might write a job description for a position on your team, fill out stickies for job responsibilities, qualifications/capabilities, and culture description for the content council.

Responsibilities (i.e., what do we do?)

Qualifications/capabilities (i.e., what skills and expertise do we need?)

Culture (i.e., how do we work together?)

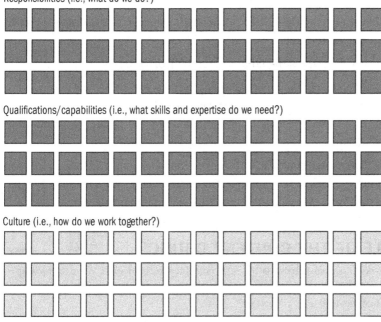

Themes

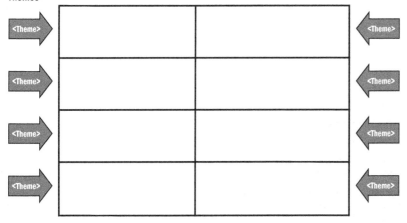

For this exercise, I first ask participants to think about the role of the content council as they might a job description for an employee. Then with that framing in mind, I ask participants to brainstorm in three categories:

- Responsibilities or *What should the content council do?*

- Qualifications/capabilities or *What skills or expertise does the content council need to have?*

- Culture or *How does the content council work together?*

Once everyone has filled out sticky notes in those categories, we work together to organize them into themes. As with most working sessions, the conversation during this process is just as, if not more, enlightening than the output of the working session.

After the workshop, I synthesize the discussion of insights and themes into a job description for the content council. Here's an excerpt from a content council job description to give you an idea of what you might create:

HINT
Take another peek at Chapter 4, "Assemble Your Cross-Discipline Team" under the heading "Kick Off for Clarity" for some reminders about facilitating these types of activities.

ROLE OF THE CONTENT COUNCIL

Our content council helps deliver the right content to the right people, in the right places, at the right times.

To do that, we need to:

- Align all teams working on content toward audience focus, messaging, content themes, and measurable objectives

- Provide visibility to past, current, and future content work across the enterprise

- Provide mechanisms to reduce duplicative efforts and create efficiencies

- Learn from our efforts and use learnings to inform future content work

Key Responsibilities of the Content Council

The responsibilities of the content council fall into four key categories:

- Strategy and Planning
- Insights and Measurement
- Content Design and Implementation
- Collaboration and Facilitation

Strategy and Planning

Strategy and planning responsibilities include:

- Set and refine content principles that guide all content efforts

- Set and refine standards for content across the ecosystem

- Contribute expertise and insights to set the global content strategy and how it propagates to brands and regions

- Align on time-bound strategic content themes and provide guidance for implementation across brands and regions

- Vet content ideas and requests outside of themes for strategic integrity

- Prioritize vetted content ideas and requests that fall outside of strategic themes

RESPONSIBILITIES OF IMPLEMENTATION DECISION-MAKERS

The implementation roles and responsibilities are likely to be spread across multiple people or job titles. Whenever possible, assign related tasks or sets of tasks to the same person or position.

Here are examples of implementation authority responsibilities:

- Manage content requests from business partners and communicate decisions
- Schedule and facilitate day-to-day content creation, review, and publishing
- Review content before publishing and provide feedback to content creators
- Mentor business partners on content best-practices guidelines
- Develop and maintain editorial calendars for timely content distributed through the website, application, or other distribution channel
- Manage the content-maintenance process and train business partners to audit their own content

THE ROLE OF A COMMUNITY OF PRACTICE

Communities of practice can be a productive way to align people who work on content on common standards, guidelines, templates, tools, and processes, and to create a space for ongoing sharing and feedback. The concept of communities of practice comes from Etienne Wenger-Trayner's 1998 book, *Communities of Practice* (www.wenger-trayner.com/books). It defines community of practice as "a group of people who share a concern or a passion for something they do, and learn how to do it better as they interact regularly."

In 2019 Kristina Halvorson wrote a blog post called "How to Build Your Community of Practice" (www.braintraffic.com/insights/how-to-build-your-community-of-practice). The post provides several examples of content communities of practice at various types of organizations, from government to education to business.

I recommend that you split among several people the job of defining the community of practice and the principles that will guide its work. You can use the same exercise I talked about for content councils earlier in the chapter. I also like to do an exercise to co-create guiding principles. That exercise might look like the following image:

Content Principles

What is challenging about how content is ideated, prioritized, planned, created, approved, distributed, measured, and managed?

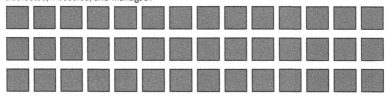

What rules or suggestions would you make around how content is ideated, prioritized, planned, created, approved, distributed, measured, and managed?

Themes

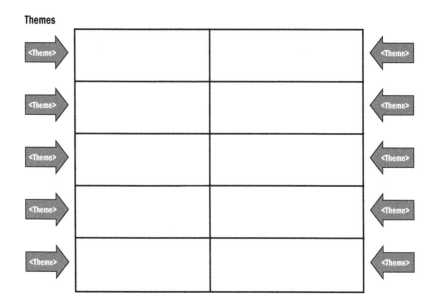

The principles that come out of this exercise tend to fall into one of two categories:

■ Example principle for how we do content work

We are collaborators and champions.

We break down silos to create a connected content experience that empowers supporters, champions, and allies. We assume positive intent when working with our colleagues and partners.

■ Example principle for the content itself

We prioritize impact over quantity.

We do fewer things well. We don't measure the value of our role or expertise on how much we produce, but rather the effects of what we produce on the organization and our audiences.

With my synthesis of the workshop exercise discussion and themes, I like to provide some context for how the content principles will be used.

Here's an example:

We use our guiding principles to validate that the content we create is on-strategy and provide feedback in constructive ways by asking the following questions:

■ How does this content contribute to our goals?

■ How does this content add value for our audiences?

■ How will we know if this content had the desired impact?

■ Have we considered what other information our audiences are receiving from us elsewhere before distributing this content?

TIP *When doing co-creation exercises like these, it's beneficial to ask others in the group to help synthesize themes into principles, either in the same working session or separately.*

DECISION-MAKING PROCESS

Content governance requires two key types of planning decisions: content product and editorial planning. *Strategic content planning* is the kind of planning done to set and articulate a roadmap for content on your website, in your application, or across your ecosystem (depending on your sphere of influence). *Editorial planning* is more campaign focused to dictate where and how you will talk about things like product promotions, events, thought capital (such as position statements, reports, and blog posts), and so on.

Content product planning informs editorial planning. For example, in Chapter 7, "Learn About Your Audience and Users," we used a dental practice as an example for analyzing audience needs. Let's say that based on their content purpose, the dental practice decided to include a series of video tutorials about how to teach children to brush their teeth at various ages. That's a strategic content decision. But then, you need to decide how you will promote or feature those videos on your website and in social media. That's an editorial planning decision. Make sense?

STRATEGIC CONTENT PLANNING

If you've gone the route of a content council, that group should be gathered for strategic content planning.

Bring this group together at least twice a year specifically for strategic content planning. Start this meeting by reviewing the content purpose and asking, "Has anything changed?" If the changes render your content purpose no longer relevant, your next step will be to go back to discovery to fill in gaps in knowledge and adjust it.

If the business environment is largely the same, make a plan for what content work to do next.

You'll need to generate a list of possible projects, which shouldn't be too hard. People always have ideas. You can have stakeholders submit those ideas ahead of time via something like a content brief, or they can present them to the group in your planning meeting.

The next step is to evaluate the ideas. Chapter 11, "Set Your Content Compass," went through a similar exercise when you said yes or no to a list of projects using the content purpose as the litmus test. You'll do much the same thing here, but with a little more rigor.

1 Ask people to present only ideas that they believe pass the core strategy statement litmus test.

TIP

If you can effectively integrate content product planning with other strategic planning processes, do it. It's efficient. And your stakeholders will thank you for reducing the number of meetings they have to attend.

2   Make sure everyone understands each idea before moving on to the next. Have someone summarize each idea on a sticky note.

3   Ask the group to work together to evaluate the ideas.

I like to do this with a scoring system or a four-quadrant scheme. Let's assume you go the quadrant route.

4   Draw a rectangle with four quadrants on the board or show one on the screen.

5   Label one axis with Business Impact and the other with User Need. If you want, you can also add the level of priority for each quadrant, as shown in the image. Or you can talk about how the level of priority corresponds with each quadrant.

If this sounds familiar, it's because you did almost the same thing to prioritize content in Chapter 13, "Organize for Intuitive Wayfinding."

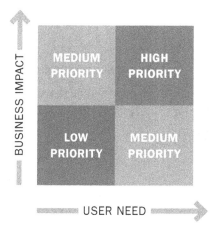

Have stakeholders work together, with as much discussion as they need, to place each idea on the quadrants. Listen for disagreement and facilitate conversations to reach alignment. Make sure everyone feels comfortable with the result.

6   Set aside anything from the lower-left quadrant. In fact, just throw those away.

7   Draw another four-quadrant rectangle with the axis labels Value and Effort.

Note that the priority labels are slightly different here because of the axis for effort.

8   Take the ideas from the high business value/high user need quadrant and put them in one of the top quadrants, depending on their level of effort.

9 Take the ones that were either high business impact/low user need or low business impact/high user need and map those according to effort in the bottom two quadrants.

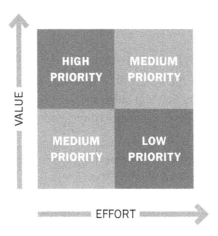

Now you'll draw on the board or project a calendar for the planning timeframe.

10 Plotting ideas on the calendar, put sticky notes for planned maintenance work in the appropriate places to ensure that those efforts are considered.

11 Plot the prioritized ideas on the calendar in this order:

- High value/low effort
- High value/high effort
- Low value/low effort
- Low value/high effort

You'll probably run out of time in the calendar by the time you get to the fourth bullet, maybe even the third one. Save those ideas for the next planning session.

The hard part is finished. You have alignment on the content efforts to pursue. Now it is time to make a plan and execute like you know you can.

EDITORIAL PLANNING

Editorial planning helps you publish or share content at the right times for the right people. Think about it the same way you might think about an editorial calendar for a fashion magazine. They create and publish content based on the time of year or season, projected trends, timely topics, and so on. Your organization likely does the same.

Having a calendar that's thought out in advance is beneficial for a couple of reasons: It provides content creators with advance notice of what needs to be produced and published, and it gives the people managing the calendar backup when they need to tell a business partner that the unplanned editorial request can't be accommodated.

Here, you're going to focus on the calendar itself. Your content strategy, marketing plan, and other inputs will help you determine what to feature when.

Let's say you want to create a calendar to ensure you are coordinating messages and featured content throughout your website. The first step is to document the places where your site can feature timely content. I like to do that with a simple wireframe that includes specifications for each available area. In the homepage example shown in the next image, the boxes are used for product promotions, thought capital content, and so on.

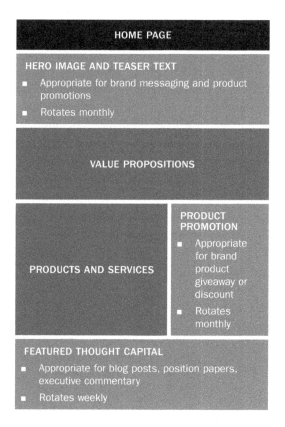

Next, you'll want to create a calendar that includes all the available placements and what's going in each one when. You probably need to track other information, such as who is creating the content and when it's due. I recommend doing that in a separate sheet so that the calendar view is clean and clear. The next image shows an example of what a calendar might look like for the homepage.

HOME PAGE		MONTH			
LOCATION	CONTENT	WEEK 1	WEEK 2	WEEK 3	WEEK 4
Hero	Children's Dental Health Month message				
Featured Product	Kid's Sonic Toothbrush promotion				
Featured Thought Capital	"Teaching Toddlers to Brush" video				
	"Telling Your Kids What to Expect at the Dentist" blog post				
	"Getting Your Grade Schooler to Floss" video				
	"Does Your Baby Need a Dentist?" blog post				

Depending on how you've defined the role of your community of practice, this process can also be collaborative, with people working on content across the organization. One way to collaborate on the calendar is to hold quarterly planning meetings to "rough out" your calendar for the upcoming quarter. You can use a digital or physical space to add campaigns, known news announcements, events, and other items that influence what you communicate and when. Then, you can collectively add any tactics that teams are working on and probably even find opportunities to make connections between planned content that improves the experience for your audiences. Your planning "wall" might look something like this image:

Quarterly Calendar

APPROACH TO CONTENT OWNERSHIP

One of the key decisions regarding content ownership is to determine which of these three models makes the most sense for your organization:

- A **centralized model** typically means that all content production and publishing is managed by one department or team. The central team—which includes job titles like writer and editor—creates, edits, and publishes all content with input from subject matter experts (SMEs) and other reviewers (such as legal and brand).

- With a **decentralized model**, teams throughout the organization are charged with creating, editing, and publishing their own content. These teams may or may not include members with *specific* content-creation expertise or experience.

- A **hybrid model** combines aspects of centralized and decentralized models. For example, each team throughout the organization may be responsible for creating and publishing their own content, but a central team edits all content before it is published. Or a central team may be responsible for all marketing content, whereas decentralized product teams own support content.

Decentralized models can pose more risks to keeping your content consistent and on-strategy, whereas centralized ones may allow you to run a tighter content ship. I find that most of my clients end up with a hybrid model. Which model is right for your organization depends on several factors, including the usability of your CMS, resource availability, comprehensiveness of a content playbook, team member skillsets, content volume, and timelines.

Here is another four-quadrant scheme that you can use to dig into additional details about what options might be best for your organization. In the image are an axis for centralized versus decentralized and an axis for prescribe versus guide and labels describing types of ownership for each square.

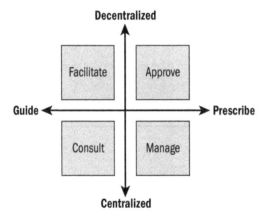

The squares within the four quadrants mean the following:

■ **Facilitate** is a decentralized approach in which teams that work on content use the content purpose and content playbook to implement their content without oversight from the people or teams tasked with strategic or implementation decision-making. (They do hopefully have a representative on the content council and participate in the content community of practice.)

■ **Approve** is a decentralized approach in which teams use the content purpose and content playbook to implement their content, and that content is reviewed by a person on the centralized team tasked with implementation decision-making.

- **Consult** is a centralized approach in which the people or teams tasked with strategic and implementation decision-making operates like an internal agency (e.g., gathers requirements, makes recommendations, and implements recommendations).

- **Manage** is an approach in which the people or teams tasked with strategic and implementation decision-making do all the content tasks and rely on SMEs to ensure content is accurate and up to date.

As I mentioned, most of my clients employ a hybrid approach. To make sure everyone working on content understands which approach applies to which content, I like to prepare a matrix with the clarifying details, like **Table 16.1**:

TABLE 16.1 **CONTENT OWNERSHIP MATRIX**

CONTENT TYPE	CONTENT OWNER	EXPECTATIONS	APPROACH
About Content	Marketing and Communications	■ Create content ■ Review content as part of maintenance process ■ Keep content up-to-date as needed ■ Archive or remove outdated content	Facilitate: The content strategist can work with the marketing and communications team to develop content requirements based on the strategy; marketing and communications will create the content.
Product Content	Product Teams	■ Create new product items according to new requirements ■ Tag products with the appropriate taxonomy terms ■ Archive or remove outdated items	Approve: The Publications team creates the content based on the strategy and templates; the content manager should review entries before they are published.
Loyalty Program Content	Customer Experience Loyalty Team	■ Create content ■ Review content as part of maintenance process ■ Keep content up to date as needed ■ Archive or remove outdated content	Consultative: The content strategist and content manager should work with the loyalty team to develop and execute content requirements based on the strategy.

SMART DECISION-MAKING, FACILITATED

I hope you feel ready—or if not quite ready, excited—to define, document, and implement an approach to content governance that helps your client or your organization make on-strategy decisions throughout the content life cycle. It may seem hard, but it's some of the most important work you'll do.

In the next (and final) chapter, I'll walk through what goes in a content playbook and present examples to get you started.

CHAPTER 17

BUILD OUT YOUR CONTENT PLAYBOOK

We're nearing the end. And I'm not going to lie, I'm a little sad about it. Let's take a moment to celebrate all the amazing work you've done so far:

- Made the case for content strategy

- Set up your team and your organization for success

- Synthesized a ton of information and data about your organization, your audiences, your content, and your content processes

- Aligned stakeholders on a content compass that will guide all your content work

- Designed a user-focused content experience

- Determined an approach to make sure your content stays on-strategy

We'll expand on that last bullet in this chapter. Although this chapter isn't as lengthy as many of the others, my hope is that it gives you a head start on pulling together a playbook that will help your client or organization be successful with their content efforts.

We'll talk about what a content playbook is and what's in it. I've also provided some examples of content playbook contents.

CONTENT PLAYBOOK OVERVIEW

Your content playbook is how you codify everything your teams need to understand and do to strategize, plan, design, create, distribute, measure, and evolve your content. In some ways, this book is a content playbook. (And content strategist Scott Kubie suggested I call it that, but you know a second edition isn't really a second edition if it doesn't have the same title.)

In this image, I've laid out the high-level anatomy of a content playbook.

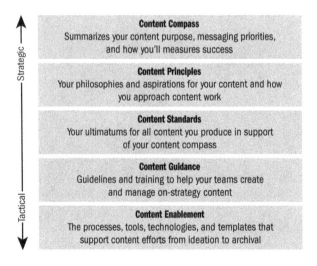

Note that the playbook includes both strategic information such as your content compass and tactical information such as content guidance. The content compass should look familiar because we talked all about it in Chapter 11, "Set Your Content Compass." We also talked about content principles in Chapter 16, "Define How You'll Govern Your Content," as something your content community of practice might set to guide content work.

The more strategic aspects enable you and your teams to make smart decisions about content and how to approach content. We're not going to focus on those aspects here. We're going to jump right in to the more tactical elements of your playbook—the elements that help you and your teams make smart implementation decisions about your content to create an on-strategy content experience. You can use **Content Strategy Tool 17.1: Content Playbook Outline and Examples** to begin pulling together a playbook of your own.

CONTENT STRATEGY TOOL 17.1

CONTENT PLAYBOOK OUTLINE AND EXAMPLES

Get a content playbook outline in a Google Doc with lots of examples from various places you can pull from.

TIPS

- Take stock of what you already have that could become part of a playbook. Most of my clients have bits and pieces of standards, guidelines, and enablement throughout the organization.

- Put the content council and community of practice to work setting standards, defining guidelines, and documenting templates, processes, and so on.

- Use yourself and your team as user research subjects to determine what will be most helpful as you do content work.

WHERE TO GET IT

Download the collection of templates at www.peachpit.com/register.

WHERE IT CAME FROM

Meghan Casey (www.dobettercontent.com) and a lot of smart content people

CONTENT STANDARDS AND GUIDANCE

Content standards are the ultimatums for all content you produce in support of your content compass. As ultimatums, they should be quite firm, although there may be some flexibility in how they are met. I find it helpful to brainstorm these standards (and organize the tactical part of your playbook) by the phases of the content life cycle we covered in Chapter 16.

Content guidance refers to the guidelines and training that team members need to meet the standards you've defined. Here are some examples of standards and related guidance for each phase in the content life cycle:

- Strategize

  - The content council meets quarterly to decide what content efforts to pursue in the following quarter.

    Guidance: Content purpose (see Chapter 11 for an example)

  - The content council reviews the content purpose annually to adjust for changes in business priorities.

    Guidance: Content purpose working session guide

- Define

  - We don't launch anything without at least one method of user testing to shape the experience.

    Guidance: Choosing user testing methods guide

  - We employ a content-first approach to experience design.

    Guidance: Core model facilitation guide

- Create

  - We are judicious in our use of subject matter experts' time in the content creation process.

    Guidance: Pair writing guidelines

  - We follow established best practices for usability, inclusivity, and accessibility.

    Guidance: Best practices training modules

- Measure

  - We don't publish or distribute any content without first defining how we will measure its success.

    Guidance: Choosing appropriate metrics article

  - We conduct user testing at least once per year on each user task designated as a priority.

    Guidance: Task-based user testing protocol

- Evolve

  - We conduct a rolling audit and maintenance process.

    Guidance: Audit criteria definition

  - We use the results of quarterly measurement reports to propose future content efforts to the content council.

    Guidance: Turning testing data into insights and recommendations blog post

---

🔧 **TIP**   *Guidance can take many forms, from bespoke guides to blog posts to videos to on-demand training to hints and requirements in the CMS forms themselves. Consider the types and formats that will be most useful to the people working on content in the context of their tasks when the guidance applies.*

CONTENT ENABLEMENT

Content enablement is a big bucket that can include quite a lot, such as process documentation, the technologies used to get the work done, and templates. **Table 17.1** pulls content standards, guidance, and enablement together for a few of the examples listed earlier.

📏 *HINT*
It's likely you will have overlap in guidance and enablement across phases and standards. That's a-OK. You can cross-reference and cross-link in your playbook.

TABLE 17.1 **EXAMPLES OF STANDARDS WITH ASSOCIATED GUIDANCE AND ENABLEMENT**

STANDARD	GUIDANCE	ENABLEMENT
We are judicious in our use of subject matter experts' time in the content creation process.	▪ Pair writing guidelines ▪ Content review guidelines	▪ Content creation process documentation ▪ Pair writing content worksheet
We don't publish or distribute any content without first defining how we will measure its success.	▪ Choosing appropriate metrics article ▪ Setting up conversion tracking tutorial	▪ Content scorecard template ▪ Google Analytics
We use the results of quarterly measurement reports to propose future content efforts to the content council.	▪ Turning testing data into insights and recommendations post ▪ Preparing your quarterly planning brief submission video	▪ Measurement report template ▪ Quarterly planning content brief

CONTENT PLAYBOOK EXAMPLES

OK, with a broad overview behind us, let's get into a few more detailed examples. Keep in mind that there are a lot of methods, guidelines, and templates right here in this book that could be a good starting point for a playbook.

CONTENT CREATION PEOPLE AND PROCESS DOCUMENTATION

Let's begin with some baseline content creation process guidelines and enablement available for your consumption. This can be a great starting point in documenting your content creation process in the context of standards you define with your teams.

ROLES AND RESPONSIBILITIES

Here is a core set of roles and responsibilities that apply to most content we create.

EDITOR

The *editor* is ultimately accountable for the strategic and brand integrity of the content. Responsibilities include the following:

- Assigning content creation work to writers
- Reviewing content and providing feedback to ensure that it is on-strategy and on-brand
- Creating and communicating editorial standards for content creation
- Ensuring that all people working on content have the tools necessary to create on-strategy and on-brand content
- Bringing in and managing outside resources to work on content when needed

OWNER

The content *owner* is responsible for ensuring that specific content is accurate and updated. Responsibilities during content creation include the following:

- Identifying SMEs and source content for writers
- Reviewing content from the perspective of the owner's business area
- Serving as the primary contact for content-related questions that come up during the creation process

WRITER

The *writer* creates content based on the strategy and requirements outlined by your content design. Responsibilities include the following:

- If necessary, defining content specifications or outlines for the content to be written

- Assessing available source content to determine whether there's enough information to write the content

- Collaborating with SMEs to gain an understanding of the subject matter

- Drafting content for review by SMEs and the editor

- Revising content based on reviewer feedback

- Submitting content for publishing

SME

The responsibilities of the *SME* (subject matter expert) include the following:

- Participating in interviews or pair writing sessions with content creators to provide expertise and knowledge

- Reviewing content for accuracy and provide feedback

PUBLISHER

The *publisher* is responsible for publishing or distributing the content and performing quality assurance.

PROCESS

The following is a standard process for content creation. You may find that some steps aren't necessary. Be sure to consider these content standards when making decisions about what might be OK to skip.

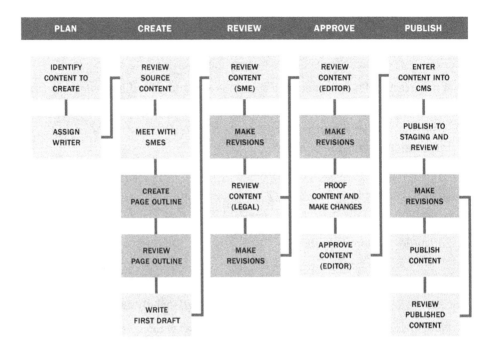

I recommend including a bit more detail than just a workflow diagram to describe the who, why, when, and how of each step in your process. In **Table 17.2**, I've included an example of what "more detail" might look like for the Create column.

TABLE 17.2 **EXAMPLE PROCESS DOCUMENTATION**

	STEP 2: CREATE		
TASK	Review source content.	Meet with SME.	Write first draft.
WHO	Writer reviews source content and consults with content owner if gaps are found.	Writer interviews SME or conducts a pair writing working session.	Writer creates draft for review by the SME.
WHY	Ensure writer has the information necessary to create accurate content.	Fill gaps in existing source content.	Provide a draft for SMEs to review and validate.
WHEN	Within three business days of receiving assignment.	Within one week of receiving assignment.	Within two weeks of receiving assignment.
HOW	Content owner provides source content via email.	Writer interviews SMEs using the interview guide template or pair writing worksheet.	Writer references the content compass, voice and tone guidelines, content specifications, and best practices guidelines.

FEEDBACK FORMS AND CHECKLISTS

The following templates help streamline the SME and editorial review process.

SME Feedback Form

REVIEWER INSTRUCTIONS

- Before reviewing the content itself, take a moment to read the page objective and primary use cases that the content is meant to address.
- As you're reviewing, make notes about whether the information is accurate and complete. It's not necessary to edit the content. We'll incorporate changes based on your feedback as appropriate in the next draft.
- Provide the feedback using the comment functionality in Microsoft Word or in the comments sections of this form.
- Please do not modify the text in the Word document.
- You don't have to worry about grammar or typos; the editor will take care of that.

QUESTION	YES	NO
Does the content accurately reflect the features and benefits of the product?		
Comments:		

QUESTION	YES	NO
Is any important information missing?		
Comments:		

Editorial Checklist

Writers and editors should use a checklist like this one to ensure content is on-strategy before publishing or distributing:

X	REVIEW ATTRIBUTES
	The content supports our strategy to <do this> for <these people> so that <this happens>.
	The content demonstrates one or more proof points from our messaging framework.
	The content addresses users' likely tasks or information.
	It is clear what action(s) the user can or should take next.
	The call to action is prominent and appropriate.

MAINTENANCE PROCESS EXAMPLE

Table 17.3 shows an example process for planned content maintenance. It includes the details of the process and who completes each step, and it points to guidance and templates that people participating in the maintenance process will need to review their content.

TABLE 17.3 **EXAMPLE MAINTENANCE PROCESS DOCUMENTATION**

STEP	DESCRIPTION	WHO
1	Set maintenance schedule.	Web Manager
2	Prepare process tools: ■ Content inventories ■ Assessment criteria ■ Reviewer instructions	Web Manager
3	Hold reviewer briefing and training.	Web Manager, Content Owners, SMEs, Legal Reviewers
4	Complete review and record data in the content inventory.	Content Owners, SMEs, Legal Reviewers

STEP	DESCRIPTION	WHO
5	Consolidate inventories and prepare a project plan to make the updates.	Web Manager
6	Approve the project plan.	Director of Content Strategy
7	Assign resources.	Web Manager
8	Make updates in the staging environment.	Writer, Publisher
9	Review and approve updates.	Editor, Content Owners
10	Publish updates.	Publisher

STYLE GUIDE AND CONTENT CREATOR TRAINING

This example is a case study of something I collaborated on with the fine folks at Contentious Ltd (http://contentious.ltd) in London—namely, Laura Robertson, Julius Honnor, and Ettie Bailey-King—for their client Internet Society. Before I joined the team, Contentious Ltd worked with the Internet Society to set their content strategy, including defining their content compass and helping them evolve their content to support their strategy.

I joined the team to help with governance and develop parts of a content playbook. Laura and Julius led the development of a style guide, and Ettie and I worked together on a style guide and best practices training program.

The content style guide (https://assets.internetsociety.org/Styleguide/#page/ FA2D1D25-DA14-4DB6-BE4B0E2A7E1560A5) that we worked on with our Internet Society partners is made up of 10 sections that empower and enable anyone writing for the Internet Society to create amazing content in support of its mission.

This section describes who should use the style guide and how it provides value, as well as excerpts from the guide itself.

EDITORIAL ESSENTIALS

These essentials contain some key usage choices for the Internet Society as well as some fundamental best practices for writing like the snippet in this image.

---

2. Assume no prior knowledge, but not stupidity.

The Internet Society often talks about technical concepts. This doesn't mean it should exclude a non-technical audience. Our vision, the Internet is for everyone, applies to everything we do and everything we write.

To make complex subjects accessible to all, use real-life examples. Provide context for everything except widely understood concepts. If you're speaking to a specific group of people and you have in-depth knowledge of their understanding of the topic, you can tailor to their level of expertise.

> **Tip:** Ask a non-expert to read your content and summarize it verbally. If they struggle, you probably need to include more explanation.

3. Use the active voice.

Avoid the passive voice.

In the active voice, the subject of the sentence does the action. In the passive voice, the subject of the sentence has the action done to it.

✗ An important role is played by community networks.

☑ Community networks play an important role.

> **Tip:** Unsure if you're using the passive voice? Add "by botnets" to the end of your sentence. If it still makes sense, you're using the passive voice.

TONE OF VOICE

This section of the guide provides an overview of the four voice pillars with examples that demonstrate their use . Here's an example from that section of the guide:

Knowledgable

We're the experts. We've been here since the beginning of the Internet, and we're excited to share what we know.

We Bring Clarity to Complex Issues

Anyone can write about a complex topic in a complex way. It takes skill to present technical subjects in clear, plain, and engaging language.

> ✖ Internet encryption appears complex and convoluted, but we can provide examples to facilitate your comprehension.

> ☑ Want to learn how encryption affects you? Here are five examples.

We break down complicated topics into simple statements.

> ✖ We feel that the digital divide is detrimental to society at large.

> ☑ The gap between people who have the Internet and those who don't is bad for everyone.

We Write Like We Speak

Using plain language and commonly understood words helps our diverse audience understand our content.

> ✖ Passwords must be a various amalgam of characters, including numbers and letters (uppercase and lowercase).

> ☑ Secure passwords are a mix of everything you find on your keyboard. That means letters in upper and lower case, numbers, and symbols like !@?".

GRAMMAR AND STYLE

This section of the guide provides direction on their "house" style guide and highlights direction for common style considerations, like capitalization.

Capitalization

We only use capital letters for proper nouns. There are three exceptions:

- We capitalize Internet when referring to the global, open Internet.
- We use title case for titles and headings, see below.
- We may capitalize defined terms in legal documents, depending upon the legal conventions.

Don't capitalize specific Internet Society terms unless they're part of a proper name.

> ✕ The Internet Society's new Communications Manager will support the Community Engagement Team on the Chapter Style Guide Update Project.

> ☑ The Internet Society's new communications manager will support the Community Engagement Team on the chapter style guide update project.

> ✕ The keynote will cover the themes of Diversity, Equity, Inclusion, and Integrity.

> ☑ The keynote will cover the themes of diversity, equity, inclusion, and integrity.

When talking in general terms about everyday documents, like "content plan" or "policy briefing," don't use capitals.

> ✕ The team created a Content Plan for the year ahead.

> ☑ Read the Internet Society 2021 Action Plan.

Tip: See more about specific Internet Society terms in the Terminology and vocabulary section.

LIST OF ACRONYMS

This section of the guide lists acronyms that are acceptable to use without spelling out, acronyms that should be avoided, and acronyms that need to be spelled out. **Table 17.4** includes a few examples.

TABLE 17.4 **ACRONYMS**

ACCEPTED ACRONYMS	ACRONYMS REQUIRING EXPLANATION	ACRONYMS TO AVOID
API (Application Programming Interface)	ARP (Address Resolution Protocol)	ISOC (always write Internet Society)
FTP (File Transfer Protocol)	DHT (Distributed Hash Table)	SIG (Special Interest Group)
URL (Uniform Resource Locator)	LIR (Local Internet Registry)	IWN (Internet Way of Networking)

APPROVED SOURCES

This section of the guide lists the websites and other sources that the Internet Society deems to be trustworthy and reputable and specifies that no sites without an encrypted connection should be linked to. Speaking of encrypted connections, here's an example from the style guide about how to use metaphors to clarify complex processes and be approachable:

> **We Use Metaphors to Connect**
>
> Metaphors can help explain complex processes. We use them to make abstract ideas more concrete.
>
> ✖ Encryption is the process of converting information or data into a code to prevent unauthorized access.
>
> ✅ Encryption is like sending a sealed letter instead of a postcard.

KEY MESSAGES

This section of the guide details how they bring values, ambitions, and impact to life through carefully constructed and curated messages as demonstrated in the excerpt shown in the image.

---

1. The Internet Is for Everyone

We Champion the Internet as a Force for Good

The Internet has changed our lives for the better. We support it to keep transforming lives.

> **Tip:** We appeal to intrinsic values (like equality, justice, and community) rather than extrinsic values (like wealth, prestige, and social status).

Our Mission Extends Around the World

The Internet Society works all over the world to make sure the Internet has a positive impact on people's lives.

> **Tip:** In this context, "all over" is better than "around the world" or "globally." It suggests equality and justice by emphasizing that *all* people deserve access.

We are a global nonprofit organization empowering people to keep the Internet a force for good: open, globally connected, secure, and trustworthy.

> ☑ Whoever you are and wherever you live, the Internet belongs to you.

TERMINOLOGY AND VOCABULARY

This section of the guide provides direction to help people writing for the Internet Society avoid internal jargon that might not make sense to people outside the organization.

ACCESSIBILITY

This section of the guide states the Internet Society's commitment to accessible content and provides guidelines for ensuring content is accessible, as shown in this image:

Images

Alt tags help people with visual impairments. They appear in place of an image on a webpage if the image fails to load on a user's screen. This text helps screen-reading tools describe images to visually impaired readers and allows search engines to better crawl and rank your website.

Images or videos should always be described. There are some exceptions, such as purely decorative or sensory content. See W3C's Web Content Accessibility Guidelines (WCAG) 2.1 for more information.

Avoid using images containing text. It's not possible to resize the text in the image and screen readers cannot read text which is part of an image.

Links

Accessible links describe where they go or what they do. Text should also make sense if the link wasn't there. So never use "click here," "this," or similar phrases.

✕ Click here to download our Internet impact assessment toolkit.

✅ Download our Internet impact assessment toolkit.

INCLUSIVE LANGUAGE

This section of the guide states the Internet Society's commitment to inclusive language and provides principles for writing inclusively, as shown in this snippet:

Don't Assume What Is Normal

We don't all have the same background, values, or experiences. Try not to define people by comparison with another group.

You could say	Don't say
Speakers of English as an additional language, people whose first language is not English	Non-native English speakers
	Non-citizens, illegal immigrants
	Non-Americans
People living in [named country]	
People from [named countries]	

HINT   *A lot of great content style guides are available for all to see. I particularly like Shopify's (https://polaris.shopify.com/content), Intuit's (https://contentdesign.intuit.com), and Mailchimp's (https://styleguide.mailchimp.com). Mailchimp was one of the first publicly available content style guides.*

STYLE GUIDE AND BEST PRACTICES TRAINING PROGRAM

Once the style guide was approved, Ettie and I worked together on a three-part training series to present to the people at the Internet Society who work the most with their content. The three parts were

- Best practices for digital content

- Writing for the Internet Society

- Spotlight on Accessibility and Inclusive Language

That training series was a pilot for what we eventually delivered as a series of video modules with accompanying worksheets that people working on content for the Internet Society can access during onboarding and whenever they might want a refresher.

This image is an example of a module on their intranet site:

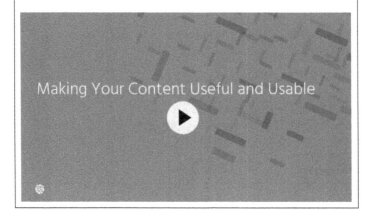

And here's the worksheet that went with that module:

Content Training

Internet Society

Module 3: Make Your Content Useful and Usable

Practice

Exercise 1 – Mini Content Brief

Part A: Think of some content you've worked on in the past and answer the following questions.

Why is it important for the Internet Society to produce this content?

Who is this content for and why do they need it?

What action would we want people to take after reading this content?

Exercise 2 – Sketch it Out

Revisit the content you used in Exercise 1, Part A. Sketch out (or write out) what content you would include on that page to make it useful and usable for the intended audience. Use as many boxes as you need to represent the content.

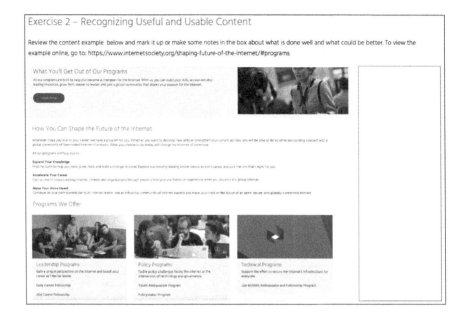

HOW'S IT GOING AT THE INTERNET SOCIETY?

The latest assessment report that compared the audit of the top viewed pages of the website for strategy, style guide, and best practices reflects a substantial improvement since the baseline assessment. They haven't had a chance to recalibrate all their content (understandably), but the great strides are exciting to see!

FAREWELL, CONTENT FRIEND

I'm not crying. You're crying. We have come to the end of our time together. My hope is that this book has—and will continue—to serve you well as you navigate content projects, launch your content strategy career, or get that promotion for being amazing at your job.

Use it as the beginning of a playbook, drop it off casually on the physical or virtual desks of colleagues who should read it, tear it apart and make something better. Seriously, maybe you will write the next book to shape our field for the future.

I believe in you.

APPENDIX

LIST OF TOOLS

This appendix lists the tools from the chapters with explanations of how they apply to that chapter's tasks. You can find them easily because the pages containing tools will have shading that will be visible when you flip through the book. Or, you can use this appendix to find out which tools are in each chapter, what page they appear on, and how you can use the tools.

To access and download the tools:

1. Go to www.peachpit.com/contentstrategy.

2. Sign in or create a new account.

3. Click Submit.

4. Answer the question as proof of purchase.

5. Download the Bonus Content from the Registered Products tab on your Account page.

If you purchased a digital product directly from peachpit.com, your product will already be registered.

CHAPTER 1

1.1 AUDIT PLANNING TIPS AND TEMPLATES

page 8

Download the audit template workbook so you don't have to start from scratch. It contains templates for the audit sheet (where you can collect your data) and a fancy summary sheet with formulas that pull in data from your audit sheet(s). If you've fallen in love with Airtable like I have, start with the Airtable template.

1.2 A SUPER SIMPLE USER TEST

page 9

The fine folks at GOV.UK have been rocking content strategy and content development for several years now. This super simple user test gives some great insights about your content.

1.3 PEOPLE AND PROCESS MINI-ASSESSMENT

page 14

Use the worksheet to jot down findings from your conversations and observations for each characteristic for people and process optimization.

CHAPTER 2

2.1 MAKING THE CASE PRESENTATION STARTER DECK

page 23

Use the presentation outline deck to provide some inspiration and get you started. I've even included a whole separate example there about why an organization should audit member communications content, structure it for reuse, and develop voice and tone guidelines to make it consistent, accessible, inclusive, and clear.

CHAPTER 3

3.1 STAKEHOLDER MATRIX

page 33

Download the stakeholder matrix to list and label your stakeholders, record how you'd like to get information from them, and make notes about topics, concerns, and your pitch. The last page is a table where you can record stakeholder interview times and key takeaways from your discussions.

3.2 STAKEHOLDER COMMUNICATIONS PLAN AND TEMPLATES

page 37

Find Airtable and Google Sheet templates for stakeholder communications planning and recording what you communicated when and to whom.

CHAPTER 4

4.1 ROSTER AND RESPONSIBILITIES TEMPLATE

page 45

Download the template or check out the Airtable database to document your team roster, roles, responsibilities, and activities.

4.2 KICKOFF AGENDA AND EXERCISES

page 49

Use the agenda template to summarize your working session plan and share it with your team. Then, use the Miro or Mural templates to facilitate the session.

CHAPTER 5

CHAPTER 6

CHAPTER 7

7.1 USER UNDERSTANDING MATRIX

page 92

Download the matrix and use it to record your user research questions and rationale for answering them so that you can start a conversation with your stakeholders.

7.2 USER UNDERSTANDING WORKSHOP ACTIVITIES

page 99

Download the sample workshop plan to get more specific instructions for conducting the workshop described in this chapter's templates (including a Mural board for remote workshopping).

CHAPTER 8

8.1 CONTENT ECOSYSTEM MAPPING GUIDE

page 106

Download the guide and spreadsheet/Airtable template to document your content properties and types and relevant details about them.

8.2 SAMPLE USER TESTS

page 117

Download the sample user tests for descriptions of tests (and instructions) that you can use to get user insights about your content.

CHAPTER 9

9.1 PROCESS ASSESSMENT GUIDE

page 124

Download the guide to get step-by-step guidance and templates for assessing content processes against the four factors outlined in this chapter.

CHAPTER 10

10.1 STRATEGIC ALIGNMENT WORKSHOP GUIDE

page 143

Download the guide and get links to the online collaboration boards (Miro and Mural) to plan and facilitate a strategic alignment workshop.

10.2 STRATEGIC ALIGNMENT SUMMARY STARTER DOCUMENT

page 150

Download the starter document so you don't have to start from scratch. It contains an outline based on this chapter's discussions along with some questions and considerations to help you put your document together.

CHAPTER 11

11.1 MESSAGING FRAMEWORK TEMPLATE

page 162

Download the template for examples and editable versions of the three ways I have documented messaging frameworks for my clients.

11.2 CONTENT MEASUREMENT FRAMEWORK AND SCORECARD TEMPLATE

page 173

Download the sample for ideas on how to put together your own content measurement report.

CHAPTER 12

12.1 CONTENT PRIORITIZATION TEMPLATES

page 187

Download the templates to think through and communicate content priorities to your team.

CHAPTER 13

13.1 SITEMAP EVALUATION WORKING SESSION EXERCISES

page 200

Grab the exercises from the Miro or Mural board to run your own sitemap critique session.

13.2 TAXONOMY DOCUMENTATION TEMPLATE

page 205

Grab the Google Sheet or AirTable template for a starter template to document your taxonomies.

CHAPTER 14

14.1 COLLABORATIVE DESIGN STUDIO WORKSHOP PLAN

page 224

Get links to the online journey and pathway mapping working session exercises in Mural and Miro and all the updated material for the Core Model.

14.2 CONTENT EXPERIENCE DOCUMENTATION TEMPLATES

page 229

Get examples and templates to help you document your content experience.

CHAPTER 15

15.1 CONTENT MODELING TUTORIAL FOR CONTENT PROFESSIONALS

page 246

Get access to my content modeling workshop, an Airtable template to document your content model, and examples of other ways you might communicate your content model to your team and stakeholders.

15.2 CONTENT SPECIFICATIONS TEMPLATES AND PAIR WRITING RESOURCES

page 250

Find templates and guidance for documenting content specifications and an overview of the pair writing process with links to lots of resources.

CHAPTER 16

16.1 GOVERNANCE DEFINITION AND DOCUMENTATION GUIDE

page 256

Get a host of exercises, instructions, and templates to set up governance that helps your organization make smart decisions about content.

CHAPTER 17

17.1 CONTENT PLAYBOOK OUTLINE AND EXAMPLES

Page 277

Get a content playbook outline in a Google Doc with lots of examples from various places you can pull from.

INDEX

PEARSON'S COMMITMENT TO DIVERSITY, EQUITY, AND INCLUSION

Pearson is dedicated to creating bias-free content that reflects the diversity of all learners. We embrace the many dimensions of diversity, including but not limited to race, ethnicity, gender, socioeconomic status, ability, age, sexual orientation, and religious or political beliefs.

Education is a powerful force for equity and change in our world. It has the potential to deliver opportunities that improve lives and enable economic mobility. As we work with authors to create content for every product and service, we acknowledge our responsibility to demonstrate inclusivity and incorporate diverse scholarship so that everyone can achieve their potential through learning. As the world's leading learning company, we have a duty to help drive change and live up to our purpose to help more people create a better life for themselves and to create a better world.

Our ambition is to purposefully contribute to a world where:

- Everyone has an equitable and lifelong opportunity to succeed through learning.

- Our educational products and services are inclusive and represent the rich diversity of learners.

- Our educational content accurately reflects the histories and experiences of the learners we serve.

- Our educational content prompts deeper discussions with learners and motivates them to expand their own learning (and worldview).

While we work hard to present unbiased content, we want to hear from you about any concerns or needs with this Pearson product so that we can investigate and address them.

Please contact us with concerns about any potential bias at https://www.pearson.com/report-bias.html.